AN INCONVENIENT PLACE

Jonathan Littell was born in New York, and grew up in France. He now lives in Spain. His best-known novel, *The Kindly Ones*, was originally published in French in August 2006, and won the most prestigious literary prize in France, the Prix Goncourt, as well as the Académie Française's Grand Prix de Littérature. He has since published books on Chechnya, Syria and Francis Bacon, as well as a novel and several novellas. He has written for *Le Monde*, the *Guardian* and the *London Review of Books*.

Antoine d'Agata is a French photographer born in Marseille in 1961. He studied photography at the International Center of Photography in New York City, under the tutelage of Larry Clark and Nan Goldin. D'Agata joined Magnum Photos in 2004. He has published more than a dozen books, and directed three films.

Charlotte Mandell has translated over fifty books of fiction, poetry and philosophy from French, including works by Marcel Proust, Maurice Blanchot, Abdelwahab Meddeb and Jean-Luc Nancy, and the majority of Jonathan Littell's work, including *The Kindly Ones*. Her translation of *Compass* by Mathias Énard was shortlisted for the International Booker Prize and was the recipient of the 2018 ALTA National Translation Award in Prose. She was recently named a Chevalier de l'Ordre des Arts et des Lettres by the French government and has received the Thornton Wilder Translation Prize from the American Academy of Arts and Letters.

'Of the three ways of observing – as witness, whose meticulous, dispassionate descriptions become the fabric of the past; as voyeur, devouring the sight of the present with limitless appetite; as seer, finding in the now intimations of things to come – Jonathan Littell chooses all three at once. He doesn't flinch from the bare, intimate detail of Russia's visitation of death and destruction on Ukraine. Although sometimes the reader might prefer it if he did, it's not because Littell's visions are naked of euphemism, but because it falls to the reader themself to clothe these events in meaning. With his companion d'Agata, Littell, so fascinated by monuments, has made one with this book.'
—— James Meek, author of *To Calais, In Ordinary Times*

'In *An Inconvenient Place*, Jonathan Littell takes us on a journey into the most disturbing of modern human landscapes, from the jumble of horrors that were the ravines of Babyn Yar, into the cellars of Bucha. In chiselled, uncompromising prose, accompanied by haunting photographs by Antoine d'Agata, Littell's unforgettable account is nothing less than a moral triumph over the wilful amnesia imposed on history's savageries by its perpetrators.'
—— Jon Lee Anderson, author of *Che Guevara*

'An impressionistic rather than analytical book, [*An Inconvenient Place*] is not intended as a definitive account of Ukraine's recent history. That will be for historians to provide, and Jonathan Littell knows how quickly words can be reduced to irrelevance. He and Antoine d'Agata have produced an insightful and frequently terrifying document whose reflections on depravity and resilience are likely to prove durable, come what may.'
—— Luke Warde, *Times Literary Supplement*

Fitzcarraldo Editions

AN INCONVENIENT PLACE

JONATHAN LITTELL
& ANTOINE D'AGATA

Translated by

CHARLOTTE MANDELL

'The place of the absence of place,
the non-place, the nowhere.'
—— Georges Perec, *Ellis Island*

Note on spelling

In this book, I've favoured Ukrainian spellings of
the names of people or places. Thus 'Kyiv' and not
'Kiev', 'Babyn Yar' and not 'Babiy Yar' or 'Babi Yar',
'Volodymyr' rather than 'Vladimir,' etc. It is true that
many of my bilingual interlocutors, when speaking
Russian, used the Russian form of their name to identify themselves; but most of them, if they spoke to me
in Ukrainian, would also have quite naturally used the
Ukrainian form of their name. Since the latter is the one
that figures on their identity papers, it's the one I've kept.

Two exceptions: when a Russian person or city is
concerned I of course use the Russian spelling; I also
preserve original spellings, often Russian, in quotations,
whether by Ukrainian authors writing in Russian,
Russian authors or foreign authors.

J.L.

ONCE AGAIN

1. In 1990, a woman who was close to me at the time asked Maurice Blanchot to contribute to a journal she was editing. His reply took the form of two letters: one, hand-written and personal, the other, typewritten and public. I translated the latter (under a pen name) for the journal. It began: 'Dear Madam, please forgive me for answering you with a letter. Reading yours, in which you ask me to write a text for inclusion in an issue of an American academic journal (Yale) on the topic: 'Literature and the Ethical Question', I was frightened and nearly in despair. 'Once again, once again,' I said to myself. Not that I pretend to have exhausted an inexhaustible subject, but on the contrary with the certainty that such a subject returns to me because it is intractable.'[1]

2. An intractable subject that returns to me. One could just as well say a stone thrown at my head that stuns me, makes me stupid. Even before I began I was already exhausted. Blanchot again: 'To want to write, how absurd: writing is the decay of the will.'[2]

3. It was early 2021, when Europe was emerging with difficulty from Covid. A friend proposed I write about Babyn Yar. 'Why don't you write something about Babyn Yar? You should write about Babyn Yar.' Again? Oh no, not again.

4. This friend was very persuasive. 'Listen, you're working on Chernobyl,' he said. 'Babyn Yar is the same, it's a Zone.' The idea was not uninteresting. All the more so since the term 'Exclusion Zone', used in both French and English, is not an accurate translation: *Zona*

11

vidchuzhennya, the Ukrainian term, as well as the Russian term *Zona otchuzhdeniya*, is closer to 'Alienation Zone'. For a while, I vaguely thought about making it my title. But that was a dead end.

5. Antoine d'Agata happened to be in Kyiv. 'What if we did it together?' I asked him. When in dismay and confusion, it's always better to have company.

6. We visited the place together. This was in April, it was grey, the trees were bare. There wasn't really much to see. I drew up an inventory: two parks, a forest, one large ravine and two small ones, an underground river, monuments (lots of monuments), three churches (one very old, two new), a synagogue, also brand-new, a psychiatric asylum, a psychiatric prison, an unfinished psychiatric institute, two cemeteries (one Orthodox, the other military), the traces of two other erased cemeteries (one Jewish, the other Orthodox), the Ukrainian television offices, the Ukrainian television tower, apartment buildings, shops, schools and nurseries, an abandoned cinema, a metro, a maternity ward, a hospital, a morgue. Antoine was just as unconvinced as I was: 'You want me to photograph what, exactly?' Better to drop the whole thing, I said to myself. Forget this story, move on to something else.

7. John Steinbeck also went to Kyiv with a photographer, Robert Capa, in 1947. They didn't go to see Babyn Yar. Steinbeck doesn't mention it in his book. He must not even have known of its existence.[3]

8. Almost twenty years later, in 1965, at the request of an Israeli newspaper, Elie Wiesel visited the USSR. He knew very well what Babyn Yar was, but he couldn't locate

12

the site on any map of Kyiv. It was as if the place had disappeared.

> The official guides at Intourist refuse to take you there.
> Even to talk about it. If you insist, they reply: "It's not worth
> visiting; there's nothing to see." And they are right. No
> point bothering. You'll discover nothing there. No mon-
> ument, no commemorative plaque. In Babi-Yar, the main
> thing is evaded. What you see with the naked eye you can
> also see anywhere else. Anywhere in Kiev. In every square,
> every public place. It's as if Babi-Yar extended to the entire
> city.... [T]he guides at Intourist are right: Babi-Yar is a place
> just like any other.[4]

9. Two things can be said about Babyn Yar: it's not just an idea, but it's also not entirely a place.

10. Perhaps you could also say it's a monad? In his course on Leibniz, Gilles Deleuze defines the monad as a subject insofar as it expresses the totality of the world. 'My soul expresses the entire world but it clearly expresses only a small part of the world, which is my *département* [my territory, Leibniz writes elsewhere]. My *département* is *limited*.'[5] What Leibniz says about the subject is also true for the place: Babyn Yar (as well as other places that we will also visit) expresses, if not the whole world, then at least a certain dimension of the world much vaster than its few acres folded under a banal neighbourhood of Kyiv.

11. The problem is history. In Babyn Yar, history too is folded. On the surface, it acts like a gendarme with his cape and kepi, waving his white truncheon: 'Move on, there's nothing to see here.' Which might encourage

13

someone slightly resistant precisely to move on, to move on endlessly.

12. To survey, to list, to photograph, to describe. Day after day, season after season. Sometimes together, sometimes alone.

13. It wasn't easy, but I finally wrote a first version of this book. While I was writing, the Russian Federation was massing its troops at the Ukrainian border and launching manoeuvres in Belarus, deploying hundreds of assault tanks two hours by road from Kyiv. According to my notes, I finished the manuscript on 22 February 2022. On the 24th, at 5.07 a.m. local time, Russia launched a series of strikes on Ukraine and began its invasion. I learned the news when I woke up, at around 9 a.m. Already, the text I had written became entirely irrelevant. But that was the least of my concerns. Today I'm starting over, from an entirely different perspective. Once again. It is 8 November 2022, the 258th day of the war, and nothing is the same, not the cities of Ukraine, not the lives of my friends, not the questions that matter. To speak about Babyn Yar no doubt still has meaning, but no longer the same one.

SITUATION

14. I'm speaking to you about Babyn Yar, Babiy Yar in Russian, as if you knew what it was. But perhaps you don't. Here are the essential points. The Nazi armies invading the Soviet Union occupied the city of Kyiv on 19 September 1941. On the 26th, the high command, including officers of the Wehrmacht as well as of the SS, made

the decision to liquidate the city's Jewish population. The 'final solution' hadn't yet been decided on, that would come a few months later, and this was an *ad hoc* decision, logical to the Nazi mind, whose purpose was to avenge the dynamiting by the Soviets, in the preceding days, of a number of buildings housing German soldiers and officers, especially along Khreshchatyk, the central avenue of the city. A place was chosen on the city's outskirts, in a derelict zone scattered with factories, cemeteries, a few houses, and crisscrossed by deep ravines. The one chosen for the *Grosse Aktion* was locally known as Babyn Yar: the 'ravine of the old lady', in the most widely accepted sense, even though this etymology is contested (the word *yar*, commonly used in Ukraine for a ravine, is of Turkish origin). On 29 and 30 September, the German forces shot, according to their own obsessive reckoning, 33,771 Jews of all ages. The killings would continue, in this ravine, throughout the entire occupation, turning little by little into a regular procedure, on Tuesdays and Thursdays according to some sources. In total, the number of victims is estimated to be a hundred thousand – sixty thousand Jews and forty thousand other people, Red Army soldiers, sailors from the Dnipro fleet, political commissars, NKVD agents, civilians taken hostage, Roma, Ukrainian nationalists, priests, psychiatric patients, and many others who had the misfortune of displeasing the occupiers. These are the facts between 1941 and 1943.

15. As for the massacre itself, I've already described it elsewhere. I won't repeat it here.

16. You can go to Babyn Yar by metro. You take Line 3 and get out at the Dorohozhychi station, northwest of the centre. When this station was dug out, in the 90s after independence, the workers, rumour has it, hauled truck-loads of bones to the surface. The authorities had to call in an expert, Ilya Levitas, director of the Jewish Council of Ukraine, who finally determined that the site of the massacre was fifteen metres to the right of the worksite.[6] Apparently I met this Ilya Levitas once, in 2002, when I was already carrying out research in Kyiv. His name and his contact details appear in my notes of that time, dated 20 August, along with some fragments of information he provided me, especially on the participation of Ukrainian collaborators in the massacre. Unfortunately, I don't re-member him, and he is dead now.

17. The scandal stifled thanks to Levitas' intervention, the station was inaugurated in March 2000. Move on, move on. But the repressed always returns. The friend I men-tioned above is named Ilya Khrzhanovskiy; he is a filmmaker, and for some years now has been the artistic director of the Babyn Yar Holocaust Memorial Center (BYHMC), a private memorial foundation which we will return to, founded after the Maidan Revolution by a group of Russian, Ukrainian, American, but above all Jewish oligarchs and businessmen. Ilya Khrzhanovskiy tried, for a while, to have the station renamed 'Babyn Yar'. In vain. The neighbourhood revolted, the authorities panicked, he quickly had to back down. Everything has its limits.

18. One day in June 2021, the year before the Russian invasion, Antoine and I took the metro on Line 3 to go

to Babyn Yar. In Dorohozhychi, the doors slammed open and the dense crowd poured out of the carriages, surging in little streams separated by the marble arches before merging on the platform in a compact flood surging towards the escalators. They were people of all ages, distinguished by their clothing, their hair, their bags, their possessions, the shapes of their bodies. Channelled, they flowed towards where they thought they had to go, without wondering much about what was awaiting them there. Antoine photographed them with a thermal camera: the images showed a line of orange ghosts in human shape, advancing in a line against a blue background.

19. Dorohozhychi station, like all metro stations in the former USSR, was designed to serve as a shelter in case of war; and so it was in its depths that the neighbourhood took refuge on 22 February 2022 and on the days that followed. The great marble concourse was transformed into a camp; the people, wrapped in their parkas and surrounded by a few possessions, bags of food and bottles of mineral water, slept lined up on mattresses or on the benches of the carriages parked there, amongst the echoes of crying children, yapping dogs and the murmur of anxious voices.

20. I love taking the interminable escalators of the Kyiv metro. The one in Dorohozhychi station takes at least three minutes to haul you up to the exit. This gave me plenty of time to contemplate the illumined advertising boxes, one every eight seconds, the perspective of the vaulted ceiling's arches slipping by, the weary shoulders of the person perched on the step above mine, the closed-off faces of people lost in their thoughts or their

telephones on their way down the opposite escalator, a rare, fleeting smile.

21. At the top, you had to push one of the heavy glass doors. It was massive, it resisted, I wondered how children and old people managed it. It opened onto a *perekhid*, a covered but not entirely underground passageway that linked together several ramps or stairways leading to different sides of the intersection on the surface. In this *perekhid* there are: a Big-Burg, an Arabik Shaurma, a Kolo mini-mart, a nameless hair salon, two florists displaying their bouquets on the floor, a kiosk selling electronics, a bargain shop called Bonus, a Watsons pharmacy, and four kiosks selling coffee and cake: Kaviarnia-Konditerska, Premium Coffee, Energy Coffee and Aroma Kava. Antoine somewhat at random elected Aroma Kava, I ordered tea, he an espresso, and we gulped them down standing there in the midst of the locals and the homeless people huddled in the corners. Later we often went back there; sometimes we offered coffee for the homeless people, the ones they call *bomzh* here. In the winter it warmed you up, it did you good.

AT GROUND LEVEL

22. Behind Aroma Kava, the *perekhid* opened right out into a vast park. This is what we were looking at while we blew on our scalding drinks. Designed in the 1970s and completed in 1980, it is divided into three large sections: the first two are flat, with few trees, criss-crossed with perfectly straight lanes, and separated by Yurii Illienko Street and the *perekhid* of the metro. The third section is higher up, bordered by little ravines and merging with a

19

large forest called the Kyrylivskyy Hai. During the day, it's quietly bustling with people jogging and strolling, solitary retirees, teenagers in groups, local residents walking their dogs, young women pushing strollers, often in pairs or accompanied by their own mothers. These people are drinking beer, talking into their phones, laughing, chatting, and royally ignoring the dozens of monuments scattered every few feet throughout the park. If you venture a little into the woods to the side, you quickly come across the remnants of small campfires, piles of rubbish and empty bottles. At night, the main lanes are lit by LED streetlights; behind them, dark, stand the trees, the mass of forest. The park doesn't empty out; you can hear footsteps on the flagstones, muffled, banal conversations, laughter, then crickets and, further away, the constant throb of vehicles on Illienko and especially on Olena Teliha Street, the main axis separating the park from the Syrets neighbourhood. At night, the woods are the domain of the *bomzh*, and few people venture into them, except solitary drinkers and lovers in need of intimate space, who scatter their condoms between the trees. But my favourite time there is winter. When the snow falls from the grey, overcast sky, light, magical, it gently carpets the park, and everything is still just as busy, the passersby, well-wrapped phantoms, continue strolling along the footpaths, the children in fluorescent snowsuits flee their annoyed parents or else play with their sledges with shrill cries of happiness, forming a series of colourful little blotches on the thick white layer blanketing the expanse.

23. I had been told: Babyn Yar is here. But Babyn Yar was a ravine, and here it's completely flat. What a funny non-place, even the ravines have disappeared. It started

immediately after the killings: already on the night of 29 September, the Germans dynamited or knocked down with mechanical diggers parts of the slopes of the *yar* to cover the bodies. Look at the famous colour photos taken, probably on 1 October 1941, by a certain Johannes Hähle, the official photographer of *Propagandakompanie* 637: in three of them, you'll see dozens of Soviet prisoners of war, guarded by soldiers from the Wehrmacht, busy flattening with shovels the mass of earth poured onto the corpses. And the German camouflage attempt continued until the end. Starting in mid-August 1943, not long before the retaking of the city by the Red Army, the SS mobilized several hundred prisoners from the concentration camp in Syrets, Jews and others, to dig up the victims' remains and burn them on huge bonfires built with train tracks as well as the wrought iron railings and the headstones of the nearby Jewish cemetery. On 29 September, the day of the second anniversary of the initial massacre, 327 of these prisoners, knowing they too would soon be liquidated, rose up; eighteen of them survived to testify about this clean-up operation. The Soviet authorities continued and completed their work. In 1950, a Kyiv municipal commission decided to entirely level Babyn Yar by pouring through it the muddy water run-off from the many brick factories in Syrets or on Kyrylivska Street (most of whose former owners and workers, Jews, lay at the bottom of the ravine). Pipes were laid down, and the muddy water filled one branch of the ravine after the other, resting for many months and drying out as the water evaporated before another layer was poured. The common people of central Ukraine – called, in reference to the Dnipro, which cuts the country in half, right-bank Ukraine – used to believe that 'God created smooth ground and Satan made the ravines, dark thickets, and unlit places where spirits hid.'[7]

21

In Kyiv, Germans and then Soviets continued the work of God, erasing that of the devil.

24. The filling of the ravines of the Shevchenko district continued all throughout the 1950s. But the winter of 1960-61 was unusually snowy, and in March torrential rain poured down on the city; what's more, for once the brick factories were exceeding their plan and thus producing a surplus of waste. On 13 March 1961, a poorly built dam, unable to withstand the pressure, gave way in the early hours of the morning, and millions of cubic metres of liquid mud flooded below, inundating the Kurenivka neighbourhood and drowning residents in their ground floors, their basements and their vehicles. The official reckoning of the victims counted 145 dead; the actual number is probably closer to 1,500.[8] The images of the neighbourhood filmed after the disaster show an endless sea of mud from which emerge low houses, the cabs of trucks, tramways, trees, poles, and through which the men mobilized to help are slowly slogging. The Soviet authorities compensated the survivors and covered the whole thing up. They also discreetly put an end to the operation of filling in the *yary*; with the work unfinished, some of the ravines subsisted, the ones that still border or cut through the upper reaches of the park.

25. This place seems smooth. The memory of Babyn Yar, like the remains of the bodies, is underground (Leibniz would have said 'folded under'). It is a grey, ghostly, hidden memory, but which wells up everywhere, even from a cardboard cup brimming with hot tea at Aroma Kava. You have to scratch the earth, then turn it over under your fingernails, roll it between your fingers, smell it, taste it, see what minuscule clues you can extract from it.

MONUMENTS

26. On 30 May 1955, the Soviet writer Vasily Grossman, 'after walking along Volkhonka past a cordon of Moscow militia regulating a crowd of thousands of people wanting to see the paintings of the great artists', entered the Pushkin Museum in Moscow to approach Raphael's Sistine Madonna, seized in 1945 at the Dresden Art Gallery by victorious Red Army troops and, ten years later, about to be sent back to the GDR.[9] The painting made his head swim. 'Afterwards, as I walked down the street, stunned and confused by the power of this sudden impression ... I realized that it wasn't a book, or a piece of music that the spectacle of the young mother with a child in her arms had brought me close to ... [but] Treblinka...'[10] Grossman goes on to cite his own work, passages from *The Hell of Treblinka*, a long text written under the shock of his discovery in July 1944 of the traces of the extermination camp. First published in *Znamya* in November of that same year, the book was introduced as testimony by the Soviet prosecutors during the Nuremberg trials, and was quickly translated into many European languages, including French in 1945.[11]

It is these pines, this sand, this old tree stump that millions
of human eyes saw from their wagons slowly coming up
to the platform.... We enter the camp, walk on the earth of
Treblinka.... Here they are – the half-rotted shirts of those
murdered, shoes, cogwheels from wrist watches, penknives,
candlesticks, children's shoes with red pompoms, lace un-
derwear, a towel with Ukrainian embroidery, pots, canteens,
children's plastic mugs, children's letters written in pencil,
volumes of poetry...
    We walk further over the bottomless, swaying earth of

24

Treblinka and suddenly we stop. Yellow, wavy thick hair gleaming like copper, the thin, light, lovely hair of a girl, trampled into the ground, and near it some equally blond curls, and then black, heavy braids on the bright sand, and further on more and more...[12]

Grossman, however, in *The Sistine Madonna*, does not quote the entire passage, and omits the following phrases from his original text:

The earth undulates under the feet, soft, rich, as if copiously soaked with linseed oil, the bottomless earth of Treblinka, unsteady like the depths of the sea. This wasteland, surrounded by barbed wire, has swallowed more human lives than all the oceans and the seas on the globe since the human race has existed. The earth rejects crushed bone, teeth, objects, papers – it does not want to keep secrets.[13]

27. *You talk to us about secrets. But what are you talking about? What secrets? Look around you.* Yes, it's true, wherever the eye falls in this pretty park, it meets a monument, a stele, a plaque. Yet it hasn't always been this way. In 1961, despairing of the official refusal to commemorate the site, Yevgeny Yevtushenko began his famous poem thus: '*Nad Babim Yarom pamiatnikov niet.* Over Babiy Yar there are no monuments.' I met him as well, it seems: looking for the poem in my library, I came across a copy of *Predutro* (*Before Dawn*) inscribed to me by the author. It surprised me, I'd always thought it was Voznesenskiy I'd met, at a poetry reading with Allen Ginsberg around 1988, but no, it was Yevtushenko. Be as it may, monuments now proliferate in Babyn Yar, they teem even, and it's far from over, new ones sprout from the ground all the time, Marina Abramović's wall today, a kurgan of memory tomorrow.

25

Is it in this jumble of monuments that the memory of Babyn Yar survives? Or do they on the contrary also contribute to making it a 'space of non-memory'?[14]

28. Let's start with a list. It opens with the large bronze monument to the Citizens of the City of Kyiv and the Prisoners of War shot by the German-Fascist invader, inaugurated in 1976. In 1981 a plaque is erected in memory of the Football Players of Dynamo Kyiv, victims of the famous 'Death Match', a lovely Soviet fiction we won't dwell on here.[15] The first monument raised after independence, by the Jewish community, is the Menorah, in 1991. Then come: the plaque in memory of the Prisoners of the Syrets Concentration Camp (1991); the cross in memory of the Executed Members of the OUN (1992); the plaque in memory of the Employees of the Podil Tramway Depot who died during the Kurenivka disaster in 1961 (1995); the monument to the executed Prisoners of War and Football Players (1999); a symbolic cemetery, with a memorial cross, dedicated to the German Prisoners of War (1999); the iron crosses for the Executed Priests (2000); a cross in memory of the Executed Priests (2000); a monument to the Children shot in Babyn Yar (2001); a monument to the 751 Patients of the psychiatric hospital who died at the hands of Hitler's regime in 1941-1942 (2001); a cornerstone of the Jewish Heritage Community Centre lain on the 60th anniversary of the Babi Yar massacre (2001); a stela to the 752 [sic] Patients of the psychiatric hospital who died in 1941 at the hands of the Hitlerian occupiers (2003); a plaque in memory of the Specialists of the psychiatric hospital who devoted themselves to their patients (2004); a wooden cross for the 752 Patients as well as the nurses, doctors and interns of the 'Pavlovka' psychiatric hospital shot by the Hitlerian occupiers between 1941

and 1945 [*sic*], with a list of witnesses (date uncertain); a memorial to the *Ostarbeiters* or deported workers (2005); a plaque to the memory of the Victims of the Kurenivka tragedy of 1961 (2006); a monument to the Jewish heroine of the Kyiv underground Tetiana Markus (2009); a monument to the writer Anatoliy Kuznetsov (2009); a memorial stela to mark the raising of the monument to the Victims of the Romani genocide (2011); an information panel on the 'Plan-Scheme of the National Historical Memorial Preserve "Babyn Yar"' (2011); a stela at the starting point of the 'Walk of Death' of the Jews on 29 September 1941 (2011); a cross to the memory of the Victims of the Kurenivka disaster of 1961 (2011); crosses in memory of the Soviet prisoners of war shot in Babyn Yar (2011, 2012); a monumental chapel for the Victims of Babyn Yar (2012); a plaque on a stone ceiling with an inscription near this chapel (2012); a monumental chapel for the Victims of genocide and of the Holocaust of the Ukrainian and Jewish peoples (2012); a memorial panel reading 'Eternal sorrow. In eternal commemoration of the victims of Nazism, shot at this place in Babyn Yar in 1941-1943' (2016); a 'Roma Caravan' monument (2016); twenty-three information panels on the history of the Babyn Yar tragedy (2016); a memorial sign reading 'Metasequoia trees donated by RememberUs.org in memory of the Jewish children killed at Babi Yar' (2017); a monument to Olena Teliha and her colleagues who died for the independence of Ukraine (2017); an alley called the 'Road of Sorrow' (2017); a temporary monument called 'Field of Mirrors' (2020); four stones with inset photographs called 'A Glimpse into the Past' (2020); a monument to the Kurenivka tragedy (2021); a symbolic Synagogue (2021); a 'Crystal Wall of Tears' (2021).[16] The construction of the 'Kurgan of Memory', planned for

2022, has been indefinitely interrupted by the Russian invasion.

29. If the Germans had won the war, would they too have erected in Babyn Yar a monument to their 'great work'? It's entirely possible. In his history of the extermination camps of eastern Poland, Yitzhak Arad writes:

> ... in August 1942, when asked by visiting SS officers whether it would not be better, for reasons of secrecy, to cremate rather than to bury the corpses of the victims of Operation Reinhard, [Odilo] Globocnik [the commander of the said extermination operation] had answered: 'We ought, on the contrary, to bury bronze tablets stating that it was we who had the courage to carry out this gigantic task.'[17]

30. Thus has the memory of Babyn Yar become entirely fragmented, forming a kind of kaleidoscope in which everyone contemplates their own dead, while the image of the others remains muddled, diffracted, indistinct.[18] Hence the clashes between factions, the polemics, the quarrels on the internet that pollute any attempt to grasp this place in its entirety. Rare are those Ukrainians who can say, like Anton Drobovych, director of the Ukrainian Institute of National Memory (UINP in the Ukrainian acronym), 'Babyn Yar is a tragedy of the entire community. They killed your neighbour who brought you *vareniki* [a kind of traditional ravioli] when you were sick, the grandmother who told you fairytales, your *dvirnyk* [superintendent], your dentist, your teacher... Babyn Yar touched all the inhabitants of Kyiv.'[19] If each group claims its piece of Babyn Yar, then the place indeed belongs to everyone, but not to all.

31. Having finished our coffee break, Antoine and I were walking along the park's straight, poplar-lined main alleyway. Many of the monuments in my list are lined up here, on the central divider. Antoine didn't try to photograph them, they didn't interest him. As for me, I was gazing at the cottony down masses of poplar seeds, which in both Ukrainian and Russian they call *pukh*, white streaks rolled up against the edges of the pavement by the breeze, and itching to take out my lighter and set fire to them. *Pukh* is extraordinarily flammable, and burns so quickly that there's no danger, the flame runs along the trail of seeds, and the game consists of making it go as far as possible before it dies out. But I was afraid of getting scolded by one of the fierce neighbourhood grandmothers, even though they had probably all done the same thing with their girlfriends back in the days of Brezhnev or Khrushchev, or even Stalin.

32. In front of us, to the right at the end of the lane, rose the fencing surrounding the site of the future kurgan. We headed that way, towards the hill. Our friend Dima Stoikov had shot at this very spot a funny little film for his *Babyn Yar Diaries*, a series commissioned by the BYHMC and quickly terminated. In this film, two rather decently dressed *bomzh*, one about fifty, the other younger, rummage about in a concrete pipe emerging from a recess in the grass to extract cans and bottles which they pack into plastic bags. 'We're just working,' the older one insists in Russian while the other one crushes a can. His mirrored sunglasses, masking his eyes, are aimed directly at Dima's camera: 'It's work. It's real work.' Women pass calmly by with their strollers in the background while he waves his

cigarette butt. 'Living in this country and doing what we do... They should build a monument to us, like that one over there.' 'Yes, like that one,' the younger one interjects. 'Well,' the first one continues, 'not for gypsies, of course.' 'We're not gypsies, pfff.' 'Just raise a monument to us, because to survive... to know how to survive...'

33. The monument the *bomzh* with the sunglasses was pointing to out of the frame stood there, just in front of us. Antoine didn't want to photograph it either, but I did, with my phone, to keep a record of it. It must be said that it's pretty hideous. It represents, in bronze, a *kybytka*, a large canvas-covered caravan, life-sized and decorated with links of flower garlands, leaning on a pile of rocks and dedicated, as indicate the two plaques hanging from chains, one in Ukrainian, the other in Romany, to the Roma exterminated by the fascists between 1940 and 1945. Like those it commemorates, this caravan wandered a long time before finally finding its place here, not far from the place where three Romany *taboras* (clans) were shot in 1941, possibly even before the Jews. It had been cast in the late 1990s, financed by private donations, but the municipal council of Kyiv – one might wonder why – resolutely refused its installation under the pretext that its design 'was incompatible with the overall design of the memorial ensemble' which at the time did not yet exist. It finally ended up in Kamianets-Podilskyy, to the far west of the country, where it remained for many years.[20] In 2004, at the initiative of President Kuchma, the Ukrainian Rada, the parliament, instituted a 'Day of Memory of the Romany Holocaust'. The date chosen was 2 August, the anniversary of the sadly infamous 'Night of the Gypsies' at Auschwitz-Birkenau.[21] Obviously, this again set the Roma people apart: as Zemfira Kondur, a Roma activist

employed by the Council of Europe, pointed out to me, 'On 29 September, when the president comes to place a wreath at Babyn Yar, it is for the Jews. The Roma people aren't even invited.' In 2009, the municipal authorities erected a stela at Babyn Yar on which was written: A MON-UMENT TO THE VICTIMS OF THE ROMA HOLOCAUST WILL BE INSTALLED ON THIS SPOT; a year later, it was destroyed by unknown people. It wasn't until 2016 that the 'Roma car-avan' was moved from Kamianets-Podilskyy to Kyiv to join the other monuments in the park.

34. Even though the Nazi persecution of the Roma and Sinti peoples, a subject that obsessed Himmler but did not interest Hitler at all, remained much more haphaz-ard in western Europe than that of the Jews, it seems to have been methodical in the occupied territories of the USSR as well as in Yugoslavia. The Ukrainian schol-ar Mykhailo Tyahlyy has inventoried 140 mass killing sites of Roma on the present-day territory of Ukraine. But after the war, as he shows, the Soviet memory of the persecutions and massacres of the Roma people took a different turn from that of the Jews: rather than erasure, an insidious form of blame. Whereas during the war many Roma had fought in partisan units as well as in the Red Army, the representations in the Soviet press, after 1945, 'formed, albeit inadvertently, the widespread no-tion that the Nazis had persecuted the Roma because of their supposed "asocial" character. This in the end con-tributed at least to the partial shifting of blame for their persecution onto the victims themselves. Such notions ... were preserved until the collapse of the USSR and were inherited by the mass consciousness of the population of independent Ukraine.'[22] The government is making some efforts: before the Russian invasion, the Ministry

of Education had asked for the help of the Council of Europe to codify the Romany language in Latin characters, so as to be able to begin to educate the children in their own language. But discrimination is still intense, especially in Transcarpathia, a mountainous region of the Carpathians adjoining Hungary and Romania: 'You can recognize them from the colour of their skin, their names, their clothing,' Zemfira Kondur told me. 'They don't have the right to leave their camps, the children don't go to school, they're not allowed into bars...' In 2018, anti-Roma pogroms, proudly uploaded on YouTube, still regularly took place in Kyiv, organized by S14 and other neo-Nazi groups.

35. From the *kybytka* we headed towards the hill. On our right, in the little copse, stretched a long wall made of wooden beams and black cloth, a full-scale model representing the future anthracite wall by Marina Abramović, still seeking its definitive placement. Workers were busy behind it, shadows visible against the light – now that interested Antoine, and I waited a while as he took some pictures. Beyond the copse, below the hill, lay the 'Field of Mirrors', the first creation of the BYHMC, but we'd already seen it and so we climbed the hill, straight ahead to the Menorah, a large bronze seven-branched candelabra raised on stone steps often decorated as tradition will have it with little pebbles, carnations (which are not Jewish at all), Israeli flags and stuffed animals, and flanked by two stone tablets, one in Hebrew, the other in Ukrainian, bearing the Biblical inscription THE VOICE OF THY BROTHER'S BLOOD CRYETH UNTO ME FROM THE GROUND. Ah, Cain, his resentment, his anger, his wandering: what then was he doing here? Would the Jews killed in Babyn Yar have been the brothers of their murderers? A curious

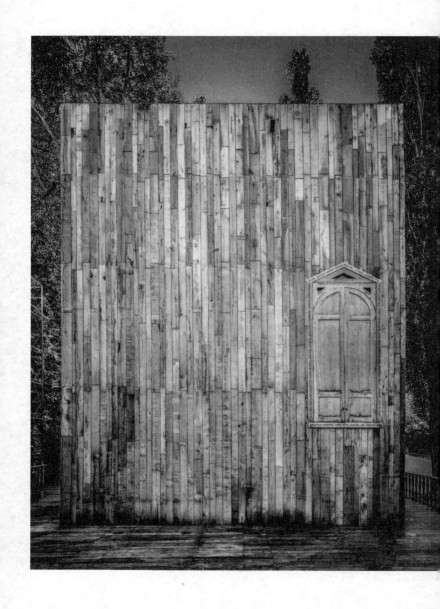

interpretation. To tell the truth, and let me be forgiven for saying so, this monument isn't much better than the *kybytka* or Marina Abramović's wall, finally inaugurated in October 2021. Oh sad fate of monuments in Babyn Yar, strewn throughout the setting only to blend into it straight away, as unremarkable as a wastepaper basket, and less useful than a public bench. At least this one has the honour of being both the first post-Soviet monument and the first Jewish monument installed here.

36. And what about the Jews, then? We'll get to that. Let us simply note for the time being that during the long memorial desert of the Soviet era, the Jewish communities of Kyiv were champing at the bit at the idea of finally erecting their own monument as soon as circumstances allowed. The Rada's ratification, on 26 August 1991 (a few days after the failed coup in Moscow), of a Declaration of Independence of Ukraine provided them with the opportunity they were waiting for. The Menorah was erected even before this independence came into effect, in December with the official dissolution of the USSR. At the same time as democracy, unregulated capitalism and the reign of the oligarchs, memorial competition was slowly taking root in Babyn Yar.

FOLDS (IN THE LAND)

37. I'm being harsh about all these monuments: it's true, their clumsy pathos offends me. But right behind the Menorah stood a very beautiful one, the fruit of a BYHMC project about to be inaugurated a few days after our walk: a little wooden synagogue designed as a children's pop-up book, which, like a giant toy, opened and closed with

a crank-powered handle. A dozen artists, scattered about on scaffolding, were still putting the finishing touches on the decorations of the walls and ceiling, naïve traditional paintings of the vanished synagogues of Ukraine. A few days later we would come in the evening for a test run as a guard slowly turned the wheel in front of a handful of spectators, it was beautiful to watch the ceiling folding in half while one of the walls closed against the other, the soft orangey light of the interior slowly shrinking in the dark blue of the twilight before finally disappearing.

38. Antoine photographed the synagogue, its very simple façade seemed to please him. I left him there and walked around the building. Just beyond it opened up the end of a little ravine, not very long but with steep, deep sides, a wooded gash ripping into the hill. I went up to the edge and contemplated it, dreaming of hurtling down the side but finding it too steep. Antoine, who had joined me, proved to be bolder than me, and thus, hanging from one tree to another and taking photos all the while, did he reach the bottom, having scattered part of his equipment on the way, but unhurt. Later, examining an outline of Babyn Yar superimposed over a contemporary map, I realized that this little ravine and the long cliff that continued it to the right used to form the eastern crest of the filled-in *yar*, north of the western spur where the massacre took place. Vasily Grossman – a Ukrainian Jew from Berdychiv whose mother was murdered, along with the city's entire Jewish population, two weeks before the *Grosse Aktion* of Kyiv – has described this ravine as it existed before the massacre. Krymov, a political commissar who has come from Moscow, reaches Kyiv on the eve of the fall of the city.

The driver stopped the car at the edge of the city, and Krymov continued on foot. He walked alongside a deep and long ravine with clay scree and stopped, involuntarily rejoicing in the silence and charm of the early morning. Yellow leaves covered the ground, the morning sun illumined the autumn foliage. The air that morning was exceptionally light. The cry of the birds seemed only to ripple the deep and clear surface of the transparent silence. The sun shone on the clay slopes of the ravine. Darkness and light, silence and birdsong, the warmth of the sun and the coolness of the air all created a marvellous sensation – it seemed as if the kind old men from a children's fairytale were climbing the slope with quiet footsteps.

Krymov turned off the road and walked sweating between the trees. He saw an elderly woman in a dark blue coat climbing the hill, a white canvas bag on her shoulders.... Krymov asked the way to Kreshchatik, and the woman told him:

'You've gone the wrong way, from the ravine, Babiy Yar, you should have gone left, but now you're headed towards Podol, go back to the ravine and go by the Jewish cemetery, along Melnika Street, then down Lvov Street...'[23]

39. I slowly walked around the little ravine, going down the hill on the left to join Antoine at the bottom. The synagogue, from here, was no longer visible, there were only the trees, ranged in tiers to the top of the ridge and leaning towards each other to hide the sky. I felt very small, I had the impression, for the first time here, that I was almost touching something. This desolate fold of land spoke to me in a quiet voice, yet far clearer than the jabber of the monuments.

40. Finally we climbed back up, going back the long way around. We passed the Menorah and the synagogue and just after there was a cross, a tall wooden cross topped with a triangle and decorated with a lantern and a little sculpted Christ, standing in the centre of a circle of flowers. I lingered there while Antoine continued to follow a path between the trees, along the ridge of the little *yar*. I soon lost sight of him and stayed there for a moment, trying to decipher the gilt text, partially erased archaic letters engraved in the marble at the foot of the cross. But already Antoine was calling me and I followed him under the trees to join him. He was pointing to a hand-painted inscription on a small black cross made of metal tubes, its base decorated with plastic flowers. I translated for him: 'Protoierey Pavel Ostrensky shot 6 November 1941.' A little further on there was another, dedicated to the Skhimonakhinya Esfir (Esther), shot on the same day 'by the fascists'. The ridge of the *yar* was now curving inwards to form a long cliff overhanging the lower part of the park. The woods, here, were denser, the path snaked between the trees, slippery. Further on, a third metal cross, almost hidden in the middle of a copse, presented, in Ukrainian, a more general commemoration: IN THIS PLACE PEOPLE WERE KILLED IN 1941. MAY GOD GIVE REST TO THEIR SOULS. Here the path forked, disappearing to the left into the trees to follow the cliff, or looping back towards the large wooden cross. Behind the forest, on this side, a group of wooden structures was visible: a church, a chapel, an open belfry with a dozen little bronze bells visible on the upper floor.

41. A plaque on the chapel gave the name of the place: 'Memorial church in honour of the icon of the Mother of God "Joy to all those who weep".' The door of the church opened onto a large wooden hall flooded with light, its walls covered with modern icons in gilt frames. A lady in a scarf, immersed in her phone, guarded a little shop at the entrance offering books, pamphlets, crucifixes and reproductions of icons. Opposite it, in the midst of various posters and leaflets, there was a sign in Russian printed from a computer and placed under plastic in a cheap frame. I'll take the trouble of translating it here:

NOT COMMEMORATED IN THIS CHURCH:
→ **For health**
  · **The Unbaptized**
  · **Followers of Other Faiths** (Roman Catholics, Greek Catholics, Catholics)
  · **Sectarians** (Baptists, Adventists, Jehovah's Witnesses, the sect of Olga Asauliak)
  · **Schismatics** (followers of the Kyiv Patriarchate)
  · **People who follow** extrasensory therapists, witches, healers, 'grandmothers'
→ **For repose**
  · **Suicides** (and also those who die of an overdose of alcohol, of drugs)

42. Maksym Yakover, the director of the BYHMC, had already told me about this church. It had been built illegally in the early 2010s, during the presidency of the pro-Russian Viktor Yanukovych, and the authorities at the time had chosen to close their eyes to it, since it was affiliated with the Ukrainian Orthodox Church, subordinate to the Moscow Patriarchate – not to be confused with the Orthodox Church of Ukraine of Metropolitan

Epiphanius I, the 'schismatics' of the above sign, to which the Patriarch of Constantinople Bartholomew I granted autocephaly in 2018, thus withdrawing the recognition bestowed in 1686 of the jurisdiction of the Russian Orthodox Church over the Ukrainian Church, and provoking a vast politico-theological upheaval.

43. Meeting the priest of this church took time, he was a busy man. For weeks, an assistant harassed him with phone calls, appointments were set up and then cancelled at the last minute. A curious man, this Father Sergey. When I finally met him I had the strange sensation of finding myself face to face, not with a character from Dostoyevsky, but with a man who inhabits the role of a character from Dostoyevsky, or who at the very least has been so marked by Dostoyevsky in his earliest youth that he doesn't realize how much his entire presence, his manner of being, is shaped by a novelist rather than by the Gospels: the stained black robe, the long stringy beard, the thin body, the lame leg, the piercing, almost crazed eyes haunted by a mission incomprehensible to the layman. A native of Luhansk, in the Donbas, he had moved to Kyiv in 1995, and in 1999 began to come here, to Babyn Yar, to pray at the foot of a little wooden cross (now replaced by the large one in the middle of the flowered circle) for the repose of the priests murdered in this place.

44. There were apparently many. But as the archives have been destroyed, only three names are preserved: Pavel, Esfir and the Archimandrite Oleksandr Vishnyakov. Speaking about them, Father Sergey slipped from the register of Dostoyevsky to that of Voragine and his *Golden Legend*: 'Vishnyakov and the others refused to pray for the victory of the Germans. They were arrested and brought

to the Gestapo. The *Polizei* [Ukrainian collaborators] offered Vishnyakov a way to buy his freedom: he called them traitors. Then they tied him to a cross, poured gasoline on him, and burned him alive before throwing him into the ravine.' The only website that mentions the death of these priests, that of the National Historical Memorial Preserve 'Babyn Yar' – the *zapovidnyk* in charge of managing and maintaining the site – indicates more soberly and without any other clarification that Vishnyakov and his companions were executed.[24] 'It helps us when we pray and we remember the Archimandrite. He hears and it helps. We would like him to be canonized.' The process, unfortunately, has been blocked by some *kompromat* found in the archives of the SBU, the Ukrainian Security Service. Father Sergey didn't specify the nature of these 'compromising pieces of information', but it was easy to understand that Vishnyakov, like all the priests authorized to oversee and manage a church under Stalin, had been an agent of the NKVD. The priest was talking to me now about the construction of the church. The first Mass was celebrated on 6 May 2012, under a tent. The Metropolitan supported them, but gave no money: 'We were helped by people we knew, good people.' In October of that year he and his followers completed the little chapel; the church itself was built immediately after, and they were able to inaugurate it in December, just in time for the cold. The bells came from Voronezh, in Russia. 'The government wanted to expel us, but they saw that we were feeding the neighbourhood's poor. God made them understand our mission, and since then they've left us alone.' Max Yakover had told me that the BYHMC was trying to have the church closed. 'And what about the Jews,' I asked Father Sergey, 'the rabbis who come to pray over there at the Menorah, do you know them? Do you

sometimes perform ceremonies together?' His feverish eyes remained fixed on me: 'No, never. Everyone prays in his own way, on his own side.'

UNDER THE TREES

45. We had left the church and entered the forest. There, we were plunged into another space, rougher, wilder, which suddenly brought us back to what this place might have been before it was transformed into a mass grave and then erased. It was the Kyrylivskyy Hai, the 'Copse of Cyril', dense, hilly, crisscrossed with asphalt paths and mountain bike trails. Under the trees, here and there, we could glimpse old tombstones bearing more or less legible dates, 1830, 19**, the remains of the old Orthodox cemetery that used to fill these hills. One of the graves, to the side of the path, had recently been decorated with a wreath of dead branches and plastic flowers; further on, at a crossroads, stood the grey ruins of the small mausoleum of the Kachkovskiy brothers, Anton Erazmovich, a law student who died in 1898, and Piotr Erazmovich, a medical doctor and lecturer at the University of Kyiv: I went in, but there was nothing there, just an almost erased sculpted medallion and the remains of a wood fire. We continued our stroll. By the edge of the cliff, three teenagers in black hoodies were smoking and chatting in a thicket. Behind them were intertwined the branches of the last trees, through which you could glimpse the buildings of the Kurenivka neighbourhood. 'Hey, guys, can we photograph you?' One of them, without waiting, began by refusing outright: 'No, no. I don't like to be photographed.' But his pimply friend protested shyly: 'Come on, photos are cool...' Suspicious, the one who had

positioned himself as the group's natural leader asked me: 'Will you send them to us? On Telegram?' 'Of course.' His face lit up: 'Fine, go on then. How do you want us to pose? Like this? Like this?' But Antoine didn't want them to pose, photos like that held no interest for him.

46. We often returned to walk in this forest; sometimes, when I didn't know what to do with my day, I'd go back alone, surveying it from one side to the other, I really liked the place, and every time I go back to Kyiv I still go there for a stroll. In January, if there's no snow, the paths are muddy, the puddles shine and reflect the bare trees, their branches laden with ghostly clumps of mistletoe; clouds pass in front of the pale sun, letting fragmented light filter through. Between the trees, you can clearly make out the old gravestones that are almost invisible in the summer; there aren't many other people about, you have the forest to yourself. In April, the trees are still bare, the first buds barely emerging; then very quickly, in a month, they're covered with leaves, enclosing the lanes under a roof of greenery. In summer there are more people, you frequently pass cyclists and people walking or strolling, joggers, hyperactive teenagers, and also more singular individuals, their expressions inscrutable, muttering under their breath or hiding behind a tree trunk and only emerging from their inner worlds to beg for a cigarette, patients from the asylum at the end of the forest who have come out for some air. One day, Antoine photographed one of them who had folded himself into a V in the fork of a tree, his feet in rubber flip-flops at the level of his head, and who, eyes bulging, was strangling himself with both hands, as if the very place were suffocating him.[25] The last time I went back to this forest was in June 2023, over a year after the beginning of the war. It was still just as welcoming, gentle

49

in its curious roughness. I saw almost no one.

47. After taking leave of the three teenagers, we wandered around, now to the right, now to the left. At a bend in a path we suddenly came upon a vast abandoned structure half-hidden behind a little wooded hill. We walked to the top of the knoll; the ruined building was spread out below, divided up into several wings five or six storeys high, a vast ensemble of yellow brick walls, the brick so typical of Kyiv, pierced with gaping windows exposing the bare interior of the rooms, no doors, no window frames, nothing. We walked down around the knoll. Below, everything was open, large raised entrances covered with concrete overhangs, but without any steps to reach them. We finally found a little opening on one of the sides and entered the building, going down a few steps and then walking through the expanse of the labyrinth. A dirt floor that smelled of dust and mould, graffiti-covered walls, bare cement staircases with no railings, sections of white light piercing the darkness of the rows of rooms, a silence barely punctuated by birdsong outside. One last staircase leading to the roof had collapsed, but we managed to climb it and hoist ourselves up so that we could go out to explore the extent of that wing. The tops of trees jutted up all around, we could glimpse the roofs of the asylum a little further on, then the city beyond. A long wooded ravine dominated the other side of the building, beyond which rose a high hill crowned with a huge building surrounded by cranes, under construction.

48. We finally learned that this vast abandoned complex had been intended for a psychiatric institute, built on land rented from the asylum and then abandoned during construction in the 80s. Until the Russian invasion, it

was a favoured playground for graffiti artists, paintball enthusiasts, bored teenagers, lovers, the curious, and even – as Antoine one day discovered, confronted with a fully armed soldier hanging upside-down from one of the empty windows – the army, which used it for training exercises. We often returned to this place as well. One day, in the autumn, we followed two kids in fluorescent jackets cutting through the woods there. We lost sight of them by the ruin, and began looking for them on the different floors, listening for the sound of their footsteps or voices, catching a glimpse of them at the end of a hallway and then losing them again. Having reached the top floor of the wing we'd climbed, we went over to an opening and saw them a little lower down on the roof of the other wing, inaccessible from the place where we were. They had put on masks and rubber gloves, and were hurriedly spray-painting a large image, a sort of blue octopus if I remember rightly. During the time it took for us to go down one floor, cross the building and climb up to the roof where they were, they'd already disappeared. This game of hide-and-seek was becoming fun, they were crafty little things; suddenly their voices echoed beneath our feet, through the cracked slabs of the roofs. Then everything fell silent again and we stayed there smoking and contemplating the landscape, dominated by the building under construction across the way, which hadn't progressed for months and must also have been abandoned. Leaning on the edge, I saw the two kids leaving the institute and heading into the forest. I cupped my hands around my mouth and called to them: 'Hey, guys! Can we take your picture?' Their return shout echoed through the trees: 'No, we don't have time. Have a good day.' During one of my last walks in the forest, I also returned here, drawn by the almost erotic charm of the vast dilapidated halls. The knoll backing the building was now marked by a series of holes dug out in the clayey soil, individual shooting positions with their back to the institute, which must have dated from the siege of Kyiv in March 2022. But I couldn't see what they were supposed to be defending. Maybe it had to do with another training exercise.

IN PRAISE OF FOLLY

49. The first time, we'd gone out the back of the abandoned institute. It was a mistake, we found ourselves tangled up in the undergrowth, floundering in the mud. Finally we reached a path. It led a little further on to a long sad grey wall, flanked at each end by a guard tower with windows covered in blue wire mesh, obviously some kind of prison. It was in fact a psychiatric prison, where, it is said, were held the most dangerous psychotics in Ukraine – rapists, murderers, serial killers. We spent weeks trying to gain access to it, in vain. The story is long and slightly absurd, very Ukrainian in some ways and also completely ridiculous, and not worth retelling here. In any case – after a change of legislation, or from lack of funds, nothing is clear when it comes to this institution – it would be closed once and for all on 21 February 2022, three days before the Russian invasion, and emptied of its charges, who were scattered throughout the country.

50. Just after the prison, the territory of the asylum proper began with another abandoned building, *korpus* 26. The doors were open and we visited dusty rooms that had been used for art therapy, still decorated with some paintings and potted plants, we examined dilapidated bathrooms, and we stroked some cats well fed by an invisible guard,

finally ending up in a little interior garden surrounded by windows partly covered with plywood, overgrown with more or less moribund plants that a devoted hand was obviously struggling to save. Upstairs, in one of the therapy rooms, workers were building a structure out of pine boards. 'What is it for?' we asked. They had no idea. A few days later, walking by this *korpus* in the other direction to reach the forest, we came across a film shoot. Surrounded by projectors, several cameras and a crowd of technicians, a man in a leather jacket, standing in front of a luxury car, was aiming a gun at another man lying on the ground, his T-shirt soaked with fake blood. An assistant, catching sight of us, started bawling at us to clear out, but instead of turning back we hurried around the set and continued towards the grey wall of the psychiatric prison, along which a few technicians were sipping tea next to their equipment trucks. A gunshot resounded behind us, the only one we'd hear in Babyn Yar. That night, an acquaintance showed me some photos on his phone of the inside of *korpus* 26, which he had visited the day before: the upstairs rooms had been turned into a 1990s psychiatric asylum with beds, an office, lots of crockery and equipment – a fake asylum inside the real one.

51. After the abandoned *korpus* we headed towards the administration building. This is normal, every visit to an institution should begin with a courtesy call to its director. At the entrance, the guard made us wait, and I absent-mindedly contemplated his four large screens covered in a mosaic of views of the asylum, each little rectangle formed from a slightly different combination of grey and green, crossed sometimes by the dark grey of asphalt. Upstairs, we were made to wait again in a hallway decorated with portraits of the past directors of

the asylum before finally being led into the office of the present one, Vyacheslav Danylovych Mishyev. It was a luminous space with pale-green walls decorated with paintings by one Volodymyr Slepchenko, with shelves full of books, African sculptures, orchids, Chinese vases. The affable director served us Armenian cognac and cookies as he told us the story of his asylum. At the time of the fall of Kyiv, in 1941, there were about 1,500 patients at the 'Psychiatry Clinical Hospital', which everyone still calls the Pavlovka, its pre-1937 Russian name; the asylum was placed under the authority of the occupying forces' Department of Health, rations were drastically reduced, and the patients started dying of hunger. Then, two weeks after the massacre of the Jews, the Germans began to liquidate the patients. On 13 October 1941, 308 Jewish patients were shot by members of *Einsatzkommando* 5 above a mass grave in the Kyrylivskyy Hai. In 1942, they moved on to non-Jewish patients, hundreds of whom were gassed in trucks, about 300 in January 1942, then the rest between March and October, when the killings stopped, due to a lack of victims probably. The precise numbers are given in a series of *Einsatzgrüppen* reports which survived the war.[26]

52. As we left Vyacheslav Danylovych's office, well-lubricated after our meeting, I went back to study the row of portraits in the hallway. They were all there, from 1941 to the present day, but one was missing, between the one whose term of office ended in 1942 and the one who had started in 1945. Immediately I thought they'd removed the portrait of a collaborationist director. The head doctor of the hospital, a certain Musii Tantsyura, had indeed been tried for collaboration in 1946.[27] Yet in the portrait gallery in the hallway, Musii Dorofiyvytch Tantsyura, a

slightly thickset man with a firm gaze framed by round glasses, and sporting a small, very late-nineteenth-century goatee, appears as the first director of the Pavlovka, from 1941 to 1942, just before Pylyp Danylovych Pashchenko, 1945-1959. 1941 and 1942 are precisely the years of the killings; the missing years, 1943 and 1944, are those of the return of Soviet rule. So my initial hypothesis seemed incorrect. Had there been a vacancy in management during the trials of Tantsyura and many other staff members? I was unable to find an answer to this question. Tantsyura and his colleagues had at first gotten two to ten years in a labour camp, before being found innocent and freed by decision of the Military Council of the Ukrainian Supreme Court; it had in fact turned out that, far from collaborating, Tantsyura had used his position to save many patients, urgently sending over five hundred of them home after the first massacre and altering the medical records of many others to make their condition appear less serious.[28]

53. Just before we left Vyacheslav Danylovych had called a nurse into his office, who was also treated to a drink. 'The hospital is open to you,' he had obligingly declared in front of her. 'Svetlana Mikhailovna, show them anything they want to see.' The complex is vast: dozens of buildings spread out over the long hill that ends the Kyrylivskyy Hai between Olena Teliha Street and the big ravine that borders the forest to the east, the Repyakhiv Yar. Svetlana Mikhailovna first showed us a *korpus* dating from 1919 and restored in the neo-Classical style, with paintings depicting Christ, Pontius Pilate and unclad women, closed and guarded by massive, authoritarian nurses as it was reserved for patients deemed at risk for self-harm, under 24-hour surveillance. Then we moved on to the

10th department, also situated in a Tsarist-era *korpus* close to St. Cyril's church. In a dark room, a half-naked young woman was getting dressed; she came out to welcome us in a short, form-fitting blue dress; when we asked her permission to photograph her, she went back into her room and first posed standing, then sitting with her legs crossed on her bed, as if for an Instagram selfie. Further on, a small elderly lady addressed me in French with a perfectly good accent, a little old-fashioned perhaps; her first sentences were very clear and comprehensible, but then suddenly became confused, dissolving into gibberish, then once again becoming good French for an instant; it was unsettling. 'Are you my son, Monsieur?' 'No, Madame, I am not your son.' 'I studied at the Sorbonne, did you know? At the Sorbonne, Monsieur. Tell me, is Édith Piaf still alive?' All this, despite the sadness of these broken lives, was very pleasant, very neat, very nice, and we'd have liked to see something else, the wards crowded with clusters of patients pressing up against the windows, for example, beneath whom we'd passed on the way. But Svetlana Mikhailovna remained extremely evasive. 'It's too late today, you'll have to come back. I'm sure there won't be any problem.' She was being a little optimistic. Antoine especially returned many times to this asylum to try to take photos there, but constantly came up against a wall of passive obstruction: when he arrived, smiles, cognac, friendly chats, after which they arranged for him to see only clean, orderly wards, full of calm, smiling patients on their well-made beds. It was frustrating. This little game continued during the war, in February 2023, when Antoine returned to the Pavlovka on commission for the *New York Times*, to photograph traumatized soldiers being treated there: one day, open access, red carpet; the next, existential crisis, absolute ban on working.[29] On the

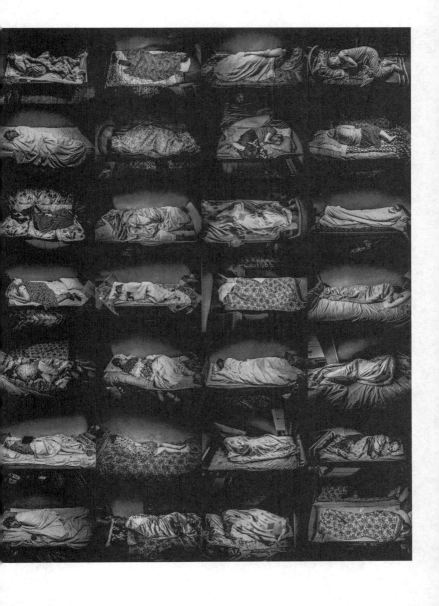

eve of his return to France, I asked him to greet Mishyev for me. He wrote in reply: *He was cool today because I was leaving and he was happy to get rid of me...*

54. On the first day, Svetlana Mikhailovna had at least allowed us to visit the asylum's morgue, a pretty little Tsarist-era building with cracked fuchsia plastered walls. In the first room, large cabinets made of old wood enclosed thousands of glass plates, biological samples still constantly collected from the patients and preserved for five years before being thrown out; the next room, even vaster, was used for autopsies. There was actually one in progress, a young bearded doctor was cutting up the cadaver of a very old woman, smooth and yellow as a wax sculpture. One hand was clenched upwards, her breast was hanging under her armpit, her chest was open in a triangle, and between her feet lay her brain, which had been taken out of her skull, the upper part of which had been completely cut off. With the delicate light entering through the opaque windows, it would have been a picture to make with a large-format view camera, a huge image in the manner of Jeff Wall, fixed in its absolute perfection and made so that the eye could roam endlessly over all the details, as ours were doing. But in the morgue you can't take photographs with a view camera. You can't take any photographs at all.

55. Svetlana Mikhailovna ended our visit at St. Cyril's church, one of the oldest in Kyiv, situated inside the territory the Pavlovka. This isn't by chance: for a long time, the monks of the fortified monastery attached to St. Cyril's took care of the mad, those close to God, and in 1787 Catherine the Great had the monastery closed to transform its quarters into a hospital. The church remained as

the hospital grew, preserved but transformed into a museum by the Bolsheviks, who knocked down the belfry in 1936. On the way, the paths were swarming with patients, strolling in ordinary clothes or bathrobes, alone or accompanied by relatives. A bearded monk, very elegant in his perfectly cut long black robe, suddenly emerged, smartphone glued to his ear, from an administrative building only to dive into a brand-new Mercedes; a little further on, a hospital employee, perched on rickety scaffolding, was carving a wooden sculpture in the middle of a large lawn. In the lane running alongside the little wooden church built for religious patients – St. Cyril's is still a museum, you can't go there to pray – a panic-stricken woman was gripping the waist of a muscular young man, shirtless and a head taller than her, and was trying to drag him back while he was struggling, step by step, to move towards the stairs down the end leading to the avenue. '*Sinok, sinok! Stoi!*' the mother cried, sobbing and embracing him frantically: 'Stop, my darling boy!' On the ground a creased purple shirt lay forgotten; another man, paunchy and looking at a loss, also obviously part of the family, stood close to them waving his hands, vainly trying to calm the young man down. The latter was stubbornly struggling, fleeing determinedly, dragging his clinging mother with all his strength while Antoine discreetly took some photos; mother and son still clinging together, the three moved away, passed St. Cyril's, disappeared. A little later, walking around the large church's metal fence, I found the mother below, lying between the trees on the stone incline of another staircase, exhausted, overwhelmed. The man and boy had disappeared; Antoine, again, took a picture of her, as did I. Then we returned to St. Cyril's to buy our entry tickets. In the courtyard in front of the church, the mother caught up with us and raged at us, furious that we had photographed her. While she was venting her anger I translated for Antoine: 'Who are you, what right do you have to photograph people, we're not Africans...' Finally, accepting my explanations, she calmed down and started talking with Svetlana Mikhailovna. Her son, committed to the 6th department, had decided to leave, and the hospital was refusing to prevent him. Patiently, Svetlana Mikhailovna explained the law to her: the hospital could only accept patients who had come voluntarily; they had no right to keep them by force without a legal injunction; if the boy was dangerous, his mother should ask for a decision from a judge, otherwise she could do nothing but persuade him. The mother, again, was sobbing quietly: 'You can do nothing? Nothing at all?'

56. Finally we entered the church. The outside, white with green cupolas, had been completely remodelled in the Baroque style after a major fire in 1734, but the inside was still close to what it had been in the time of Vsevolod Olhovych, Prince of Chernihiv, its founder in the twelfth century. The tall columns were still covered with period frescoes in faded colors, sublime in their delicacy; but among them another series of brightly coloured frescoes stood out, painted in the Symbolist style of the 1880s by the great artist Mikhail Vrubel. The Soviet writer Konstantin Paustovskiy describes Vrubel as a man nearly as tormented as the patients of the asylum surrounding the church. One day in 1904 or 1905, Paustovskiy's father took him to meet Vrubel in a hotel in Kyiv:

> My father knocked on a low door. It was opened by a thin man in a shabby jacket. His face, hair and eyes were of the same colour as his jacket – grey with yellowish flecks....
> He grabbed my father by the arm and led him to a table.

I timidly looked around the room. It was a garret. Several watercolour drawings were tacked onto the dark wallpaper. Vrubel poured some cognac for my father and himself, quickly downed his and began pacing around the room. He tapped his heels loudly. I noticed that his heels were very high. My father said something laudatory about the watercolours pinned to the wall.

'Rubbish!' Vrubel replied. He stopped pacing around the room and sat down at the table.

'For some reason I keep whirling around all the time like a squirrel,' he said. 'I'm tired of myself. How about we go to Lukyanovka, Georgiy Maksimovich?'

'To St. Cyril's church?'

'Yes. I want to look at my work. I've completely forgotten it.'

[In the fiacre,] Vrubel and my father smoked. I looked at Vroubel, and felt sorry for him. He twitched, his eyes kept shifting, he spoke incomprehensibly, he lit cigarettes only to throw them away immediately. My father spoke to him gently, as if to a child....

Inside St. Cyril's church Vrubel silently examined his own frescoes. They seemed modelled out of blue, red and yellow clay. I found it hard to believe that such large images on the walls could have been painted by this skinny man.

'Now that is painting!' Vrubel exclaimed when we left the church.[30]

Several cats were quietly sleeping in corners, others stalked by along the walls. On a pillar, half-effaced, a medieval angel a virile pose, his head tilted, was unrolling a scroll that furled out and curled back onto itself like a long sheet carried by the wind. Our guide was commenting the frescoes, Vrubel's and the old ones. The young man we'd seen earlier, in a T-shirt now, entered the church.

Shaking, nervous, twitching all over, he began pacing around the nave, drawing one large circle after the other while our guide, without interrupting her explanations, eyed him with the same anxious look Paustovkiy must have had at this place over a century ago, watching the painter Vrubel contemplate his work.

57. Beneath the church, it is said, are grottos, occupied centuries ago by the monks, then walled up in 1953. It may have been in one of these dens, or in any case in one of the grottos in Babyn Yar, that the corpse of Andrii Yushchynskyy, a 13-year-old boy who had disappeared a few days earlier, was found in March 1911. A vague denunciation led to the arrest of a Jewish foreman at the nearby Zaitsev factory, Menahem Mendel Beilis, and, at the instigation of anti-Semitic prosecutors, to accusations of ritual murder. The trial had immense repercussions, dividing Ukrainian society the way the Dreyfus affair had split French society some years earlier. A jury composed mainly of Ukrainian peasants finally acquitted Beilis (who ended his days peacefully in New York), but accepted the authorities' argument that the child's murder was a ritual one.[31] Thus Babyn Yar was already linked to the Jews. But the place has always seemed complicated, problematic, dangerous. During the Upper Paleolithic era people had already settled there, mammoth hunters who must have used the ravines slicing through the clay to the back of the large cliffs bordering the western shore of the Dnipro to hem in and trap their prey. These ravines have long formed a kind of *limes* to the rear of the city, a labyrinth that could easily serve as a natural defence; during the centuries of the Kyivan Rus', it was the area through which rival princes of the reigning Rurikids launched their attacks on the city, too well defended on the river's

side, offensives that usually ground to a halt against the defences of the fortified monastery and the walls built along the crests of the ravines, filling them with the corpses of the assailants.[32] Paustovskiy also found the place unsettling. In November 1918, as Kyiv was falling to the forces of the Directorate of Symon Petlyura, he deserted Hetman Skoropadskyy's army, into which he had been drafted by force, and walked through the neighbourhood to return to his house:

> I arrived at St. Cyril's hospital, where I had once been a long time ago with my father and Vrubel. At that time all these places around the hospital, the deep ravines, full of hawthorns and gnarled elms, seemed to me mysterious and sinister. Now I slowly and heavily climbed the steep and dusty road to Lukyanovka, and I felt nothing, not only about the strangeness of these places, but even about the times.... The dull sky hung over the shabby outlying lanes and hovels, just as it had hung thirty years ago.[33]

IN THE DEPTHS OF THE RAVINE

58. Beyond St. Cyril's, a wide staircase leads down to Olena Teliha Street and the trolleybus stop from where one can head back to Podil and the centre along Kyrylivska Street. But after taking our leave of Svetlana Mikhailovna, we preferred to go have a bite at the asylum's canteen, a tiny space painted pink where they serve *kotlety* and stuffed peppers warmed up in a microwave. Our meal over, we went back out to smoke while we examined the monuments lined up on the lawn opposite the canteen. Then we took an asphalt road that led down, winding between the trees. At the bottom it forked, the

asphalt continued to the left towards Kyrylivska and the Spartak stadium; to the right, it became a dirt path that led into the Repyakhiv Yar, the only great ravine in the neighbourhood to have survived the levelling operations of the 1950s. We were full, not yet too tired, we decided to head that way. The ground was muddy, with deep ruts and boot prints, and strewn with debris, plastic bottles, cans, dozens of old tyres. The tall branches, pale grey and loaded with clumps of mistletoe, intertwined, blocking the sky where crows circled, cawing mournfully; the ravine's grey sides rose behind the trunks, everything was grey, beige, brown with little touches of green. We passed the abandoned institute, high up on our right, to our left on the crest stood the mass of the building under construction, then a handful of other recent buildings, with, lower down, a series of private garages and sheds for automobile repairs. In the nineteenth century, these hills were dotted with villas, somewhat isolated but very sought-after by a certain section of the middle class (Vrubel had his there); to connect this outlying, difficult to reach neighbourhood to the city, a charming little tramway line was built at the bottom of the ravine, which can be seen on postcards of the time illustrating what they called 'The Switzerland of Kyiv'. On these photos, curiously, as on the photos of Babyn Yar taken by Johannes Hähle, the sides of the ravines are bare, dry and bald, and even the hills aren't very wooded; I have no idea where today's overgrown vegetation comes from, but it covers everything. We passed iron manhole covers, one after the other, through which we could hear water gurgling in a pipe; other sounds reached us from afar, clear, detached, a chainsaw, snatches of birdsong, the vague distant murmur of cars. We passed by the concrete remains of old drainage collectors, a few shacks apparently occupied by

bomzh; Antoine photographed the trees and the earth, I took a few notes, looked at the sky or the crest of the *yar*, deserted. My mind wavered between contemplating the present ravine and vain attempts at imagining the other past ravine, the men and the women, the cries, the gunshots, the white bodies, the blood, the stench. I was at the bottom of a *yar* and reality, in all its banality, formed a screen even more impenetrable to thought than all the efforts of those seeking to erase this inconvenient place.[34]

DRUMS (OF WAR)

59. Every morning, while I was writing the first version of these pages, I would read the news. The Russian forces massing at Ukraine's border numbered 100,000, then 135,000, then 150,000. Their tanks were manoeuvring in Belarus and nine landing crafts were arriving at Sebastopol, having come from northern Russia after sailing past Sweden and Ireland, pausing in Tartus, and crossing the Bosporus. Biden called Putin, Macron met with Putin, Truss met with Lavrov, Biden called Putin again, Macron also called Putin. Warnings were issued, alarms were raised, threats were made. My journalist friends wondered how they could get to Kyiv if the Russians attacked from the north and the airport immediately closed; my expatriate friends wondered whether they should evacuate or not; my Ukrainian friends drank beer, went on vacation to Egypt or Turkey, and, if they had some foresight, prepared grab bags with their essential possessions and documents in case of bombardments. As I was describing Babyn Yar, I imagined Russian tanks stationed near the Dorohozhychi metro station and Russian soldiers patrolling the park lanes, haughtily

ignoring the mothers with their strollers and the rare joggers (only women, since the men would be in the army,
in prison or in hiding). The Ukrainian TV headquarters
nearby, bombed, would have been reduced to smoking
rubble. And many Ukrainians would be dead.

60. This is not quite how it happened. The Russians did
indeed invade from Belarus, passing through Chernobyl,
and tried to take Kyiv. But the Ukrainians were far braver
than everyone thought, and especially far better prepared.
President Zelenskyy refused to flee his capital and his
men stopped the enemy forces dead in the suburbs of the
city, Irpin, Hostomel, Horenka, Moshchun. Frustrated,
the Russian soldiers turned against the civilians who
hadn't been able to escape.

ANTOINE D'AGATA'S JOURNEY

61. The invasion of Ukraine began on 24 February 2022.
Kyiv rapidly emptied of its inhabitants, a huge traffic jam
filling the westbound motorway for days; a large number
of those who stayed, both men and women, joined up and
took up arms, and many of those who had left returned to
do the same once their families had reached safety. On 1
March, in the midst of other strikes on the city, two missiles fell on Babyn Yar, aimed at the television tower, which
they failed to bring down. On 8 March, Antoine decided to go; for various reasons, I couldn't go with him. He
bought a bulletproof vest and a helmet and set off alone.

62. The Kyiv airport had been bombed on the first day
and the Ukrainian airspace was closed. Antoine flew to
Warsaw and managed to be taken to the border by other

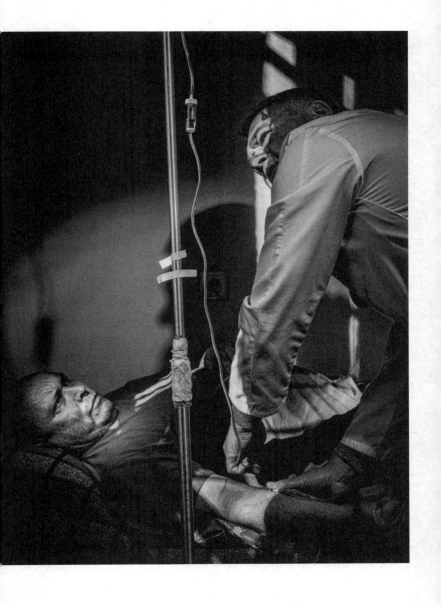

photographers better off than he. They left him there and he crossed on foot. A bus driver who had just dropped off some refugees and was returning empty agreed to take him to Lviv. On the evening of the 11th, at the train station, he came by chance upon Dima Stoikov, our videographer friend who had filmed the two *bomzh* in Babyn Yar, and took the night train with him to Kyiv.

63. When he arrived on the 12th, he set off immediately for Babyn Yar, to photograph the damage from the strike on the television tower. Before he could even take a single image he was arrested by a patrol. I sent him through WhatsApp an outdated assignment letter from the BYHMC, and they let him go, but with strict orders not to photograph the tower or its surroundings.

64. He tried to go to the front line below Irpin. There was heavy shelling in both directions; shaken civilians were steadily pouring in from the combat zone. But the checkpoints made it difficult for journalists to pass the Kyiv city limits; beyond the Irpin River, and the bridge dynamited by the Ukrainians beneath which civilians were fleeing via a makeshift footbridge, it was impossible. *Lousy day*, Antoine wrote to me. *A mess*. An American journalist, Brent Renaud, was killed between the city's last checkpoint and Irpin, possibly by Ukrainian fire, and Antoine saw his corpse being brought back. He also observed body searches being carried out, out of fear of infiltrators, on refugees arriving at the checkpoint. One of these refugees showed up with severe burns on his hands and face. He was trembling like a leaf and they brought him to a Red Cross tent to be treated. After a little while he came back out to smoke. When he finished his cigarette, he made as if to throw down the butt, paused, looked around

him, got up and went to find a bin to dispose of it. Antoine watched him with astonishment.

65. He went back to Babyn Yar. In the Dorohozhychi metro station, about forty people were still sleeping in the centre of the platform, gloomily settled in there, but traffic had started up again, even though there weren't many trains running. He visited the nearby morgue and had tea with the director whom we had met the previous year, who explained to him that the basements were full of corpses, but refused to let him visit them or take any photos. He went to the Pavlovka, where he met Vyacheslav Danylovych in the street, in a hurry. They let him enter a hallway where the patients, having deserted their rooms, were huddled together for warmth or company. There were many patients brought in from Kyiv *oblast*, the part of the region surrounding the city invaded by the Russians; they seemed much more afflicted than the ones we'd seen together. He was able to shoot some portraits.

66. The curfew ordered on the 16th confined him to his hotel all day. He had no army press card and no car, and was completely isolated from the other journalists. *I'm going to lose it*, he wrote to me. Through a friend I tried to find someone to help him, but the Ukrainian journalists were reluctant, they'd already had enough bad experiences with foreign journalists, especially the photographers of the big media outlets who treated their fixers with incredible arrogance. That evening Antoine called me to tell me he was leaving by car for Kharkiv with a mutual friend, another photographer. Kharkiv was being heavily shelled and I tried to dissuade him, in vain. *Understood and I'm aware of what's involved,* he wrote to me. *But important for me to touch the event as close as possible.*

74

67. On the 18th, after a night in Poltava and about thirty checkpoints on the road, they arrived in Kharkiv. *A little tense. A fair amount of artillery. We're getting our bearings*, he wrote to me at midday. That night he wrote again: *It's pretty much shit here. We haven't managed to find an angle, a perspective from which to photograph. City deserted, checkpoints paranoid, war impalpable. Defeats [sic] everywhere but nothing worth photographing, broken glass, gutted façades and — Well, maybe it's time to leave. Still there's a feeling we did well to come, even if it's completely pointless. Still there's the incessant noise of artillery, I never really know who's shooting...* He stayed for three days, hovering between tension and boredom. On the 21st, at dawn, our mutual friend dropped him off at the train station. There weren't any trains and he waited there till evening; finally he managed to leave. It took him over forty-eight hours to reach Warsaw. As far as I know, he kept no photos of that journey. In any case he never showed me any.

LOW TIDE

68. Taras Shevchenko, a poet and painter born serf and Ukrainian, is regarded as the founder of the Ukrainian literary language, the one that barely two years after his death would be banned by the Tsarist authorities. In 1850, exiled in the terrible penal colony of Novopetrovsk[35] on the Mangyshlak Peninsula in Kazakhstan, he secretly wrote the following lines:

Takii, bozhe nash, dila
My tvorymo u nashim rai
Na pravednii tvoii zemli!

My v rai peklo rozvely,
A v tebe drugogo blagaem.[36]

This, our Lord, is what
We are doing with our paradise
On your blessed earth!
In Paradise we have raised Hell
And we beg you for another one.

69. At the end of March, with their offensive on Kyiv still blocked in front of Irpin and Moshchun by the bitter Ukrainian defence, the Russian high command acknowledged its failure and decided to withdraw its forces to redeploy them towards Kharkiv and the Donbas, where they were also struggling. The Ukrainian soldiers who entered the liberated towns, and then, a day or two later, the international press, discovered with horror what the Russians had left behind: hundreds of civilian corpses scattered throughout the streets, the courtyards of apartment buildings, the gardens of homes, alongside the country paths and the motorways. The little occupied towns and villages were in ruins, there was talk of systematic rape, and everywhere appeared mass graves, dug by volunteers or by the occupiers. With these revelations, and the thousands of images that flooded the world, the conflict took on a different meaning. It was no longer a matter of a brutal, unscrupulous imperial army, but of a horde of criminals, rapists, sadistic murderers. Bucha, a quiet suburb of 37,000 inhabitants just beyond the capital, surrounded by forests and not far from the large artificial reservoir called the Sea of Kyiv, is the name that came to designate all these atrocities.

70. In May, I was finally able to return to Ukraine with Antoine. A commission for a major French newspaper gave us the means to work and the freedom that goes with it. Bucha was already ancient history, yet we wanted to see things for ourselves. Vain hope, but not for lack of trying. The Russians had just been pushed back from the outskirts of Kharkiv, and we visited several freshly liberated villages. Rubble, desolation, glum melancholy. A few rare individuals who had come back to rebuild a little or recover whatever could be salvaged. Burnt, rusted Russian tanks, their turrets hurled to the side by the power of the detonations. Sometimes a corpse, a soldier who had dragged himself into a hen house to die, without it being possible to tell if he was a Ukrainian or a disguised Russian trying to flee. We visited the morgue in Kharkiv. Civilian corpses had been lined up behind a tarpaulin to be returned to their relatives: all photography was forbidden, categorically. At the back of the courtyard some soldiers were standing around other bodies in black bags, Russian corpses. I walked over and began talking with an officer. He was extremely annoyed: each body had to be photographed before being stored in a refrigerated train with an eye to a possible exchange; however, fortunate stroke of luck, their camera was broken. I offered Antoine's services, and the officer agreed. A forensic pathologist in a blue lab coat, in charge of writing up the report, opened each bag and Antoine had to follow a rigorous protocol: label number, face, profile, whole body, distinctive marks. Some were nothing more than shapeless, mouldy packages of flesh, blown apart by an explosion; one of the corpses, in a better state, wore one of those wool sweaters crocheted with black and white patterns you usually see in ski resorts; an officer, Gerasimov V.O., still had a chain with a cross and a ring around his neck, and was in

such a state of decomposition that there was no flesh on his skull. Another of these corpses had his body covered in tattoos, old-school designs in black ink you could see had cost time and money, and the doctor grabbed a rag to roughly rub the clay-incrusted skin, trying to make them more visible. The front side fully photographed, he got up and grasped a foot to flip the body over; the entire leg remained in his hand, which didn't keep Antoine from conscientiously continuing to take his images.

71. When I look at a corpse, what do I see? Strange question, which I find difficult to answer. The closest I can come to the truth of the experience might be these words of Maurice Blanchot: 'The corpse is its own image.'[37] For whether I contemplate a dead body or contemplate the image of that dead body, what is the difference? There is the smell, so tenacious, foul, obstinate, which seems to penetrate your pores even if you hold your nose: there is indeed no image, no representation of that stench. But when it comes to the visual aspect it's another matter. When I examine this body, here, lying in front of me, nicely made up in its coffin like a recently deceased grandmother or with its greenish flesh and mouldy rags in the mass grave from which it's being extricated, what happens? If it was someone I knew, immediately memories come to me, themselves images. If it's a stranger, as in the case of these anonymous bodies spewed out by the war, then I examine the clues, the marks, the distinctive signs, the objects, to attempt to represent to myself what this person may have been, what their life was like before it so violently came to an end; I try, according to the state of the body, to imagine their final moments, the manner of their death, and from there, as my imagination lets itself be carried away, I dream of what their thoughts

might have been, their fear, their pain, their refusal of the incomprehensible as the instant drew near, no longer able to be put off, that would dispossess them forever of themselves. Yet it's no different from when I look at a photograph of a dead body: as I scrutinize it, I carry out the same mental operations, it's the same thoughts, the same images that come to me. Thus the corpse is never entirely there, is never fully real: at once a material object that the mind objectifies in order to chase it far away, and an image it greedily seizes hold of. Blanchot again: 'What we call mortal remains escapes ordinary categories: something is there in front of us, which is not the living person, or an ordinary reality, or the same as the person who had been alive, or someone else, or something else. What is there, in the absolute calm of that which has found its place, nonetheless does not actualize the truth of being fully here.'[38]

72. Back in Kyiv, we finally went to Bucha, along with other towns in Kyiv *oblast*. We spent a lot of time there. It was like in Babyn Yar: apart from the ruins, there wasn't much to see, almost no remaining trace of the countless killings. The bodies had been buried, the abandoned dogs spayed and adopted, the destroyed tanks sent to the scrapyard, the infrastructure repaired, the streets cleaned, the potholes filled in, the street signs replaced. One month later, everything was already underground, hidden, on the way to erasure. Folded back under a normality that could nonetheless not be any such thing.

73. Already the authorities were talking about monuments. In Kyiv, on the square in front of St. Michael's monastery, they had placed a collection of Russian tanks to commemorate the battle for the capital, and it was immediately extremely popular. Apart from the

smartphones and the selfies, the spectacle was the same as the one described by John Steinbeck after his return from Moscow in 1947:

> On Sunday we went to the war trophy display.... And walking among the weapons were soldiers with their children and their wives, explaining these things professionally. The children looked with wonder at the equipment their fathers had helped to capture.[39]

Capa, who accompanied him, took many photos of these trophies, and published in their book the picture of a heavy 'Elefant' tank destroyer, with the inscription BRONIA 200MM ('200 mm armour') painted on it in Cyrillic. But Antoine wasn't with me the day I visited the exhibit at St. Michael's Square. In any case these tanks wouldn't have interested him any more than the monuments at Babyn Yar.

74. We went to the morgue in Bucha, but that didn't help us much. Behind the little building, six metal stretchers, each loaded with a large black or white plastic bag, were quietly warming up in the sun and filling the spring air with the sweetish odour of decomposition. I photographed a foot sticking out from a badly closed zipper, wearing a black sneaker covered in fine sand, the ankle's flesh marbled and red. Inside, in the hallway, a yellowish old man, his legs covered in bruises, lay waiting his turn on a stretcher; in the little dissection room, a doctor was finishing opening the thorax of a woman who had died of natural causes. A recently exhumed body, entirely green and looking almost melted, lay on a second table. 'A civilian killed by the Russian Nazis,' said Serhii, the young forensic pathologist who had welcomed us. He

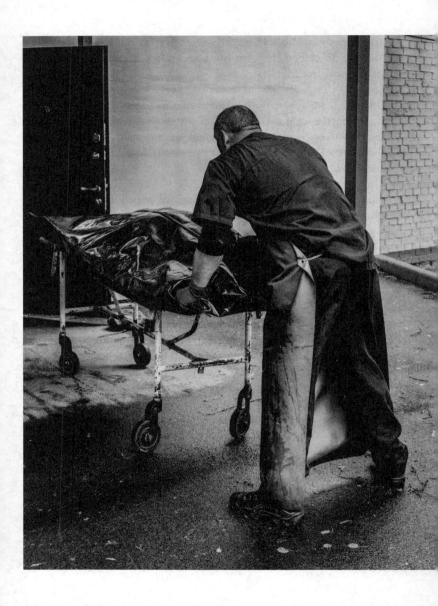

allowed Antoine to photograph it, provided the face wasn't visible. The dead man, ill-shaven, must have been in his fifties, and a large hole went through the centre of his putrefied chest; his eyes, wide open in the middle of a face deformed by rictus and decomposition, gave him an alarmed look, as if he were still overwhelmed with astonishment at what had happened to him the instant the piece of shrapnel had sliced into his back.

75. Serhii didn't want us to come back to the morgue. Running out of ideas, we went to visit the municipal cemetery. Fresh graves were lined up all along the main path, dug in the flowerbeds bordering the preexisting enclosures, each one with its little plaque bearing the name and dates of the person buried there along with large mandorla-shaped wreaths of plastic flowers, sometimes hiding a dish full of offerings, eggs or sweets. At the back was another enclosure for the unidentified dead, 76 graves when I returned to count them a few months later; on each one a cross had been placed, a very simple plastic wreath, and a little plaque with a hand-painted number along with, sometimes, code letters indicating where the corpse had come from: *Obl* (*Oblast*), *B-Ts* (Bila Tserkva), *Bo-a* (Borodianka). Beyond lay dozens of empty graves, beside which was parked an ambulance with a sign reading GRUZ 200, 'Cargo 200', the Soviet military code, now common slang, for the transport of dead bodies (the wounded are '300'). Rather loud music was pouring from the open window and I walked over. The vehicle hid two gravediggers with shaved heads, heavyset but muscular, their bare, tattooed chests tanned down to the white line of their hips; they were exchanging bawdy, idiotic jokes as they piled earth up on a fresh grave. I greeted them and they put down their shovels and introduced themselves.

The one named Serhii Matiuk shot me a wily look and said calmly, 'All the questions come to us. And you know why? Because these bodies, we're the ones who collected and buried them.' 'All the ones you saw over there,' his comrade Vladyslav Minchenko went on, 'they come from behind the church.' When the city was liberated, a colossal mass grave, with over 240 bodies inside, had been discovered behind the pretty little St. Andrew's Church in the heart of Bucha: it had been dug by these two men, who during the occupation had collected the bodies in the streets. 'We buried a lot, along with Artiom Mykhailov too. The Russians had men based here, at the cemetery, who were shooting at Kyiv and Irpin. They wouldn't let anyone get close. That's why we put them behind the church.' While Matiuk was telling his story, Minchenko had gone back to work and was methodically finishing the grave, carefully boring with the handle of his shovel three holes in the mound of sand to plant some plastic flowers in them. 'Our humour doesn't bother you, does it?' he asked as he worked. 'You see, we joke a lot.'

THE SURVEYORS

76. This was the strange thing: like Babyn Yar in 1941, Bucha is an outlying suburb of Kyiv, a peripheral zone, far from the centre, from the places of power, from the gazes that could matter. It always happens in the suburbs. This time, the capital itself hadn't been occupied, but its integrity had been threatened, and on the margins the wounds remained open. There may not have been much left in the way of visible traces, but in people's memories, the wounds had not healed. Scattered, individual,

86

completely random damage, dictated by chance and topography. So it was the latter we had to rely on: survey, photograph and take note of the insignificant as well as the essential.

77. The *New York Times* had published an initial map of the killings, and I chose a path through the town somewhat at random, according to the concentration of bodies found.[40] With the map printed out and folded as a viaticum in my pocket, I came one morning to park our car in the centre of the small town, on Vokzalna Street where it crosses the railroad tracks, looping a bit to skirt round the long elevated platform of the train station before plunging straight down towards Irpin, farther to the south. The crossing led, on this side, to a roundabout adorned, on top of a pole, with large steel snowflakes, lamps probably. Below the embankment of the station were bus shelters with wooden benches turned grey with age; their metal roofs and blue posts, covered with superimposed layers of tattered posters, were pockmarked with the impacts of bullets. On the other side of the roundabout stood a long white building with a blue roof and three to four floors, full of various shops; behind it, well back from the street, to the left as you look towards Irpin, rose two lines of new apartment buildings with traces of artillery strikes and some burned apartments; the last two, the ones furthest to the south, were unfinished, with bare bricks and gaping windows, dominated by a tall green crane, its broken shaft hanging down lamentably, held up by cement counterweights twisted almost horizontally. A blue and white suburban train was gently braking at the platform, cars were circulating in both directions around the roundabout, a municipal worker was cleaning his orange truck, some people, sheltering from the bright

spring sun, were waiting for their *marshrut*, a kind of local minibus, a woman was shouting into her phone that she couldn't bear it anymore.

78. After the APB supermarket on the right corner of the street, the Vokzalna was lined with old private houses, nestled among gardens and orchards behind variegated fences. This is what's called Bucha's *pryvatnyy sektor*, the 'private sector'. The very first house after the roundabout, No. 76, was on the left side; the ensuing numbers, towards Irpin, went by descending order, evens to the left, odds to the right. In the morning, as the sun slowly rose towards the station, it was the odd side of the street, lined every few metres with tall linden trees, that offered the most shade; the trees opposite, much smaller, seemed recently planted. Cars passed, a few trucks as well; the trees and electrical poles were covered with missing-pet signs – cats, dogs, even an Amazonian parrot, that had disappeared during the occupation. A Ukrainian soldier, Yehor Firsov, recently described his experience at the liberation of Bucha:

> I remember that strange feeling of walking along an empty street – it's broad daylight and not a single soul in sight. But suddenly there's a movement: The gate shakes. It's the wind, you think, but then you open it – and there stands a dog or a cat. You reach down to stroke it and ask, 'Hey, how're you doing?'... In one yard, we find the corpses of four people and a pitbull. Nearby lies a haggard German Shepherd, still alive. It has stayed with its owners, guarding their decomposing bodies and refusing to leave, even though we can tell they have been dead for some time. It won't abandon those who once gave it their love.[41]

The house at No. 76, like the ones following, old but quaint, appeared from the outside relatively unharmed. The one at No. 64 was for sale, with a garden of twenty *sotok*, 2,000 square metres. I called the number posted to ask the price: '80,000,' a woman replied. 'Hryvnias?' 'Why hryvnias? Dollars!' The one opposite, at No. 57, housed a shop for gates, roller shutters, wrought iron and awnings, along with a tyre repair shop with a separate sign. Then suddenly came No. 60 and the first signs of destruction: broken windows, a corrugated fibreglass roof almost completely blown off, exposing the framework's wooden beams.

POGREB

79. An older gentleman was bustling about in the yard of the neighbouring house, at No. 58. His house too was damaged, but far less than his neighbour's. I greeted him and he invited us in, introducing us to his nephew Vyacheslav, who had come to help him with the repairs. His name was Volodymyr Ivanovych Shepitko.[42] During the occupation, some Russian soldiers had moved into his house, positioning a high-calibre mortar in the back garden to bomb Irpin. The inside of the house was in chaos, everything had been overturned, ravaged, broken, soiled, all the valuable objects had been looted. When the town fell in early March, Volodymyr Ivanovych and his wife had first taken refuge in their *pogreb*, the underground shelter in the back of the garden used to store preserves and potatoes. But when a Russian tank had crashed through the fence behind their house to park in the garden, they had decamped to the basement of the nearby school. Volodymyr Ivanovych had tried to go back one day to

find some food, but he had fallen upon Russian soldiers camping in the house; they started insulting him, inveighing against 'Ukrainian fascists', and tried to take his phone; his dog's furious barking made them retreat, and they let him go. On 12 March, he and his wife were evacuated by the Red Cross. During his absence, according to neighbours who had stayed, the soldiers staying at his house brought young women there, and when he returned he had found many used condoms and empty bottles of alcohol in the shambles they had left behind, as well as two necklaces, cheap costume jewellery, still hanging from a rusty pole in the garden. There was also a dead woman in the *pogreb*. It was Vyacheslav who had found the corpse, on 7 April when he had returned to inspect the house after the liberation of the city. 'She was naked, on her back, her head blown open, her legs and belly slashed with a knife. She was wearing nothing but a *pol-shuba* [a short fur coat] and she was looking up. They kept her like a plaything, and when they left they put three bullets into her face.' The police had found two of them, and Viacheslav had found the third one a little later, a long thin bullet that I turned over in my fingers, 5.45 mm. I'd already seen a photo of this woman in the *New York Times*, her body half-wrapped in the *pol-shuba* lying face down on a blanket in front of the *pogreb's* brick building, an investigator in civilian clothes with latex gloves delicately covering her with a patterned blanket.[43] Inside the little building, a trap door opened onto a dark space into which a metal ladder disappeared almost straight down. I lit up the interior with a flashlight and carefully descended. The *pogreb* was scarcely two metres wide, and I let my flashlight's beam rove over the brick walls, the wooden debris, the little shelf for the jars of berries and marinated tomatoes. There was nothing else to see, aside from a

little puddle of rotten matter swarming with maggots in the middle of the clay floor: squatting down to examine it up close, I couldn't tell if it was the remains of foodstuffs or of the poor girl. I forced myself to stay there for a moment, letting the film of events flicker in the darkness, the troopers coming and going between their mortar and the ransacked house, drinking, getting bored, bringing girls back and raping them, then deciding to keep one. I also tried to imagine the thoughts of this young woman during those endless days in this freezing *pogreb*, her terror, her pain, her anguish. But it was impossible. My thinking resisted, and just like at the bottom of the Repyakhiv Yar, that which it was capable of and the experience of this woman remained separated by a thin partition, flexible and always as if about to break but resisting everything, a wall you never go through but beyond which you find yourself one day without having crossed it, like the one that isolates the living from the dead.

80. Many months later, I saw a photograph of the corpse of this young woman as Vyacheslav had found her. The image had been taken on 8 April by Florent Marcie, a French photographer, just before the investigators lifted the body out of the *pogreb* with the blue rope you can see next to her head in the photo taken by Daniel Berehulak for the *New York Times*. It was published in October in *Paris-Match*, with an investigative report by the friend who showed me the article, Patrick Chauvel.[44] Let us look at it. The body, naked under the *pol-shuba*, rests half-seated on stacked planks up against the metal ladder, its head leaning on its right shoulder, right leg outstretched, left leg bent outwards. Part of the face, the breast showing through the *shuba*, and the right leg, as well as the striped blanket pushed back next to her, are covered in

white mould, and the right leg also bears the red marks of wounds, just below the groin. A demijohn of water wrapped in plastic rests on the ground, a red bucket full of objects on a wooden chair appears at the edge of the image; one's gaze, if it lingers, might also notice a green sack of potatoes, another polyester flowered blanket and a striped one, a burgundy red cushion, a blue plastic clog hanging from the right foot.

81. The Bucha prosecutor opened a criminal investigation into this woman's death under file number 675. She seems to have been executed by a soldier standing above the open trap door, who fired the three bullets in one blast through the opening. The corpse was sent for an autopsy to the morgue in Vyshehorod; the state of the body made it impossible to prove rape, but it's a reasonable supposition. The law forbids the prosecutor from disclosing her name; Chauvel identifies her as Oksana S.; the *New York Times* reporter, who met her parents, finally named her.[45] She was called Oksana Sulyma. She had grown up in Bucha, then after her divorce had moved to Kyiv with her daughter to be closer to her parents. She had worked for a while at the Ministry of Infrastructure, and had learned French during an exchange visit to France; Patrick Chauvel found on a social network a photo of her taken in Rouen. According to the *New York Times*, she returned to Bucha on 22 February to see some friends, and thus found herself trapped there (Vyacheslav thought she'd come back to see her grandmother). The last time her friends saw her was on 10 March, near Shevchenko Square. When she stopped answering the phone calls from her family, her mother, Larysa Sulyma, posted a message on Facebook, mentioning that her daughter was suffering from mental health issues that might have been exacerbated by the

situation: 'Her behaviour may show manifestations of anger, aggressivity or helplessness,' her post said. 'If anyone knows her whereabouts, please call us.' In reply, Larysa Sulyma anonymously received a photo showing Oksana all wrapped up at a Russian checkpoint, giving a sidelong, frightened glance to the woman examining her ID card; only the red painted thumbnail of the woman is visible. According to the police, she was killed on 17 March, one week after she disappeared; her papers were found near the railway tracks, far from No. 58 Vokzalna Street. At the time of her death, she was 34, and was the mother of a little five-year-old girl. The daughter now lives with her grandparents, who still have not been able to explain to her that her mother will never come back.[46]

82. In September, a few months after our first trip there, I returned to visit Volodymyr Ivanovych, alone, without Antoine. Oksana's parents had come to see him, and they had shared a drink together after examining the place where their daughter had died. The father was a retired military pilot, who told his host how in Afghanistan he skirted around the *kichlaky* assigned to him as targets to drop his bombs nearby, on the mountains. Volodymyr Ivanovych and his wife, since our last visit, had cleaned up, put things in order, sown and planted. The potatoes had already been gathered, it was a good year, for apples and grapes too. They still had to repair the second floor, which had been ravaged by the blast that had destroyed the house next door. They had also cleaned and disinfected the *pogreb*, in order to store the crates of potatoes there. The reserves from the previous year had of course been looted, and they hadn't been able to plant enough to get them through the winter, but they planned on buying what they lacked, along with half a pig or even a whole

pig to prepare preserves if their shared pension of 6,500 hryvnias per month, 140 pounds at the current exchange rate, allowed. The Russian ammunition crates we'd seen in May scattered across the field behind the house were now neatly piled up near the *pogreb* and partly cut up with a chainsaw, to save on heating gas. The apples weighing down the branches were still green; in one corner lay a gutted safe, from which all their daughter's savings had disappeared, over 8,500 pounds in Turkish lira, hryvnias, dollars and gold. The *pol-shuba* going mouldy on Oksana's corpse had also belonged to this daughter who, having married a Turkish man, was living in Ankara and had just given birth to her first child. Volodymyr Ivanovych was not from Bucha: he was born in 1955 in Lviv, where his parents had been sent after the war to occupy one of the apartments left empty by the Nazi extermination of the Jews and the Soviet deportation of the Poles. When their contract expired, they had returned home to Vinnytsia *oblast*, and he had grown up there before leaving for Kyiv to study and then work as a hydraulic engineer. Not long before the fall of the USSR, around 1987, his parents had bought this house in Bucha, to be closer to their children, and he had come to live here after their death.

83. The neighbour on Volodymyr Ivanovych's right, at No. 56, was also repairing his house. This man, Anatolii, had not been so lucky, his house was badly damaged: behind the gate rose a mound of rubble, and the entire outer wall of the house had had to be demolished, exposing the wooden beams of the inner wall. When we came the first time, in May, Antoine had photographed Lilia, Anatolii's wife, from behind in a print dressing gown and with pink flip-flops, standing in front of the ruins of this brick wall, white with yellow decorative elements, and of the red

decorative woodwork of the terrace at the entrance, mangled by the explosion. The shell had fallen in front of the window, and inside, everything – the washing machine, the radiators, the lilac- and pastel-purple floral wallpaper – was shattered, riddled by the spray of shrapnel. But the couple had already cleaned everything, and gathered and piled up the debris. Anatolii was limping, a car accident in 1986 which had left him paralyzed in his entire right side, but even so, back in May, he had taken us into the field behind his house to show us the placement of the Russian mortar, the half-broken ammunition crates, the caved-in fence and the garden churned up by the armoured vehicle's intrusion. When they pulled out, the Russians had left a pipe stuck in the ground with little explosives, to make people think the mortar was still there, they'd had to call in the sappers to check and secure everything. Beyond the field, the apartment building under construction rose against the pale sky, the broken shaft of the crane dangling next to it. 'There was a Ukrainian flag up there,' Anatolii said, laughing. 'The Russians wouldn't stop shooting at it to take it down. They got the crane but the flag stayed, it drove them crazy.' In September, he too had harvested his potatoes, and was still waiting for the tomatoes, cucumbers, apples and raspberries. Near the gate stood a fine plum tree, and he picked one of the fruits to offer it to me. I ate it in the street after saying goodbye. It was succulent.

84. In May, then, we set off again for Irpin, along fences pierced with gunfire and houses in various states of damage. After No. 48, there was a little intersection leading on the left to the school No. 3 where so many neighbouring residents had taken refuge in early March. On the 7th, a couple had tried to leave, but they had quickly caught a

volley of gunfire, the husband had been killed on the spot and the wife wounded. Volodymyr Ivanovych had helped bring her back, then taken her to the hospital loaded onto a stroller. She had survived and had probably been evacuated on the same day as they were, on the 12th, when the Russians had opened for a few hours a 'green corridor' for civilians. The school was a long pale brick building with a purple roof, separated from the street by an iron gate; the only thing out of the ordinary was the plastic sheeting covering the windows.

SPARE PARTS

85. Immediately beyond the little intersection, the destruction became much worse. Even the trees had been mutilated, cut, torn up. Only a little bus stop, in yellow-painted metal with green seats too high for feet to touch the ground, had remained unharmed; a hand-written sign on a sheet of white paper, stuck on with packing tape, gave the schedule for the *marshrut* 422 Bucha-Kyiv, from 6.30 a.m. to 8 p.m. weekdays, and from 7 a.m. to 10 p.m. weekends, but less frequently. Opposite the bus stop, high up, a little sign was still attempting to attract drivers to the ATB supermarket, the one at the top of the street near the train station. Past that, the brick houses were completely devastated, burned or collapsed. The fences had disappeared along with the house numbers. A carbonized car was still nestled in the rubble at the entrance to one house; the rusted metal roofs were draped over the ruins like wet blankets. Further on, a melted van seemed curled onto itself; a piece of sheet metal, rattled by the wind, was clanking without any rhythm; the linden trees opposite were still standing, scarified by the explosions

that had laid waste to this unlucky section of the street. On 27 February, at around 7 a.m., as the Russian forces, thinking they wouldn't meet any resistance, were entering Bucha from Hostomel, Ukrainian artillery had annihilated at this spot one of their armoured columns as it was heading down towards Irpin. The Russian disaster was made public a few hours later when a video filmed by a local resident was posted online. Accompanied by an incessant stream of invective emitted by the man holding the phone as he posthumously curses the soldiers of the pulverized column, the camera, moving from the crossroads at the school almost up to the next intersection, examines one after the other the smoking wrecks, often still marked with a white V, of various BMDs, BTRs and other combat vehicles or tanker trucks scattered along the street, embedded in each other or sometimes even over each other, knocked over, overturned by the power of the detonations. 'Pederasts, bitches, you came here, you fucking faggots, fuck!' the man rages in a furious, hoarse voice. 'Used condoms! They're spare parts [now], faggots, fuck. That's what's left of them, fuck.' The translation loses a great deal of the savour of the Russian language in which this Ukrainian man insults the dead. The video comes to an abrupt end when a soldier, who seems to be wearing the white armband of the Russians but must surely be a Ukrainian, seizes the phone and barks out 'No filming!'[47] At one point, the man filming interrupts his swearwords with the word '*Kadyrovtsi*', referring to the militia of Ramzan Kadyrov, the Chechen dictator, and the media did in fact repeat that this column was a unit of *Kadyrovtsi*, perhaps the same ones as those who were supposedly charged with liquidating President Zelenskyy before being wiped out by the Ukrainian special forces. But this seems to be an unfounded rumour. A

Chechen friend in exile has told me that it was a regular army unit, the 70th regiment of the 17th Separate Guards Motor Rifle Brigade based in Shali, in Chechnya, which recruits not just among Chechens but also among their neighbours in Dagestan, Ingushetia, Kabardino-Balkaria and elsewhere. The *New York Times*, however, claims they were elements of the 104th and 234th Airborne Assault Regiments, which the preponderance of BMDs – an armoured vehicle used solely by airborne troops – among the destroyed vehicles would seem to corroborate.[48] The burnt-out vehicles remained there during the entire occupation, quietly rusting in the March rains, and were still obstructing the street when the town was liberated in early April. Western media filled with impressive images of the rust-coloured metal monsters cluttering this road, examined curiously by Bucha residents bringing their children to contemplate the spectacle. A photo by Rodrigo Abd, of the Associated Press, shows a woman walking alone in the middle of the carcasses with a cardboard box under her arm, passing by the vestiges of the houses located between Nos. 31 and 23 on her right and, to her left, the twisted arbour of No. 32 Vokzalna Street.[49] But the army and the municipality then quickly cleaned things up. In May, when we visited, the street had already been given a new coat of asphalt, and ferns, fuchsia tulips and large green plants were flourishing in the gardens in the midst of this sea of ruins.

86. Antoine and I walked up and down this section of the street, looking for what could be noted down or photographed. The first house that was still standing, beyond the devastated ones, was the one at No. 22, with a shady front lawn under a beautiful vine-coloured arbour. But the one at No. 20, a little pale-green, cheerfully decorated

house, was also almost little more than a ruin; heaps of beams and pediments carved with decorative motifs, painted blue, were piled up in front on the pavement. Opposite, behind the lindens, people had been luckier, the houses, apart from the broken windows, seemed relatively unharmed; just before another stop of the 422, a little mattress shop stood out incongruously between two houses. Orange cones protected freshly-painted pedestrian crossings. I was still looking at all this when my daughter called me on WhatsApp, and I turned on the camera to show her a panorama of the ruins: 'Oh, that's so sad!' she exclaimed. At the stop, some people were waiting for the *marshrut*, cars and people on bikes were circulating, technicians in fluorescent orange vests were pushing equipment. Coming up from Irpin, the 422 jolted towards us in the midst of the stream of vehicles.

AT THE CROSSROADS

87. The intersection the 422 was crossing was the one at Yablunska Street. Here too, a lot of things had happened. To the right of the crossroads, the soldiers who had liberated Bucha had found four corpses of civilians scattered on the asphalt, the first curled up on himself at the corner, the second on his side next to a little backpack, the third, a woman in a blue jacket, her left leg almost torn off, lying on her back with her face hidden beneath a bicycle, the fourth a little further on, face to the ground and legs crossed. A fifth body, that of a bare-chested man, lay further down on Vokzalna, stretched out in front of a little white shop selling window frames made of metal or PVC. I had seen images of these people, as well as those of the dozens of photographers massed around them, and I tried

to picture the scene as I contemplated the peaceful street, the cars, the pedestrians, the large, faded, half-collapsing ads extolling the future apartment complex Kontinent Rai and a housing estate of *taunkhaus*, little brand-new 100 square metre cottages. But I was distracted by a man in his fifties who, hurtling suddenly across the intersection on an electric scooter, stumbled and flew into the bushes lining the fence under the posters, scratching his face but then promptly getting up before I could even take a step towards him, and setting back off towards Irpin on foot, pushing his machine. I crossed the street towards the place where he'd fallen. The fence that formed the southeast corner of the intersection, made of bare, old, grey planks, surrounded the garden of No. 8 Vokzalna Street, full of fine apple trees and young corn; a little old house made of yellow brick was visible through the slits in the fencing. The *New York Times* map indicated that two sisters had been killed here. I went over and knocked on the gate; no one came, so I knocked again, more loudly. A woman finally emerged from the house and without opening asked what I wanted. I explained through the gate. She half-opened it, eyed me up and down, and spat out: 'We're sick of talking to journalists,' closing it abruptly in my face even before I could articulate the words that came to my lips: 'I certainly understand you.'

88. It was discouraging, but we had to keep going. Across the street, Antoine was photographing some wilted flowers placed on the pavement on a cloth square decorated with traditional floral patterns, held down by little pebbles. Another completely wilted bouquet rested in front of a green fence on the little corner wall. They must have been placed there for one of the dead, but which one? The person was dear to someone, that was certain, for when I

returned to that spot in September there were still flowers there, relatively fresh this time, a bouquet of red, pink and purple carnations stuck in a plastic mineral-water bottle cut in half, right next to the same piece of cloth, soaking wet now and folded on the concrete ledge. Antoine and I examined the area, but there was no one nearby. A door without any number visible stood in the green fence on the Yablunska side. I hesitated to knock, then knocked. No one answered.

89. As the months went by, quite a few investigative reports, articles and documentaries were published trying to reconstruct what had happened at the intersection of Vokzalna and Yablunska Streets. The most detailed of these is a little film produced by the *New York Times*, which is based on a vast quantity of videos gathered by surveillance cameras and Ukrainian drones to which the paper had access.[50] On 5 March, elements of the 234th Airborne Assault Regiment, the same one that had suffered so much on Vokzalna on 27 February, deployed across Yablunska from an initial base set up to the west of the street two days earlier and proceeded towards Vokzalna, with the objective of establishing a new base just before the crossroads, a little bit to the North on Vodoprovidna Street. Having learned their lesson from their losses on the 27th, they advanced carefully, positioning snipers as well as two armoured vehicles a little way back from the crossroads, in front of No. 215 Yablunska Street. Ukrainian drones observed them. A senior officer arrives, with a radio man and a bodyguard. The armoured vehicles start shooting down Yablunska, towards the east. At 11 a.m., the first civilian victim appears on one of the videos, lying on the other side of the intersection in front of No. 221. It was a man on a bicycle, Volodymyr

Brovchenko, 68 years old. Around noon, the armoured vehicle fires again and strikes a small blue van very close to the first body, in front of a house under construction. The explosion kills all four passengers of the vehicle: the driver, Zhanna Kameneva, 37, a volunteer who was evacuating friends from Bucha; her neighbour Mariya Ilchuk, 69; Tamila Mishchenko, 52; and the latter's 14-year-old daughter, Anna. The charred remains of the four women were still lying in the van a month later when Ukrainian investigators found them.[51] But the shrapnel-riddled vehicle and Brovchenko's body had already been secretly photographed on the same day they died, at 12.04, by Viktor Shatylo, an inhabitant of the street hidden in his attic at No. 344. In another photo taken by Shatylo at 12.46, we see a sixth victim next to the burning van, Mykhailo Kovalenko, 61. At the crossroads, the Russian officer has reached the position of the armoured vehicles that are shooting and watches events unfold. At the same time, the drone shows a woman slowly heading up Vokzalna from Irpin on a bicycle she had borrowed in order to rejoin her husband. When she reached the intersection, this woman, Iryna Filkina, 52, gets off the bike and turns the corner, headed towards the Russians. As the commander moves away from the scene to head up Vodoprovidna, the second armoured vehicle opens fire, and Iryna Filkina is killed on the spot. The woman with the bicycle and the ripped-off leg, found on 3 April, is her. A *Reuters* photographer, Zohra Bensemra, took a closeup of her half-putrefied, mud-stained left hand. The nails were still perfectly painted: four fingers in a proud bright red, and the ring finger pale pink with an ace of spades drawn on. The beautician who had painted her nails just before her death, Anastasiya Subacheva, survived and is now living as a refugee in Vilnius.[52]

90. The murder of Filkina took place right in front of the beautiful three-storey house at No. 342 Yablunska Street which belonged to Volodymyr Abramov, a former Chernobyl liquidator; the house next door belonged to his daughter Iryna Abramova and her husband, Oleh Abramov.[53] Shortly after killing Filkina, the Russian forces began firing on Volodymyr's house, which caught fire. Oleh shouted that they were civilians, and begged the men beyond the fence to cease fire. Soldiers entered the yard and ordered them to come out with their hands in the air. In an interview given to *Reuters* around the time we first saw her house, Iryna Abramova described these soldiers as Chechens, with tan uniforms and nubuck boots, which would seem to indicate men returning from Syria;[54] the *New York Times*, however, identifies them as paratroopers from the 234th Regiment. One of the soldiers kept asking Iryna where 'the Nazis' were hiding: 'The soldiers accused us of killing people in Donbas,' Iryna told a Human Rights Watch investigator in April. 'They accused us of killing the Berkut [the riot police unit that killed dozens of protesters during the 2014 Maidan protests in Kyiv] in Maidan as well. They concluded that we were guilty and should be punished.'[55] While the soldier continued to interrogate Iryna, the other three ordered Volodymyr and Oleh to put out the fire, which was impossible, then led them to a corner of the yard. There, they forced Oleh to take his shirt off and made him go out into the street. Volodymyr begged them to let Oleh come back and help him fight the fire; then he heard Oleh shouting 'Don't hurt me,' just before a soldier came into the yard and said curtly, 'Oleh will not return.' Iryna rushed into the street: her husband had been executed with a bullet fired point-blank in his temple, and she rushed over to the body screaming: 'Kill me, kill me too!'[56]

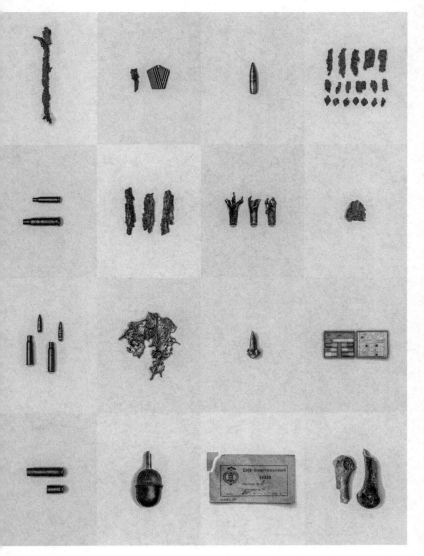

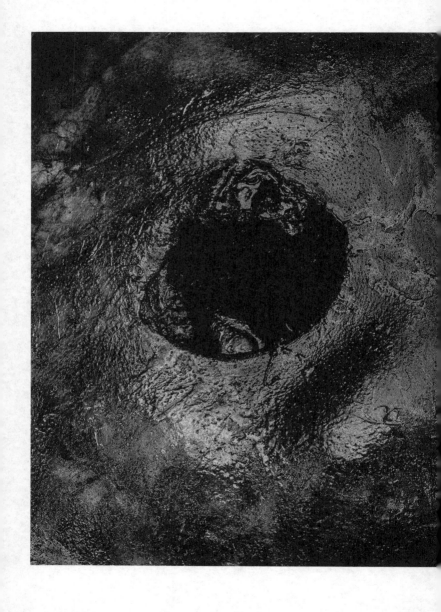

The soldiers didn't kill her. 'He was lying with his face down, and blood was pumping out of his left ear,' Iryna told Human Rights Watch. 'The right side of his face was missing, and brain tissue and blood were coming out of his wound.' A group of soldiers was standing no more than five metres away, calmly drinking water. 'They were watching the event as if they thought it was theatre.'[57] On her way out, she had also seen Filkina's corpse lying just in front of her gate, near a concrete post knocked over by the explosion. One of the soldiers asked Volodymyr: 'Is that your daughter?' 'Yes.' 'Take her and get out of here. *My tut zachistka sdelaem*, we're carrying out a cleansing operation here.'[58] The house was burning; nothing is left of it. Oleh's corpse, the shirtless man lying in front of the little white shop, also remained abandoned there; when the town was liberated, Iryna allowed herself to be filmed in front of her husband's body. At that time, the gate of her house still bore a plaque with the number and the old Soviet name for Yablunska Street, KIROVA STREET 342; I didn't see this plaque because someone had later moved it to the inside of the gate, as I noticed in Volodymyr's interview for the *New York Times*. The flowers that had so intrigued us must have been placed there for Oleh.

91. On that day, 5 March, Russian forces killed at least eight people in three hours at that crossroads.[59] Some of the other dead found there in April must have been killed later on. I only know that one of them was a 38-year-old construction worker named Dmytro Shkirenkov. He lived near Chernihiv with his Moldavian wife, Marta, and their ten-year-old son, and had come to Bucha in mid-February to work on one of the new construction sites. On 9 March, he had managed to call Marta: 'A lot of people are getting killed here. But I'm alive.' On 3 April,

Marta came across the first photographs of the corpses lying on Yablunska, and instantly recognized her husband.[60] I don't know who the other two men are.

APPLE TREE STREET

92. We turned right onto Yablunska. It looked a lot like Vokzalna, with rows of little brick or wooden houses, and, as its name indicates, gardens full of apple trees – Yablunya, in Ukrainian, means 'apple tree'. The fruit often hung over the fences, within easy reach, but unfortunately weren't ripe yet. Behind these houses, on both sides, rose little apartment buildings, and another, larger one, nine storeys high, its top two floors burned out. On the right side of the street, the first house was completely destroyed; the next, at No. 215, the one in front of which the two armoured vehicles responsible for the killings on 5 March had parked, looked very pretty behind its overturned green fence, its little garden furrowed with caterpillar treads of the vehicle that had manoeuvred there. Three girls with a large muzzled guard dog on a leash, chatting animatedly among themselves and on their phones, passed us and turned right onto Vodoprovidna Street, where the Russians had installed their second base. Another man on a scooter, wearing a cap and a parka, slid quietly through the traffic past us with much more dexterity than the first one. I paused for a moment to look at two white-and-ginger cats squabbling, the more aggressive one chasing the other under a car. They were playing in front of a long Soviet-era building, a five-storey *khrushchiovka* still bearing a plaque with KIROVA STREET 203A on it. The flowerbeds, full of multicoloured flowers, were impeccably maintained; beyond the

110

building, three children were playing on a swing hanging from a support painted long ago in yellow and blue; one of them, as I stood watching them, got very excited when he saw a large white sports car go by, gaudy and loud. Behind, at No. 203B, stood another *khrushchiovka*, built in the same style but even longer, with a little food shop named Flora in front of which had been found, his head in a pool of blood, another victim of the 5 March killings, still unidentified.[61] The bus stop on the other side of the street served the 423, which goes from Lisova to the Bucha train station. I didn't note down the schedule.

93. The street was straight and endless. In the yard of No. 203, just past the *khrushchiovka*, a dog was barking near an old beige Zhiguli still sporting a taxi light from another era. The houses here were pretty much intact, but some had suffered more than others. On the left side of the street, a mortar shell had struck the asphalt in front of No. 298, you could still see the rosette of the impact that had riddled the gate with shrapnel and apparently set fire to the attic; further on, at No. 153, the fence was similarly pockmarked, and some men were installing a new roof in the shade of a tall apple tree. Here too several people had been killed or gravely wounded. A man named Oleksandr Kovalevskyy had left his house to look for food and had been shot down in front of No. 163. Daniel Berehulak, the photographer for the *New York Times*, took a picture of his body, lying face-down fully stretched out, his feet crossed, his head, still with a woollen cap on, resting on a yellow and red plastic bag; behind him, three people are walking single file towards him, the first two leaning on wooden walking sticks, their mournful gazes fixed on the body.[62] The car of Mykhailo Hrabuliak, who was fleeing Bucha with his family, had been machine-gunned a

111

little further on, and his nine-year-old daughter-in-law, Oleksandra, had lost an arm.[63]

94. We reached the intersection with Zavodska Street, where a technician sitting on a stool next to a ladder leaning on an electric pole was repairing some thick cables. Zavodska turned to the right, and at the corner was a checkpoint with sandbags covered in hand-made camouflage netting. It looked abandoned, and Antoine photographed it. He shouldn't have. Two soldiers, weapons in hand, appeared and called out to us: 'Who are you? What are you doing? You can't take photos here.' Our army-issued press cards calmed them down a little, but they insisted on Antoine erasing his photos. 'Tell them we thought it was an old Russian checkpoint,' Antoine said. 'Not at all,' one of the soldiers replied when I translated. 'Can't you see?' Behind the checkpoint, in fact, the freshly painted building, which I had taken for a school without really paying attention, had military signs on it; further on, on Zavodska, some soldiers were emerging from a gate to see what was happening. Finally they let us go. Just after the wall around the base was a plaster statue painted a colour approximating bronze, a soldier from the Great Patriotic War with a rolled-up flag held upright next to him, set on a marble monument bearing in Ukrainian the names of five soldiers killed in October 1943 during the operations to liberate Bucha (from the Germans, that time): Kuzmenko I.K., Bondarev S.L., Plaksyn P.P., Polyakov P.Yu. and Potekha M.M., along with some unknown soldiers.

95. Next to this, on a bench, a man with a shovel and two buckets at his feet was smoking and, between coughing fits, raising a bottle of beer to lips almost invisible

beneath his bushy beard. The thought of beer appealed to us, so we headed over to the little shop behind the monument. While Antoine examined the brands lined up in the fridge, I chatted with the shopkeeper, Katia, a cheerful, outgoing woman with beauty spots and her hair in a bun. She had quite a few stories to tell. Her shop had obviously been looted, the alcohol especially. A tank had stopped one day and a guy had gotten out and asked politely for children's food; but the ones who came in for beer were less friendly: 'Open the door, if you don't want us to break your windows!' In the early days she and her family still tried to talk with the soldiers. Two armoured vehicles had parked in front of the monument to the dead, and Katia's mother had gone out and begged them: 'Please, guys, don't shoot at this monument, there are Russians buried under it, not just Ukrainians.' All in all, in the section of street between the checkpoint at the corner of Zavodska and the next one, things hadn't gone too badly, no one had been killed or even beaten. But beyond that, things had been much harsher, people had been imprisoned, tortured, killed. On 4 March, Katia had seen a large number of captives pushed on foot towards the Steklozavod, the glass factory further down Yablunska. On the same day, her uncle Konstantin had been hit by a bullet in the leg. That had happened further down, near where the Russians had captured the Territorial Defence volunteers they then massacred; a few young guys, eighteen or twenty, had shot at him just like that, for the fun of it. Katia and her family had kept him at home and taken care of him themselves, until the green corridor to Bilohorodka was open; they had then taken him to Boyarka to get medical care, and the rest of the family had gone abroad. They'd just recently come back to clean and reopen the shop. 'In two years you'll celebrate your

114

anniversary!' a girl waiting for a sandwich said. 'Yes, if we live till then,' Katia retorted. The beers paid for, Antoine went out to smoke, and I stayed to listen to the two women tell each other stories while the sandwich was warming on the grill. 'The Russians ordered people to wear light-coloured clothes. They threatened to shoot at anyone wearing dark jackets!' 'After three or four days they gave the order not to go out at all.' 'We were afraid, we stayed in the basement. There were nine of us with the children, and we really didn't have much food. In any case no one wanted to eat.'

96. After the shop, the street rose a little. At the top of the hillock a railway track crossed the road; cars slowed down and jolted across it. We turned left to take a look. Tall grass, an abandoned Russian meal ration, silence deepening as we moved away from the street. The tracks curved to the right, running alongside the wall of a factory made of prefabricated slabs with the logo of the 1980 Olympic Games printed on the concrete; then they disappeared beneath a large metal-and-wood barrier. None of this seemed to have been in service for years. Behind the wall of an enclosure, on the left, stood a rusty, dented water tank, along with a tall brick chimney with a shell hole right in the middle of it: some joker must have wanted to take a practice shot, for the hell of it. Beyond this second complex, police investigators had discovered a body in the grass of a vacant lot, a man in a thick green wadded jacket, probably a workman. But from where we were I couldn't see how to reach this lot. We turned around and out of sheer bloody-mindedness walked over to have a quick look at the other side of Yablunska. A little drainage canal flowing between two concrete walls ran alongside the tracks, which disappeared further on

among the trees to rejoin the main line. Somewhere over there, two other corpses had been found, their gloves still in their pockets despite the cold. The first had been executed with a bullet in the back of the head; the second had been decapitated, his burned head placed carefully at his feet. They were finally identified as two guards from the Steklozavod glass factory: Oleh Bilas, 55, and Vyacheslav Hordiichuk, 46, who had hidden when the Russians occupied their factory, before trying to flee three days later, in vain.[64]

NO. 144

97. We didn't go any further; we turned around again and went back to Yablunska. We were now reaching a four-storey brick building set back from the street on the left, and we entered the car park adorned with little trees and Soviet-era decorative panels, most of which, unfortunately, were missing their images. This was No. 144 Yablunska Street; the sign next to the front door indicated it belonged to the Agrobudpostach company. With our faces, shielded between our hands, pressed against the cracked windowpanes, we knocked for a long time. A man finally appeared in the deserted lobby and opened the door. I explained what we wanted. 'Tetiana Volodymyrovna!' he called, several times. A door opened in the back of the lobby and a woman in a white blouse came over. She confirmed that she had been there when the Russians arrived; there must have been over a hundred people, including thirty children, hidden there since 24 February in the underground shelters. 'Can we see?' I asked. Yes, we could see. At the foot of the stairs were two massive armoured doors, one at the foot of the stairs,

the other perpendicular to it. 'It's a fallout shelter from the 50s,' Tetiana Volodymyrovna proudly explained. I slowly nodded my head as I tapped my nails on the thick metal, then grasped the wheel in the middle to try to pull it towards me. It was too heavy, I barely managed to make it budge a few centimetres. 'It closes,' she said, 'but you need a lot of people.' Antoine was aiming his camera: 'Oh no!' she barked, suddenly severe. 'No photos.' Inside were several rooms held up by pillars, with chairs along the walls and rows of cots. 'On 3 March, they called us to tell us that the Rashists [a Ukrainian neologism formed from the words 'Russian' and 'fascist'] were coming with a tank. We closed the doors. They opened the first one and started knocking on the second, which we'd locked. "Open up!" they shouted, "open up." We were all sitting on the chairs, we didn't have any light and we were starting to lack oxygen. I put myself behind the door and shouted, "We're civilians, we don't have any weapons!" "Open up!" they kept shouting. Finally we opened it and begged them not to shoot. They didn't shoot. They were calm, they thought they'd won the war. "In two days our police will be here," they said. "And everything will return to order."'

98. The Russians, paratroopers from the 234th Regiment commanded by Lt.-Col. Artiom Gorodilov, had set up their headquarters in this building. They had kept the people in the bunker for several days before finally sending them back to their homes. Back in the greenish light of the entrance hall, Tetiana Volodymyrovna pointed to the tiled floor where, when they'd finally been let out, they saw several wounded Russian soldiers lying. 'Many wounded. They were shouting, there was blood everywhere.' Upstairs, arrows sprayed on the wall still pointed

117

to the various offices occupied by the Russians; in one of them, near a table with a pile of binders, some cables and a computer monitor on it, someone had scrawled across the wall in red UKRAINE! WHY DID YOU NEED NATO? None of the refugees from the basement had been able to see what had happened after the occupiers took control of the building; these events were pieced together by the Bucha prosecutor and by the press. When the Ukrainian artillery had decimated the armoured column going down Vokzalna on 27 February, the Russian forces had retreated from Bucha, and life had almost gone back to normal. When they came back, on 3 March, they were much more careful. Their military intelligence had observed the Ukrainian positions below the intersection of Vokzalna and Yablunska, and this time the soldiers entered Yablunska from several directions at once, quickly taking over the street and shooting at anything that moved. In a surveillance video, one can see a BMD-3 opening fire on a civilian car trying to flee; the car then crashes into a tree, instantly killing the driver, Volodymyr Ruchkovskyy; his partner, Olena, unharmed, tries to pull him from the vehicle which has caught fire, then gives up and runs away. The paratroopers advanced methodically in formation behind their armoured vehicles, destroying the security cameras and occupying the main buildings and factories. One of the cameras positioned opposite No. 144, which the Russians thought they'd broken, was still recording sound and a partial image, and on one video you can hear a soldier at 7.37 p.m. that day discussing with one of his comrades: 'Commander comes and wakes us up at three o'clock. He says, "Let's fucking go and fuck up all these civilians." And I'm thinking: "How do you do that? Kill them? Fuck that."'[65]

99. The next day, 4 March, the paratroopers pushed nine men into the car park full of tanks, trucks and soldiers. They were civilians, all local residents; eight of them were volunteers for the Territorial Defence (the *Terytoryalna Oborona*, or TO in Ukrainian), and the ninth was the owner of the house at No. 31 Yablunska Street, where their checkpoint stood. Seven other civilians, captured from houses around the base, were already in the car park. When the new captives arrived, they were in socks with their shirts pulled over their heads; the soldiers forced them to kneel down, and, according to the survivors, immediately shot one of them, Vitalii Karpenko, a 29-year-old construction worker. Two others, Andrii Verbovyy, 55, and Ivan Skyba, a 43-year-old worker, were brought inside the building. They were interrogated and violently beaten; a bucket was put over Skyba's head and his hands tied behind his back with tape. Then the Russians executed Verbovyy and took Skyba back into the car park. There, one of the nine men cracked and confessed they were members of the TO. The Russians started screaming: 'You wanted to burn us with Molotovs? We'll burn you alive!'[66] The man who had confessed was set apart[67] and the soldiers began debating about what to do with the others: 'Get rid of them,' one of them finally ruled, 'but not here, I don't want the bodies lying around.' The five remaining volunteers, as well as Valerii Kotenko, the owner of the house, a man with tousled hair and glasses who would have turned 54 before the end of the month, were taken by two soldiers into the little lane that runs to the left between the side of the building and the outer fence. The body of Andrii Matviichuk, 37, another TO volunteer who had spent the preceding days cycling from Irpin to Bucha to keep his chiefs informed about enemy movements, already lay there. His family

had lost contact with him the day before, on the evening of the 3rd, and he had probably been killed that night, or else in the morning before the others were brought there. The two soldiers opened fire. A bullet went through Ivan Skyba's abdomen and he played dead. It was cold, he could see the frosty breath of the soldiers and the dying men, he held his breath while the soldiers finished off the wounded who were still moving. The soldiers left. Skyba waited another quarter of an hour, until he couldn't hear their voices anymore, got up and fled. His four comrades lying there were named Anatolii Prykhidko, 38, Denys Rudenko, 37, Svyatoslav Turovskyy, 35, and Andrii Dvornikov, 31. Kotenko was also dead.[68]

100. At 4.57 p.m., a little over six hours after his execution, Vitalii Karpenko's phone was used to make a first call to Russia. The paratrooper calling, Vladimir Vasiliev, made seven other calls, then another two with Skyba's phone, which was also used by fifteen of his comrades to make thirty-eight calls to Russia.[69] Images filmed the next day by a Ukrainian drone show the corpses of the eight men scattered in the alley with two soldiers nearby.[70] The Russians let them quietly rot there during their entire stay, covered little by little by detritus thrown from the upstairs floors. The occupants of the building were not all paratroopers; in April, the Ukrainian investigators found the identity card of Corporal Korchunov, Konstantin Vladimirovich, a member of the Vitiaz unit of the *Rosgvardiya*, the Russian National Guard placed under the direct control of Vladimir Putin.[71] One of the houses opposite No. 144, described as the prettiest one of this section of the street – perhaps the unfinished house in white cinderblock with a garage, an arbour and a green metal roof at No. 75 – was occupied in mid-March by an

important commander whom locals nicknamed 'Long' because of his height. Every day, this officer would cross the street to work at No. 144, hiding his face if a resident was nearby and sending his bodyguards over to threaten him with death if he looked at him. After his arrival, things became even more violent here; even his bodyguards confessed to the local residents that they were afraid of him.[72]

101. Antoine and I went to look at the side of the building. There was nothing there; it was just a corner with a bare earth floor, barred windows, a door and a few steps. In the photos, the bodies lie scattered in the midst of plastic bottles and refuse, some sallow and half-naked; the hand of one of them, a man in a purple sweater, rests tenderly on the unshaven cheek of another. In September, when I went back there, their eight portraits, in blue and yellow frames, had been hung on the wall, with three plastic flowers and three little Ukrainian flags placed around them. This little memorial poses a chronological problem: whereas the *New York Times* journalists state, in their detailed reconstruction of the events, that all the men (apart from Matviichuk, who died before them, on the 3rd perhaps) were killed on the 4th, the plaque indicates that only Karpenko died on the 4th, and that his five comrades and Kotenko were killed on the 5th; Matviichuk supposedly died alone on the 30th. At the moment, I have no explanation for this contradiction. If, as Matviichuk's brother thinks – based mainly on the state of the body – he was kept prisoner and then killed later, the Russians, when they threw him there, must have taken away another corpse, for there were already eight there on 4 March, as witnesses confirm.[73]

123

102. We continued around the building, leaving the empty recess and its sad ghosts. Behind the building lay an immense warehouse, intact at the front and then at the very end burnt and collapsed. It housed several companies, including Debyut Sklad, dealing in construction materials and household items, and a company selling ceramic toilets. The guard amiably gave us access to the compound. The concrete lot had been cleared, vehicles were parked here and there, and in the middle lay a pile of debris of rockets, mortar shells and submunitions mingled with large-calibre bullets. The Russians had set up firing positions behind the warehouse, in front of a metal barrier and a half-collapsed concrete wall, behind which stretched a large green plain with a few trees and at the bottom the Bucha River, and beyond that the first buildings of Irpin. The guard had followed me and was looking along with me. 'In the winter, the trees were bare. Then they could see everything, when they shelled from here.' 'And the warehouse?' I asked as I turned around. He made a face, hovering between irony and bitterness: 'That was our guys, shelling in return.'

103. Afterwards, we continued on towards the Steklozavod factory. We walked slowly. On the way, we passed a house at No. 43 that had burned so strongly even its fencing had gone up, then at No. 39 a series of modern three-storey cottages, the first ones with their façades machine-gunned and their windows broken, the last ones intact. The word DETI, 'children', was still neatly painted in white on the gate of the next house, No. 37. On the left-hand side, behind a white concrete wall also bearing the Olympic Games logo, a large yard was being used to store sections of yellow cranes; just beyond it stood a yellow and orange two-storey apartment building, intact,

where a small shell had just left a hole in the facing, exposing the brick. Then we passed a shabby fence, almost completely hidden under the foliage of two large trees, which belonged to the house of poor Valerii Kotenko, at No. 31. It was here, just next to the bare metal gate, that the makeshift checkpoint of the volunteers massacred at No. 144 had been situated. No trace of it remained. In the photos you can see some sandbags piled up in an L shape with a little gap for shooting towards the eastern end of the street; it didn't even reach the shoulders of the men proudly posing in front of it. When the paratroopers of the 234th Regiment began their sweep of Yablunska Street at dawn on 3 March, the six volunteers who were posted at the checkpoint, and who had only a Kalashnikov and a hand grenade between them, decided to hide in Kotenko's house. Two other volunteers joined them, and they spent a tense night exchanging text messages with their loved ones. The next morning, realizing they were trapped, they sent their final words: 'Erase all my texts and get ready to leave,' Andrii Dvornikov wrote to his wife Yulia around 10.20 a.m. 'We can't get out. I'll call you when I call you. I love you.' One hour later, Russian soldiers entered the house and made the nine men come out. They forced them to remove their jackets and shoes, examined their bodies for military tattoos, and brought them to No. 144. A surveillance video shows them walking single-file, each with one hand on his head and the other holding the belt of the man in front. There is also a final video of these men, secretly taken by a neighbour from the windows of the red-roofed yellow house at No. 148, which shows them at the moment when they're taken into the car park of No. 144 and made to kneel down.[74] After that we know what happened.

125

104. At the Steklozavod too the Russian soldiers had killed many people. Investigators had found several booby-trapped bodies there, like that of Dmytro Chaplyhin, a twenty-year-old youth who since the start of the fighting had been staying with his grandmother and filming the explosions and the Russian soldiers near their house. When they searched the houses, the Russians found the videos and took him away. His grandmother went every day to the factory to beg the occupiers to let her Dmytro go. He was already dead, and his body was discovered on the gravel near a loading dock, attached to a wire connected to a mine, with his abdomen covered with bruises, his hands with cigarette burns, and a bullet in his chest.[75] But Antoine and I didn't have time to visit the Steklozavod, we had a meeting, which we set up earlier over a quick phone call as we were parking our car near the train station. We just looked at the entrance, a little building with broken bay windows. Opposite was No. 17, a large nine-storey Soviet apartment building.

105. The balconies were patched up haphazardly, many ceramic tiles were missing from the cladding, and a shell had directly struck the central stairwell, setting fire to six apartments on the top three floors but leaving the others unharmed, aside from broken windows. The young man we were going to meet lived there; fortunately for him, his apartment had been spared. I'd gotten his contact info from Mika Skoryk-Shkarivska, the deputy mayor of Bucha, and he had agreed to meet us without hesitation. He was waiting for us near the bus stop with an older woman I took for his mother but who was actually a friend he had met while working as a volunteer during the

occupation, and who had come to give him some moral support while he talked with us. He was wearing jeans, a sweatshirt and a cap, all grey; his angelic face was striking in its gentleness; he was just twenty years old, worked as a hairdresser, and was named Vadym Evdokymenko. After introducing ourselves we all started walking, leaving Yablunska and heading towards the railway tracks through a neighbourhood of quiet streets, little shops, peaceful neighbours. On the way, Vadym pointed out his primary school, the little local train station, the brick *khrushchiovki* from the 60s built for the Steklozavod factory workers, while talking to me rapidly but clearly about the people he knew who had been killed. 'I had a customer, she was twenty-three. They raped her before they killed her. She must have resisted, her father told me her hands were broken when he found her at the morgue.' He led us down a dirt path that wound between the tracks and a grassy sports field at the foot of the *khrushchiovki*. Finally, about ten minutes from his building, we reached a zone of little metal garages, the kind one sees all over the former Soviet Union. During their operation on 3 March, several units of the 234th Regiment had cut through here on their way towards Yablunska. Vadym stopped in front of a completely burnt-out garage, its collapsed roof riddled with holes. 'This is it. There were five people hidden here. When the Russians came, they refused to open the door. The Russians threw a grenade, the garage burned for a long time. My father was among them.' Halina, his friend, listened in silence. Vadym showed me photos on his smartphone that had allowed him to identify his father's remains: a piece of thigh in a scrap of blue jeans, an intact shoe, four warped credit cards, a half-burned identity card from the Antonov aviation factory on which the name, Oleksei Evdokymenko, was no longer visible

127

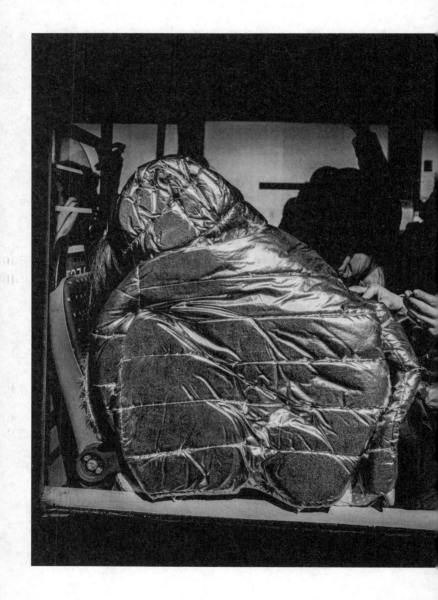

but on which the oval face of a balding man could still be made out, almost erased beneath plastic warped and made almost opaque by the fire. Little by little, in scraps, I managed to reconstruct the story. On the 3rd, unaware that the Russians had entered Bucha again, Oleksei had gone out to look for firewood near the station, and then had gone to his own garage, further down; at around 4 p.m., he had called his wife. Then the network was cut off and Vadym and his mother had no more news. Vadym had volunteered to work for humanitarian aid, in the hope he could find his father that way, but the Russians had sealed off the neighbourhood, and there was no way in. On the 8th, the occupiers finally opened a first 'green corridor', and Vadym and his mother decided to leave, crossing a field in front of Russian snipers to the evacuation buses. He thought his father must have been hiding somewhere, unable to communicate with them, and that they'd find him later on. On 10 March, when they were already in the western part of the country, a friend of his father had called him to tell him that his father had disappeared on the first day. 'He went out of his garage to get some cigarettes, and his friend never saw him again. He must have gotten stuck here and taken refuge with these people. I don't know who they were.'

106. At that moment a man with a deeply furrowed face came up to us. 'Who are you? What are you doing here?' Vadym explained and the man shook his head: 'Your father didn't die here, that's for sure.' Stunned, Vadym retorted: 'But the investigators told me it was here!' 'No, no. I've lived in this neighbourhood for forty years, I know everyone. I know what happened here better than the investigators. Come on, I'll show you something.' He led us along the alley of garages. At the end, just opposite the

raised railway, was nestled a little STO, a vehicle repair station; Anatolii, that was his name, worked here. Past the STO, the railway curved away into the distance; Anatolii guided us in this direction to show us a raised concrete slab beneath which they had found two bodies, a man and a woman. 'And look over there.' He pointed to a rectangular hole, its bottom matted in tatters of soaked cloth, an open grave under the trees just in front of the tracks. They had dug up a man there, a Russian soldier probably. Other bodies had also been found further on. Another mechanic walked up to us and started conversing with Anatolii in Ukrainian. I didn't understand everything but they obviously disagreed about the number of corpses and the place where they had been found. 'What about my father? Did you know him?' 'Aliosha? Of course.' 'So where did he die?' Anatolii hesitated, then made a motion with his head: 'Come. I'll show you.' He led us back down the alley, then turned off onto a path lined with heaps of detritus and metal bins. On the left, below the last *khrushchiovka*, stood two rows of little garages. One of them had also been burned. 'Your father died here. There was also a woman, two children and another man, a stranger. Over there, in front of the trashcans, they had parked a tank.' An overpowering burnt stench filled the little space, everything was black, charred, you could make out the carbonized remnants of a bike, a stove, a washing machine, some Christmas decorations scattered in the rubble. Antoine started taking photos, using the light from a flashlight. Vadym was all tensed up, at a loss, but he kept his calm. 'See? No one can agree about anything. I'll have to go back and see the investigators.' While he was talking outside with Anatolii, Antoine drew me into the garage again and focused the beam of his light on something on the ground, barely visible beneath the

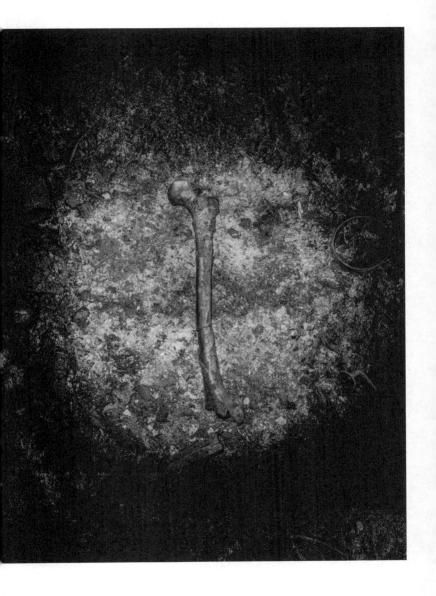

ashes. I crouched down and carefully dusted the ashes away, exposing several bones, a broken tibia, another intact one, pieces of smaller bones. I stood up and said, 'Don't show this to Vadym. I'll talk to him.' I left him to his work and went out. Vadym immediately turned to me: 'The police never wanted to tell me anything, actually. You understand? I started looking all by myself. I had to beg them at the morgue to get the photos.' Another man in blue overalls had come over. 'There were six bodies here. Five above, one below, in the pit. But it's possible that some of them were killed outside and then thrown inside.' A long discussion began between the two workers, soon joined by other onlookers, to decide who had been killed where, how, when. A man on a bicycle came up to us and stopped: 'Well I'd like to know what went on! This garage burned for three days. We would have opened it, but we'd have suffocated right away.' No one could agree on anything, they kept interrupting each other while trading horror stories about the neighbourhood, the ones who had died here and the ones who had been taken away and never seen again; they were trying to reconstruct the events, to establish a chronology, to reach a consensus, the voices were animated but calm, they kept switching between Russian and Ukrainian and I couldn't follow everything. '*Znachit tak bylo,*' one of them finally concluded. 'So that's how it was.'

107. The garages went downhill towards Yablunska. Just beyond lay a large pond, almost a little lake. We took our leave of Vadym and Halina and headed towards it. A long strip of vegetation, a section of dark green, separated the two greys, the pale grey of the sky and the dark, opaque grey of the pond. This was Bucha's former quarry, which had later been flooded; opposite stood some more private

132

houses; after the pond, the street veered right, crossed a wide road, and ended a little further on, in another outlying neighbourhood of small apartment buildings and houses. I was tired and didn't see much point in continuing. I walked over to the hillock overlooking the pond to smoke. Down below, two young blonde women, sitting on a floating dock over the water, were talking animatedly; one of them, hunched in a bright-red jacket, punctuated her sentences with huge belches. They didn't notice me and I listened to them while I smoked. Then I threw my butt away and went back towards Antoine, looking on my phone for a taxi app to go find our car back at the station.

ONE MORE LIST

108. The dead of Vokzalna and Yablunska Streets form only a fraction of the victims of Bucha; unlike Babyn Yar, it was the whole city, in April 2022, that had been transformed into a mass grave. According to the Ukrainian General Prosecutor, 637 of its residents were murdered during the month of Russian occupation, about 12% of the population who had stayed there (this number keeps going up as more bodies are discovered).[76] On Ivan Franko Street, an entire section of the neighbourhood was annihilated. The Shypilo family, Tetiana, Volodymyr and their 39-year-old son Andrii, had disappeared, along with their neighbour across the way, Oleh Yarmolenko, 47, and two other neighbours, Lidiya and Serhii Sydorenko, 62 and 65 respectively; finally, their six charred corpses, three of them with limbs cut off, were found in an empty lot before being identified by investigators from the French gendarmerie. In the same neighbourhood, two brothers, Viktor and Yurii Pavlenko,

64 and 62, were summarily executed; a man who was just passing by, Oleh Diyun, was found dead on a path near the railway; Volodymyr Sherednichenko, 26, who had made the mistake of taking a photo of the destroyed convoy on Vokzalna, was detained, tortured and then killed on 8 March by a gunshot in his ear. Elsewhere, near a supermarket, the body of Dmytro Bernastskyy, 59, was discovered with three bullets in his left leg, one in a lung, and one in his heart. Oleksandr Yeremich, 43, a volunteer for the TO, was taken out of his house by a Chechen soldier and executed by four bullets a few metres further on, behind a fence. The 32-year-old son of Lyudmyla Verhinska was killed by a bullet in his eye as he was taking out the rubbish. Vasyl Nedashkivskyy, 47, who went out in late March to walk his black Labrador, was made to kneel in the street, interrogated and executed. The body of Dmytro Fyakistava, who had gone out to look for bread, was found with several bullets in his back. Volodymyr Feoktistov, 50, was killed on 4 March when he went to ask a neighbour for bread. Roman Havryliuk, 43, and his brother-in-law Serhii Dukhlii, 46, were shot on 12 March in their garden in front of Iryna, Roman's sister and Serhii's wife; when the city was liberated, a third body, never identified, lay next to them. On the evening of 27 March, in one of the nice neighbourhoods in the northern part of Bucha, a drunk soldier accosted Oleksander Kryvenko, 75, and, in order to find something to drink, forced him to take him to the house of a pro-Russian local politician, Oleksandr Rzhavskyy, 63; Rzhavskyy offered him some wine, but the soldier, a certain Aleksey, opened fire on the two men at the dining table before throwing a grenade and wounding himself in the leg. Ivan Monastyrskyy, 43, lived in one of the apartment buildings above Yablunska and had ended up

alone at home when his wife and seven-year-old daughter remained stuck in the bunker of the Agrobudpostach building at No. 144; all we know is that he left his apartment on 7 March; his corpse was found in a field below, where a Russian unit had set up camp. Anna Noha, 36, who had stayed in Bucha to help her parents feed their eleven dogs and to collect abandoned cats, was arrested on the evening of 18 March with her friends Vladyslav and Yurii, with whom she was staying, when they were taking out the rubbish together; a week later, Vladyslav's mother finally found their three bodies in the garden of an abandoned house, each with a bullet in the eye; Anna had been so severely beaten that her face was unrecognizable. In a retirement home, six elderly people whose names I don't know died of hunger, huddled together in one room. Their neighbour, Lyudmyla Shchehlova, 81, a retired epidemiologist, was found hanging from one of her cherry trees; the police ruled it suicide, but the relatives of Shchehlova, who was very religious, assert that it's impossible. On 5 March, *Tiotya* Lyuba, an old woman, was killed on her doorstep by a sniper; her younger sister Nina, who was mentally impaired, was found dead in their kitchen, of unknown causes. On the same day as Lyuba, a sniper shot the son of Ivan X., who had gone out with him for a walk on Yablunska. Tetiana Sishkar, 46, was also killed by a sniper, on 24 March while she was going to visit her elderly parents with her husband and daughter. In the basement of a children's holiday camp at the northernmost end of Vokzalna Street, which was occupied and transformed into a military base by the Russians, five humanitarian volunteers, Serhii Mateshko, Dmytro Shulmeister, Volodymyr Boychenko, Valerii Prudko and Viktor Prudko, were discovered face-down with their hands bound with zip-tie handcuffs and traces

of torture on their bodies, executed by bullets fired point-blank to the back or the head. On 18 March, a man named Volodymyr Lisovskyy, hidden in the attic of his house on Nazarii Yaremchuk Street, filmed some Russian soldiers surrounding three men, Dmytro Shkirenkov, Maksym Kireev and Oleksandr Chumak, near a row of palettes of construction material in front of the Idilika Home Taunkhausi complex; one of them was already dead, while the other two, bound and kneeling, were executed immediately after; the same soldiers also killed an unlucky witness of their murders, a passerby who still hasn't been identified.[77]

A QUIET VILLAGE

109. I could stop here, but I will not stop here. You will say: You could go on forever. But I won't go on forever either. Just widen the focus a little. A few days after our walk in Bucha, Antoine and I went to another village in the Kyiv *oblast*, about fifty kilometres west of the city. We took the A40 motorway, the one that heads straight to Zhytomyr, along which so many people were killed while trying to flee the invasion, entire families machine-gunned or crushed in their cars. Here too the burnt-out wrecks had been cleared away, many vehicles were travelling in both directions, only the ruined gas stations bore witness to the violence visited on this road. The village lay a little to the south of the motorway, after an exit with no number.

110. The name of this little village is Motyzhyn. We were looking for a man named Oleh Bondarenko. A colleague at the *Guardian* had written an article about him,[78] and had told me we could find him at the rehab centre

for alcoholics and drug addicts. We were lucky, he was there, he could just as easily not have been. The centre was at the southeastern end of the village, at the end of a cracked road full of potholes and lined with little houses similar to those in Bucha's private sector. A gate, a yard with some gravel and grass, a pond on the left lined with a few trees, a rather large building with steps leading up to it, some outbuildings in the back: I didn't take any notes about what the place looked like, or any photos, and I don't remember much more. Bondarenko welcomed us on the front steps, a large, strapping man in a T-shirt and beige pants, with a crew cut and a wide, mischievous smile. Later, while examining a photo of him, I saw with surprise that he was missing the thumb of his left hand: I had no memory of this mutilation, and my notes don't mention it. When he understood why we came, he started by refusing: 'I've talked about all that enough already.' By chance, his daughter Rita was with him on that day, and she insisted he tell us his story. We insisted also, gently. He finally gave in and invited us into his office. Rita, a thirteen-year-old girl who looked at least fifteen, perched on a table to listen. I put my smartphone on the table and turned on the voice recorder. I also took notes.

111. Oleh Bondarenko is a minister of a charismatic Protestant congregation, the Reformed Pentecostalists; yes, there are Protestants in Ukraine, no one talks about it much and I didn't know. He had found God in prison, where he had collected the handmade tattoos visible on his arms, the word SLON ('elephant'), a flower and a cross composed of dots; if there are others, I didn't see them. For some years, he had been one of the people in charge of this rehabilitation centre founded by his church. On 24 February, he had come in for his shift, which usually lasts

two days, and had decided to stay. There were twenty-two people in all, but five chose to leave right away. On the 27th, Russian forces entered the village. They sealed off the zone and installed artillery positions in a little forest between Motyzhyn and Severynivka, to the northeast. They didn't occupy the village itself, but drove through every day to ferry ammunition to their guns. To maintain a certain level of terror, they sometimes fired randomly into houses. But they completely ignored the rehabilitation centre, Bondarenko and his flock always hid when they went by, they probably took it for an abandoned school. The centre had stocks of food, by chance they'd received a delivery just before the 24th, and it also had its own farm with chickens and pigs, enough not only for everyone there but also to help people in the village, cut off from all other provisions. Nevertheless, the patients left the centre one by one, it was only seven kilometres across the fields to reach the next village, which was still held by Ukrainian forces. By the end of March, there were only nine of them left.

112. It was at that moment, a few days before the Russian retreat, that things went sour. On 22 March, maybe, the date isn't clear, a Ukrainian unit ambushed one of the ammunition convoys passing through Motyzhyn. Furious, the Russians returned with two tanks, fired at cars and houses and killed several people. The *zachitstka*, the cleansing operation, was conducted by two military intelligence platoons that included mercenaries from the Wagner group, a private security company owned by a man close to Putin, famous for its brutality in Syria, the Central African Republic and Mali. With a drone, they spotted seven Ukrainian intelligence commandos – the same ones that had attacked the convoy – crossing a field

towards an agricultural base, a kind of farm situated beyond the rehabilitation centre, on the other side of the pond. They tried to intercept them but the Ukrainians managed to take refuge in the farm and called their comrades in the neighbouring village for an artillery strike on their pursuers. The Russians had to withdraw and it was during these operations that they entered the rehabilitation centre and saw it was in fact inhabited. Their commander, a Wagner officer who used the call sign 'Kaluga', interrogated Bondarenko, convinced he was colluding with the Ukrainian commandos who had sought refuge in the farm. He was also looking for the owner of this farm, a certain Mykola Kurach whom Bondarenko calls Mykhailych, the familiar diminutive of his surname. Bondarenko calmly explained the centre's mission to him, and the reasons they'd stayed. But Kaluga didn't believe him. 'Not a single one of my words. And he said: "Tomorrow, I'll know where you come from, who you are, what you are, and why you stayed here."' The Russians searched the centre, swiped some food and trainers and left.

113. Bondarenko immediately called Mykhailych. A few days before, the Russians had fired a rocket at his farm, destroying the garage and his car, and Mykhailytch, taking fright, had decamped with his wife to the home of Olha Petrivna Sukhenko, the head of the village. 'I said to him: "Run, they're going to your place, if they catch you now you're fucked. I heard them: *We'll put him on a bottle or a bayonet*, they said."' Mykhailych immediately fled, in a car with his wife and daughter, braving the little road that runs parallel to the motorway to Yasnohorodka and from there to Bilohorodka; the Russians machine-gunned every other car, but they were lucky and got through. But

Olha Petrivna, her husband and her son were not so lucky. They had decided to leave with Mykhailych, and had all the more reason to do so as Olha Petrivna led the village's Territorial Defence, divided into two platoons, one commanded by her husband, Ihor Vasylovych, and the other by Mikhailych. But for some reason unknown to Bondarenko, they changed their minds and stayed. When the Russian commandos reached their house, they found a complete list of the seventy volunteers of the TO, which Olha Petrivna and her husband had unfortunately kept, and arrested them. A little later on, searching through the village leader's phone, they found a video that showed her son Oleksandr climbing up a pole to hang a Ukrainian flag that had been taken down by the Russians when they arrived. They came back two hours later to find Oleksandr and took him away as well. All three were killed that same day, in the forest near the artillery positions. Their agony lasted for hours.

PIPES

114. Someone, an informer from the village or perhaps one of the Sukhenkos under torture, denounced Bondarenko. The Wagner men returned to find him the next morning. This was Thursday 24 March. First they attacked the farm. 'Those idiots thought the Ukrainians were going to wait for them there!' Bondarenko, hidden in the hallway, listened to the barrage of gunfire, without really knowing who was shooting at what. Finally he risked a glance and saw two soldiers aiming at his centre with what looked like tubes. He ran to hide in an office to the rear while they opened fire on the front steps with grenade launchers and their Kalashnikovs. The centre's

patients started jumping out of the windows and ran towards the village. 'I stayed, there was a man with no legs there, I couldn't run away and leave him, so I waited, sitting in the staircase. A rifleman came in and started shooting at the walls, the mirrors, the toilets, like an idiot. I said to him: "Listen, we are two people here, civilians, we have no weapons." He told us to come out. I said, "We can't come out, he has no legs." "Well then you come out." I came out and their commander arrived. And then it began.' Kaluga had him tied to the railing of the front steps and they began beating him. Then they attached him to a quad bike that set off at top speed towards the farm; he ran and stumbled behind, he knew if he fell he'd be dragged on the road. At the farm, the soldiers had already looted the tractors, the vehicles, and the stores of fuel and had set fire to the rest. There, Bondarenko was tortured again. 'I was lying down, they placed an AK on my spinal column and pressed down with all their strength. "Imagine what would happen if I pulled the trigger," the guy said. They dislocated two discs, my back is still in bad shape.' They could have killed him there, but a soldier intervened to say that their superior wanted Bondarenko alive. They wrapped his head in a sweater and a T-shirt, tied his hands behind his back and threw him onto a Kamaz truck.

115. Bondarenko doesn't know where the Kamaz took him. When the truck stopped they threw him outside to leave him with a soldier while the others left, saying they'd come back to get him. He was still sitting there with this soldier, with his hands tied and his eyes blindfolded, when the Ukrainians started bombing their position with Grad rockets. 'The soldier shouts at me, "You want to live?" "I do," I say. "Then run!" "Where?" "Straight ahead!" He took my hands and pushed me, and we ran. A Grad had

just exploded, it had left a crater, he pushed me inside and also leaped in. The crater was still warm.' A little later, the commandos reappeared. They lifted Bondarenko into a trailer attached to the quad and took him to their base. There, the interrogation began again. Bondarenko was tied to a pillar and beaten; they fired gunshots next to his ears and between his legs. The man who was interrogating him, a 'GBshnik' he thinks, an FSB officer whom the others called Vitebsk, yelled, threatening him: 'Who are these Patriots?' 'I don't know any Patriots. I know Jesus, but not these Patriots.' The Russians had also arrested two volunteers who were bringing food to people in the village, a young man and his father-in-law, and when they searched their phones had found a reference to 'Patriots' in deleted texts. The two men, under torture, had confessed that they gave information to the Ukrainian forces. Vitebsk threatened to crush Bondarenko's legs, he was laid out in the yard, an armoured vehicle gathered speed and then stopped short just in front of his legs. 'I don't believe you,' Vitebsk shouted. 'Your rehab centre is a cover, you actually have a group that lives there.' Bondarenko knew that the Sukhenkos were already dead and he said to himself: I'm not going to get out of here alive. At one point, the Ukrainians started shelling again; the Russians rushed to hide, leaving him outside. 'Let your own kill you!' A mortar shell struck a nearby house, some flying shrapnel nicked his abdomen, not very deep. When it calmed down the Russians emerged: 'Look, you're still alive, it's just a scratch.' The interrogation resumed, Bondarenko continued his denials, Vitebsk went on not believing him. It was then that another man who was there intervened: 'Listen, what if he's really not guilty? Why kill him if he's just a priest?' Vitebsk went mad with rage: 'I'm going to the village, I'm taking the first three on the list, I'll shoot them in the legs, they'll tell me everything about him.' Leaving Bondarenko lying there, the commandos left to round up the men from the Territorial Defence.

116. In this base or torture centre of the Russian military intelligence there were also three young conscripts. They lived in a *pogreb*, cooked, cleaned and buried the corpses. The mortar attacks had resumed all around, and between two rounds of shelling these conscripts emerged from their *pogreb* and came to get Bondarenko. 'We're going to hide you, Pastor. But you can't see anything. If you see something, you won't leave here, one hundred percent. Otherwise there is a possibility. If they don't find anything on you, maybe they'll let you go.' It was these three young men who saved Bondarenko. They threw a parka over his shoulders, tied it around him with some adhesive tape, and placed him, head still covered and hands tied behind his back, in a concrete pipe built vertically into the ground, which they closed with a cast-iron cover. It was the afternoon. Bondarenko would spend forty-eight hours in this cistern, neither sitting nor standing but half-bent over, his head resting on a little plastic pipe that came out of the concrete, his body racked with pain and cold.

117. In the village, the Russians had once again been ambushed by the Ukrainian commandos, and had had to turn back without reaching their targets, the men from the TO named on the list found at Olha Sukhenko's house. That night it started to rain, and the water seeped in around the cast-iron cover on the pipe. One of the conscripts came out of the *pogreb* and threw a canvas tarp over the cover, holding it down with stones so the water wouldn't drown Bondarenko. He prayed, sang religious songs. In this way he spent the first night. The next day,

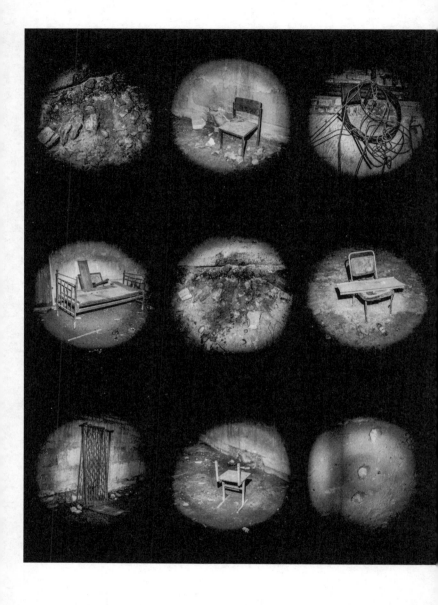

Friday the 25th, the Russians again attempted their *zach-istka* in the village. It isn't clear what happened, they were shot at again, but apparently it was by their own forces, or in any case that's what they thought when they returned to their base where Bondarenko, from his cistern, could hear them talking. One of their men had been wounded and he died there, emptied of his blood by an open artery. That only redoubled their rage. They finished off another man whom they'd already tortured and whom they'd been keeping in a ruined house next to the cistern, one of the two volunteers perhaps. He took about forty minutes to die: a relatively swift end, compared to what would follow. Between sessions, the Wagner men joked amongst themselves: 'It really is better here than in Syria.' 'We shouldn't have killed the girls, it would have been more fun.' They were talking about two women they'd murdered after raping them; the bodies of these victims have still not been found. Vitebsk was fuming: 'Here in Ukraine, I'll kill them all, women, children, men. The only thing in this Ukraine I feel sorry for are all the dogs and cats they abandoned.' From time to time, when the commandos left, the conscripts would come out to check that Bondarenko was still alive. He begged them to give him water, but they told him to wait: 'Be patient, Pastor. You don't have much time left like this. Be patient.'

118. On Saturday the 26th, the Wagnerites brought two other men to the base from the neighbouring village of Severynivka, an old grandfather and a younger man, his neighbour, who had come to help him feed his animals. When they had searched them, the Russians had found on the neighbour's phone a photo of a passing convoy, that was enough, and they set fire to the old man's house. At the base, there was another argument: 'Why did you

bring this old man? It's not his fault, the other guy was just visiting him. Where are we going to put him now?' Then they started torturing the man with the phone. They killed him slowly, methodically, shooting one bullet after another into his arms and legs, for an hour and a half. Bondarenko listened to him scream and that tortured him more than his own pain. Finally they fired a final bullet into the man's belly and threw him aside to let him die. Then they sat down to drink and eat: 'Oh, today there's mayonnaise with the salad, delicious,' Bondarenko heard. When they left after their meal, the man was still wheezing. The conscripts came to open the cistern and pulled Bondarenko out to throw in the dying man. When it was all over, a few days later, Bondarenko accompanied investigators from the SBU to the site. The man was still at the bottom of the cistern, sitting cross-legged, bare-chested, covered in blood, his bald head leaning on his shoulder. The SBU officers didn't want to touch the corpse, for fear it might be mined, and as they were waiting for the sappers Bondarenko took a photo. He showed it to me, I've kept a copy. But he still has in his head the animal-like screams of the dying man. 'Now it's OK, I'm calm, I'm getting over it. But without pills I can't sleep. The worst is the screams, when that guy's screams come back, the adrenaline rises, I shake. I can still hear him screaming.'

119. When the three conscripts pulled him out of the cistern, Bondarenko had lost all sensation in his arms and legs. They untied him and massaged him. But he still couldn't walk and one of them said: 'Let's get him out of here, otherwise they'll kill him.' They dragged him to a storehouse where there was already another old man, a certain *Dyed* Kolya who had come to the base to ask for

medicine. His daughter had been killed by a sniper, in circumstances that I don't know, and Kolya had begged the recruits not to bury her in the mass grave, but to dig a separate grave for her. There was a pile of wheat in the storehouse, spilled out of a plastic container gouged open by shrapnel, and the conscripts threw two parkas on it for Bondarenko to lie on. They came back half an hour later with a plastic bowl of hot fish soup, a loaf of bread and two bottles of water, asking *Dyed* Kolya to feed him. Shortly afterwards, they brought the other grandfather to the storehouse, the one who had been arrested with the man who was tortured to death, and then later on a fourth man, a local alcoholic who had gotten drunk and, losing his way, had walked straight into a Russian position. That night, Bondarenko started feeling a little better, regaining some sensation in his limbs. But the compressed nerves had frozen the elbow joint of his right arm; at the time I spoke to him, in May, almost two months later, he still hadn't fully recovered its use.

120. The conscripts, when they hid Bondarenko and the other three men in the storehouse, knew that their forces were about to withdraw from the zone, and had received the order to liquidate all the remaining prisoners. But they did not obey. They came to find old Kolya to show him the place where they had buried his daughter, as he'd asked them to do, and one of them said to Bondarenko: 'Pastor, God heard your prayers, we're leaving. You mustn't leave right away. The last to leave will be the snipers, and if they see you they'll kill you. Stay here at least two hours.' They went away, leaving the door open. It was Sunday the 27th. Things weren't over yet: the Ukrainian army started shelling positions in the nearby forest again, knocking down trees, destroying several artillery guns,

killing soldiers. Some shells landed right next to the storehouse, shrapnel whistled, the drunkard finally woke up, without realizing where he was. But none of the four men were hit. That same afternoon Rita and her mother, at home in Vyshniove, a suburb of Kyiv, received a phone call from an unknown number informing them that Oleh was alive. 'Every day, I pray for those guys who saved us, who showed the old man where they buried his daughter. They were normal guys. I hope they came home alive.'

THE LITTLE HOUSE

121. At the end of May, two weeks after our visit with Bondarenko, the Ukrainian prosecutors published the names and photographs of eight men suspected of being the authors of the crimes in Motyzhyn. Five were Russian soldiers, and three were Wagner mercenaries, one Russian and two Belarusians.[79] A few days later I called Bondarenko. He was doing well, his spinal column had recovered, and he was waiting for an operation on his right hand. He recognized two of the men from the published photos: 'Kaluga', the Wagner commander, and one of the Belarusians, Sergey Sazonov, the man who drove the quad bike. 'But I don't think they'll ever catch them alive.'

122. The Ukrainian forces entered Motyzhyn on Tuesday 29 March. Bondarenko, who could by then walk with some difficulty by leaning on a bicycle, guided them to the base and the place in the forest where the bodies of the Sukhenko family lay. He agreed without any hesitation to show us as well. We had to cross the village and then head east before turning north along a field. The Wagner

base was a little further on, in a property at the edge of the forest where the Russian forces had positioned their artillery. The gate was open, but no one answered when Bondarenko called; I suggested we go in, but he refused. 'Too many people have already come here. We have to ask the owner.' I looked at the forest, the hacked, burned pines, felled by the Ukrainian strikes, the collapsed remains of the large trenches dug into the sandy ground where the Russians had positioned their Grad rockets and howitzers. 'And the grave where they found Olha Petrivna and the others?' 'Come.' We left the car there to walk along the outer wall and turn left, onto a dirt path cutting straight through the plantation of pines. From there, we could see the inside of the property, where there stood a two-floor building made of white cinderblock, intact, and a completely devastated red brick house, of which only two chimneys and a few sections of blackened wall still rose to the sky. The terrain was separated from the path we were walking on by a sort of little canal or pond which surrounded it on three sides, forming a minor peninsula set between the road and the forest. On the right, Bondarenko showed us a first hole, rectangular, long and narrow, the grave where the three conscripts had buried the daughter of *Dyed* Kolya. A little further on, between the pines, behind an underground bunker covered in sandbags and branches, which in Ukrainian is called a *blindazh*, a large pit surrounded on three sides by thrown-up hills of sand had been dug with a bulldozer. Around it, towards the *blindazh*, lay leftover food, plastic forks, a Russian military jacket; in the pit there were only a few pieces of cloth, and a little fruit juice carton with its straw still stuck inside. 'There was a lot of blood here, it was full of blood. They must have killed them right here.' The first time Bondarenko had come with the Ukrainian

154

soldiers, there were four bodies in the pit, half or completely covered with sand: Olha Petrivna, her husband Ihor, her son Oleksandr and one of the two volunteers, the youngest one. The pit was much too large for them: clearly, it had been dug ahead of time for the volunteers of the TO, who would certainly have ended up in it if the repeated attacks of the Ukrainian commandos hadn't prevented the Wagner men from carrying out their *zachistka*. Ihor Sukhenko had been tied to a pine tree at the head of the pit; they had broken and bent back all his fingers, then shot bullets into his arms and legs before finishing him off. A white rope trailed on the ground, perhaps the one that had been used to tie him up. Olha Petrivna also had bullets in her legs. No one knows which of the three died first. 'Imagine a son killed in front of his mother, or a mother killed in front of her son. Can you believe? They shot into the legs of a woman... Those Wagner guys are imbeciles.'

123. While her father spoke, Rita was walking further away, wandering by herself among the burnt pines, and I took a photo of her. Finally we returned to the path and walked a little along the canal. Antoine continued taking photos, I took a few for myself as well. At the end of the canal, where it curved around to surround the property, I noticed two men fishing. 'Oleh, that might be the owner, no?' A little iron footbridge crossed the canal; we headed towards it and Bondarenko used it to go over to the two fishermen. When he returned, he motioned to us to cross over. 'They didn't want to let us enter, they're sick of visitors. But I insisted, I told him I'm sick of these stories too, but that people had to know what happened here.' The grass-covered grounds stretched open and bare between a little copse of birches to the left, the two structures, and a very tall tree down at the end, near

the fishermen. The white-cinderblock building was the storehouse where the conscripts had hidden Bondarenko and the others, with the entrance to the *pogreb* where they lived right next to it. There was a large covered porch in front of the storehouse, with two washing machines and some chairs; that was where the commandos tortured their victims. 'They closed this terrace off with plastic. When they brought me here, they attached me to the pipe there which holds up the roof. I couldn't see anything but I could feel the pipe in my back. That's where they interrogated me.' They used the red brick ruins to finish off their victims; when Bondarenko returned to the site with a French television crew on 9 April, he found the corpse of the second volunteer under a pile of rubbish, the father-in-law of the one thrown into the pit with the Sukhenko family. He had been finished off with a volley of three bullets to the back and head; his entire face had disappeared, only the lower jaw remained. The cistern where Bondarenko had spent two days and two nights was between the buildings, next to a well protected by a little roof, and a section of concrete pipe on the grass. The cover lay on the ground, along with a shoe; at the bottom, there was a little straw, some scraps of cloth or clothing, a plastic water bottle. Bondarenko looked around him, his face fully in the sun, and I took a few pictures of him with my phone, quickly. 'How did you survive all this?' I asked him. 'I already knew what it was like to die, that helps.' He started telling me about his years in prison, some of them spent in the worst penal colony in Ukraine, where he had come down with tuberculosis which almost killed him. 'The first time, in 1984, I wasn't even sixteen. I spent nineteen and a half years there in all. When I came out, the last time, I was thirty-seven. My entire youth was gone like that. I would come out, then go back for something

else. I was sentenced four times in all.' 'Four times?' Rita, who was listening attentively, suddenly exclaimed. 'Four times? You told me two!' Bondarenko spread his hands wide: 'My daughter, four times, two times, what's the difference?' 'There's a HUGE difference!' She crossed her arms, turned her back to him and set off angrily towards the large solitary tree. '*Bye, vsio, bolshe ne budu*. That's it, I won't take it anymore.' Bondarenko called after her in a half-laughing, half-bemused tone: 'My daughter, that was another life!' Finally she calmed down and walked slowly back to us, still sulking. As we were leaving, at the gate, Bondarenko turned back and contemplated the grounds one last time: '*Poka, moi domik.*' Goodbye, my little house.

LOGICS

124. In 1947, Steinbeck wrote: 'It is hard to imagine these Germans. Hard to imagine what went on in their heads, what their thinking process was, these sad, destructive, horrible children.'[80] One can endlessly report on scenes like the ones I've just described. But it's far more difficult to think about them. If I force myself to imagine a man torturing another man to death, then leaving him without even finishing him off to go enjoy a salad with mayonnaise while exchanging lewd jokes with his comrades, I'm faced with a vertigo, a black hole in thought surrounded by an impassable event horizon, near which any idea veers red before disappearing, irrevocably sucked in. All that remains is the temptation to cling to a model, an idea that could serve as a label without explaining anything. I could for example say to myself: This man is abnormal, his father beat him or he was raped as a child, he's traumatized, he's a psychotic. But if you needed to be mad to

do such things, then Ukraine would not be filled from one border to the other with Buchas, Motyzhyns and all those other small-scale Babyn Yars. There wouldn't be enough madmen, even in the Russian army. No, the man who did this is a normal man. He had a childhood, happy or not, he went to school, he played, explored forests, gathered mushrooms with his mother or fished with his father, fell in love, had children, whom he loves and protects like everyone else. He's an ordinary man, a person like you and me.

125. In the case of Motyzhyn, we can resort to a rational explanation: the two Russian intelligence platoons, Wagner and the others, tasked with the security of the artillerymen and the logistic convoys, were convinced that the attacks against their forces, which in fact came from outside, from Ukrainian commandos who had infiltrated their lines and slipped in and out, came from inside the village, from members of the Territorial Defence fighting as partisans. Armed with this conviction, they started looking for the guilty, and torturing innocent people who couldn't be anything other than guilty people who were lying, to make them confess what they wanted to hear, which is what they always ended up doing since, as Bondarenko said, 'after that, people said everything they knew and everything they didn't know.' These atrocious deaths would thus be, in this case, the consequence of a terrible misunderstanding, men doing what they thought was their work and their duty, employing on the basis of a mistaken premise the methods inculcated in them by a perverted system.

126. There is no doubt that it is a method. Neither the atrocities of Motyzhyn, or those of Bucha, or those discovered in all the liberated cities in Ukraine, Izyum,

Lyman, Kherson, are the results of mistakes or individual madness. It is a system, a strategic violence, whose aim is to eliminate, in the occupied areas, any potential opponent or partisan, and to terrorize the population to such an extent that it would be incapable of resisting Russian power in any way. There is direct proof of this, notably from intercepted phone calls of Russian soldiers carried out by Ukrainian intelligence services. On 14 March, for example, a certain Lionya – a diminutive for Leonid – declared over the phone: 'We have the order not to take prisoners of war but to shoot them all dead directly. There was a boy, eighteen years old, taken prisoner. First, they shot through his leg with a machine gun, then he got his ears cut off. He admitted to everything and was shot dead. We do not take prisoners. Meaning, we don't leave anyone alive.' On 21 March, another soldier named Vadim explained more succinctly to his mother: 'We have the order: it does not matter whether or not they're civilians. Kill everyone.'[81]

127. The violence of the first days, in Bucha, is obviously part of this logic. The Russian military hierarchy not only demands it, but rewards it. Lt.-Col. Gorodilov, the commander of the 234th Airborne Assault Regiment responsible for the first killings all along Yablunska Street, at their base at No. 144, and in the zone of garages where Vadym Evdokymenko's father was burned alive with other civilians, was promoted to full Colonel after the Russian retreat from the region of Kyiv. Many of the murders that followed the occupation of the city, like the presumed rape and the murder of Oksana Sulyma in the *pogreb* at No. 58 Vokzalna Street, are attributed by residents and investigators to one of the main units based in Bucha, the 64th Separate Motor Rifle Brigade

commanded by Lt.-Col. Azatbek Omurbekov, a native of Karakalpakstan in Uzbekistan. On 18 April 2022, not long after its retreat, the entire brigade was honoured by Vladimir Putin in person with the title of 'Guards' for 'its special merits, great heroism and courage ... The unit's staff became a role model in fulfilling its military duty, valour, dedication and professionalism.'[82]

128. There are obviously other factors, and at least some of the murders, like those, in the last days of the occupation, of Oleksandr Kryvenko and the pro-Russian politician Oleksandr Rzhavskyy, can be attributed to individual loss of control. But even in obvious cases like this, the hierarchy does not crack down. The day after the killing, while the soldier wounded by his own grenade was still lying in Rzhavskyy's dining room, his commanding officer came to find him and had him carried away, before offering his apologies to the dead man's widow and sister, who had survived by hiding, and ordering his men to bury Rzhavskyy in his garden (as for Kryvenko's corpse, it was unceremoniously thrown into a bush beyond the property).[83] It is extremely unlikely that the soldier Aleksey was tried after he'd slept off his drunken stupor. As the Russian journalist Aleksandr Nevzorov writes on his thread at the Telegram: 'Neither the commanders nor the leadership are capable of paying the personnel enough for the hardships and horror of a senseless war, or for the constant fear of injury and death. For this reason, no cases are initiated and no reprimands are even issued.... The only things that are punished are brawls and shootings over loot.'[84]

129. The loot – precisely. Let us return to the 64th Separate Brigade. This unit, based near Khabarovsk in eastern

Siberia, recruits mainly from the poorest populations of this vast region, ethnic Russians and Siberian minorities related to the Mongols, the ones the inhabitants of Bucha are referring to when they accuse the 'Buryats'. But what is at stake, when it comes to the troops' violent actions, is not ethnicity but social class: the invaders of the Kyiv *oblast* seem to have been driven to rage not just by some sort of ideological hatred of so-called Ukrainian 'Nazis', but by class resentment. Anatolii Fiodoruk, the mayor of Bucha, repeated to me the words of a Russian soldier calling his mother or wife: 'Can you imagine? They have hot water inside their houses, ceramic toilets!' A video posted online shows a Russian soldier opening a fridge and exclaiming: 'Nutella! Fuck, they've really got it all.' The fact that the village streets were paved seemed incomprehensible to them. Russian graffiti somewhere in the region of Kyiv, which several people have quoted to me, summarizes this state of mind: '*A kto vam razreshil zhit tak khorosho?* Who gave you permission to live so well?' Hence the massive looting, the thousands of computers, televisions, bicycles, household appliances carried off to Belarus in army trucks and then sent to Russia by post, as shown by numerous surveillance camera videos leaked onto the web. An acquaintance from Kyiv, Oleksandr, told me how on 3 April he found, a hundred metres from the destroyed MegaMart in Bucha, the corpse of a Buryat with thirty tubes of Sensodyne in his pockets. 'Imagine: This Buryat travelled 3,000 kilometres to come here to steal toothpaste and die on our pavements. Can you believe it?' *Der Tod ist ein Meister aus Deutschland*, wrote Paul Celan.[85] Death is a master from Germany, blue-eyed, dressed in leather, imbued with high culture, surrounded by his dogs and his snakes. Today, death comes from Russia, but it isn't a master, just a peasant drunk with rage and fear,

162

who kills because his leaders tell him it's what he has to do, who rapes because he can, and who above all sees in this disaster an opportunity to steal everything he lacks at home, as if a washing machine was worth his life and the lives of the people he kills, unbothered by the slightest thought. 'What TV do you want?' a Russian soldier named Sergey asks his girlfriend in another intercepted phone call. 'LG or Samsung?' 'Seryozha, are you bringing a vacuum cleaner, too?' 'Yeah, I already packed it.'[86]

(HI)STORIES

130. At the top of the pyramid, with the tsar and his cronies, the ones who decided on this and unleashed their dogs on Ukraine, the issues are obviously entirely different. It's a matter of ideas: Ukraine does not exist, nor do the Ukrainian people, the Ukrainian language even less so. 'A separate Little Russian language has never existed, does not exist and cannot exist,'[87] declared in 1863 already a decree of Piotr Valuev, Minister of the Interior for Tsar Aleksandr II (and model for Tolstoy's Karenin, Anna's husband), forbidding nearly any Ukrainian publication in the Russian Empire, an ultimate effort to prevent the formation, on this territory, of a Ukrainian nation aware of itself as such. The neighbours to the West also had their doubts, which is why the Ukrainian nationalists, in the first half of the twentieth century, quickly became so bitter, so violent. In *The Twilight of a World*, the Polish writer Włodzimierz Odojewski places in the mouth of a very young Piotr the following words: '... and they invented this whole Ukraine story, Aunt Barbara was talking about it the other day, I remember, but is it true or not?'[88] One might have thought the question settled by the

brief independence of the Ukrainian People's Republic between 1917 and 1921, its absorption into a federalized USSR as the Soviet Socialist Republic of Ukraine, and then by the country's independence in 1991. But Vladimir Putin, apparently, still dreams of an obedient Little Russia, appendage and granary of the Greater one. In the summer of 2021, after an initial Russian military mobilization at the Ukrainian border, he published a long essay (written, according to Russian sources, by his former Minister of Culture, Vladimir Medinskiy)[89] entitled 'On the Historical Unity of Russians and Ukrainians', in which he presents 'the idea of Ukrainian people as a nation separate from the Russians' as a fiction invented by 'the Polish elite and a part of the Malorussian [Little Russian] intelligentsia.'[90] This idea of his is not a recent one. The American diplomat Fiona Hill quotes Putin saying to George W. Bush, during the NATO summit in Bucharest in April 2008: 'George, you have to understand that Ukraine is not even a country. Part of its territory is in eastern Europe and the greater part was given to us.'[91] On 21 February 2022, three days before launching his invasion of Ukraine, Vladimir Putin gave a stunning televised speech. Tense, aggressive, enraged, he began his long diatribe against NATO, the United States and the 'radical nationalists of the Kyiv regime' with a history lesson. 'The Ukraine,' he asserted, 'is not just a neighbouring country, it's an inalienable part of our own history, culture and spiritual space,' a country that only exists in its contemporary form thanks to the insane territorial 'gifts', of which 'even the most zealous [Ukrainian] nationalists could never have dreamed of before', from communist Russia and its first master: 'It is the Ukraine of Vladimir Ilich Lenin. He was its creator and its architect.'[92] And what Lenin gave, Putin can take back.

131. The fact that the internationally recognized borders of Ukraine were drawn by Soviet colonial power, from Lenin to Stalin to Khruschev, obviously does not make them less legitimate than those of dozens of countries whose borders emerged from the European colonial adventure. It would never enter Putin's mind to question the eminently artificial and arbitrary borders of the countries where he forcefully intervenes such as Syria, Libya, the Central African Republic or Mali. The point is that his argument, even his vision, is based far more on fantasy than on historic reality. I don't intend to respond to his history lesson with another one: I'll refer the interested reader to the professionals, in particular to the magisterial book by Harvard professor Serhii Plokhy, *The Gates of Europe: A History of Ukraine*, or to the lectures posted online by the Yale professor Timothy Snyder.[93] Some facts, however, should be recalled. The political entity known under the name of Rus' of Kyiv or Kyivan Rus'[94] was founded by Scandinavian warriors who came down from the North along the rivers to trade, raid and grab slaves from the Slavic population living on both sides of the Dnipro. Little by little, through conquest and the creation of new principalities, this territory extended to the northeast, founding provinces that are now Russian such as Novgorod, Yaroslav and Vladimir. In 988, in order to marry a Byzantine princess, the Grand Prince of Kyiv Volodymyr (who according to Snyder was probably actually called Valdemar or Voldemar, and whom the Russians still call Vladimir), converted to Orthodox Christianity, which progressively brought about the conversion of all of Rus'. This state slowly fell apart as time passed, before finally succumbing in the thirteenth century to the onslaught of the Mongol invaders, giving way, in the east, to several principalities subservient to the

great Khan (the principality of Moscow was only born in 1276 from a partition of the principality of Vladimir-Suzdal), and, in the west, on the territories of present-day Ukraine and Belarus, to the Polish and Lithuanian empires. In 1648, the uprising of Bohdan Khmelnytskyy against the Polish-Lithuanian Republic allowed an independent State, the Cossack Hetmanate, to emerge along the central course of the Dnipro. Uniting Zaporozhian Cossacks and Ruthenian peasants, this state is the historic reference on which the modern Ukrainian nation is founded. But threatened in its very existence by Polish forces the Hetmanate chose, in 1654, to place itself under the protection of the Tsar of Moscow. In the years following the Truce of Andrusovo, which in 1667 decreed the partition of the territories of the Hetmanate between a right bank of the Dnipro under Polish-Lithuanian sovereignty and a left bank, as well as Kyiv, under Muscovite rule, Ukrainian monks began to propagate a new myth: that of Kyiv as the birthplace of Muscovite Orthodoxy.[95] This was a way for them to gain prestige and influence; but over the decades, the Moscow clergy appropriated this tale and amplified it, turning it into a crucial tool for secular power. When Tsar Piotr the First, our Peter the Great, took the very westernized title of Emperor in 1721, he named his new empire Rossiya, a Hellenized version of 'Rus'', consecrating the myth for centuries to come.

132. 'Vladimir Putin took upon himself ... a historic responsibility in deciding not to leave the solution of the Ukrainian question to future generations,' wrote the Russian propagandist Piotr Akopov on 26 February 2022, two days after the beginning of the invasion.[96] What does this not entirely final solution consist of? On 3

April, the day when the world was discovering the extent of the atrocities perpetrated in Bucha and in the Kyiv *oblast*, the Russian state press agency RIA Novosti posted a text online entitled 'What Russia Should Do with Ukraine', written by a certain Timofei Sergeitsev, a philosopher associated with the State University of Moscow (MGU), in which he makes explicit the meaning of the 'denazification' presented by Putin as the objective of his 'special operation'.[97] This text needs to be cited at some length.

> Today the issue of denazification has moved into a practical plane.... War criminals and active Nazis must be exemplarily and demonstratively punished. A total lustration must be carried out.... However, in addition to the leaders, also guilty is a significant part of the mass of the people, who are passive Nazis, accomplices of Nazism.... The just punishment of this part of the population is possible only insofar as it bears the inevitable hardships of a just war against the Nazi system, waged as carefully and prudently as possible in relation to civilians. Further denazification of this mass of the population will consist in its reeducation, which will be carried out by ideological repression (suppression) of Nazi attitudes and by severe censorship: not only in the political sphere, but also necessarily in the sphere of culture and education....
>
> The duration of denazification can in no way be less than one generation, which must be born, grow up and reach maturity under the conditions of denazification. The Nazification of Ukraine has gone on for over thirty years – beginning at least in 1989, when Ukrainian nationalism received legal and legitimate forms of political expression and led the movement for 'independence,' rushing towards Nazism....

Denazification will inevitably also be a de-Ukrainization – a rejection begun under the Soviet authorities already of the large-scale artificial inflation of the ethnic component of the self-identification of the population of the territories of historical Little Russia and New Russia.... Ukrainism is an artificial anti-Russian construction that does not have its own civilizational content, a subordinate element of a foreign and heterogenous civilization....

The Banderist leadership [Ukrainian nationalists] must be liquidated, its reeducation is impossible. The social 'quagmire,' which actively and passively supported it by its action and inaction, must survive the hardships of the war and internalize the experience as a historical lesson and an atonement for its guilt.

The most surprising thing is the way in which Sergeitsev candidly acknowledges that Ukrainian 'Nazism' has nothing to do with historic Nazism.

The peculiarity of modern nazified Ukraine is its amorphousness and ambivalence, which make it possible to disguise Nazism as an aspiration for 'independence' and a 'European' (Western, pro-American) path of 'development'.... There is no main Nazi party, no Führer, no full-fledged racial laws (only their pared-down version in the form of repression against the Russian language). As a result, there is no opposition or resistance to the regime. However, all of the above does not make Ukrainian Nazism a 'light version' of German Nazism during the first half of the twentieth century. On the contrary – since Ukrainian Nazism is free from such 'genre' (essentially political-technological) frameworks and limitations, it freely unfolds as the fundamental basis of all Nazism – as European and, in its most developed form, American racism.[98]

In a virulent critique published a few days later, Timothy Snyder emphasized this peculiarity of Sergeitsev's argument: 'The actual history of actual Nazis and their actual crimes in the 1930s and 1940s is thus totally irrelevant and completely cast aside.... This explains why Volodymyr Zelens'kyi, although a democratically-elected president, and a Jew with family members who fought in the Red Army and died in the Holocaust, can be called a Nazi. Zelens'kyi is a Ukrainian, and that is all that "Nazi" means.' In the minds of Putin and his regime, a Nazi is in fact, as Snyder concludes, 'a Ukrainian who refuses to be Russian.'[99] Consequently, it is perfectly legitimate, if you can't convince a Ukrainian of his intrinsic Russianness, to kill him. Starting from such a paradigm, there is nothing surprising about the events in Bucha, in Motyzhyn, and in all the Ukrainian territories occupied by Russia. 'Facts are facts,' Putin insisted during his 21 February speech. Fantasies also dictate facts.

133. 'I do not like wars. Their outcome is uncertain,' Elizabeth I is said to have declared to her Council during an umpteenth Scottish war. It's not just their similar ideas about ethnonationalism, the force of fate and the lot that should be reserved for those who oppose them that make Putin's fascist regime so similar to Hitler's Nazi regime: there is also the fact that both of them, in the name of these ideas, launched an appalling war they were convinced that they couldn't lose, but that in fact they couldn't win. Fantasies can also clash with reality, in this case with the fierce determination of the Ukrainians not to disappear as a nation (as well as with the obvious superiority of western military technologies and weaponry over a decrepit, archaic and thoroughly corrupt army). I discussed this one day, over fish soup at a cheap restaurant on Kyiv's

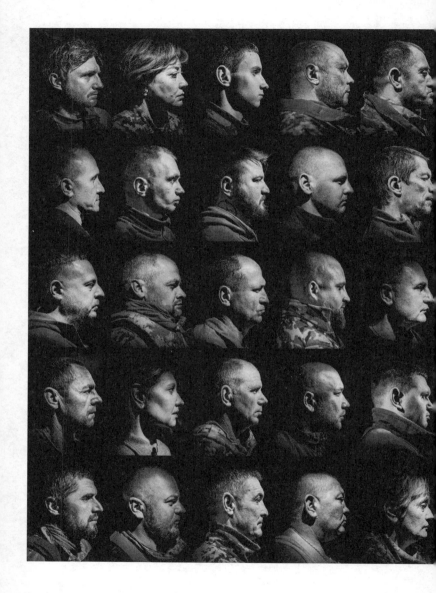

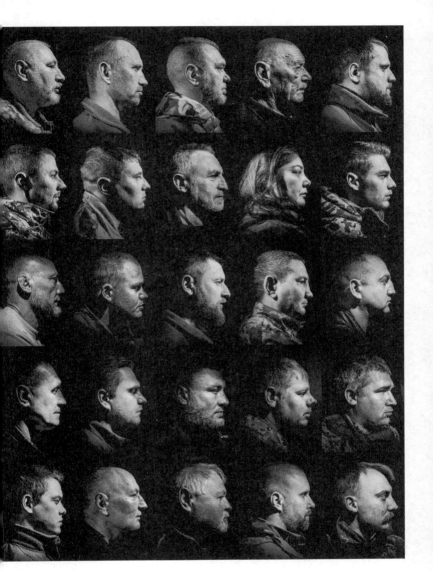

left bank, with Anton Drobovych, the director of the Ukrainian Institute of National Memory. On 25 February he had headed straight to the front to dig trenches, and had obtained an hour's leave to see me. 'Putin said: "There is no Ukraine, there is no Ukrainian people, these are our guys." But on 24 February, thousands of people lined up in front of the army offices, with bombs raining down, to say by their presence: "No, we are different guys. We are neither better nor worse than you, we are just different."'

ONCE AGAIN, ONCE AGAIN

134. We weren't done with Babyn Yar, we had to keep going. You can't do everything in one day.

135. We returned after the beginning of the war, of course, in May 2022, and I returned several more times, alone. But already the previous year we'd continued, still in June. Even if it meant starting over again, we said to ourselves that we should approach things from a different side. This time we had come by taxi. It had dropped us off at the crossroads of Yurii Illienko and Dorohozhytska Streets, east of the park, and we found ourselves in the middle of a tear-shaped roundabout where stood yet another monument, a small white rectangle covered in bare footprints. This stela commemorates the beginning of the 'road of death', the site of the *shlakbaum*, the barrier set up on 29 September 1941 to filter the tens of thousands of Jews who had come on foot from all over the city to meet their fate. On this side of the *shlakbaum*, life; beyond it, blows, screams and death. Towards Dorohozhytska stood a large glass building from the 70s, an abandoned colossus with blind or missing windows, the former offices of

the motorcycle factory which gave its old name – *vulitsa* Mototsikleta – to the street, and which today has been converted into a vast technology complex, UNIT city. At the end of the roundabout, across the street, green fences, their paint fading, hid the little garden of a building; another apartment building in the Brutalist style rose beyond Illienko Street, pale yellow in the rising light of morning before a cloud-dark sky, barred by the crossed cables of the tramway which, while we were contemplating all this, was loudly squealing around the roundabout to start again in the other direction, towards the city centre.

136. 'Which way are we going?' Antoine asked. 'That way,' I declared with certainty, pointing towards Dorohozhytska. Yes, I knew these places, fairly approximatively I must admit. I had already carried out some research here, in 2002 for another book. At the time, the topography of the site mattered a lot to me, and the sources available then gave no precise information. I'd had to make do with what I had. Thanks to a certain Ihor Kohan, president of an association of survivors of the ghettos and camps, I had met Ruvin Israilovich Shtein, one of the few survivors of Babyn Yar who had been old enough at the time to be able to testify with precision. Unlike Ilya Levitas and Yevgeni Yevtushenko, I remember Ruvin Shtein very well, a slender, elderly gentleman with whom I talked for a long time, sitting on a park bench. His red eyes sometimes misted over with tears, but he always spoke in a precise and detailed way about what he knew. It was thanks to him that I was able to recreate the layout of the massacre, with some mistakes of course, but small ones; in the end, my description was not so far from the definitive conclusions of contemporary experts. I still have my meagre notes of our

conversation, with even a little sketched map, not very precise unfortunately (Google Maps didn't exist at the time, and my map of Kyiv was not very good) but on the whole correct. Before I brought Antoine to the site of the *shlakbaum*, I had tried to find Ruvin Shtein again, but it seemed he had been dead for many years; despite all my attempts, I couldn't find his children either, the survivors' associations hadn't kept any records of them, and no one answered his old telephone number. But I unearthed a film of him, a series of six VHS cassettes of his testimony filmed in 1996, six years before I met him, and posted online much later by the USC Shoah Foundation as part of the 'Spielberg Project'.[100] This interview, much more detailed than the one I was able to conduct with my hesitant Russian of the time, shows Ruvin Shtein sitting in his apartment, surrounded by inexpensive Soviet furniture, with carpets on the floor and on the chairs. He wears a neatly ironed pale blue shirt, without a tie, and a grey suit with his service ribbons on his left chest. His eyes are moist, red, the way I remember them, and he looks almost terrified, as if trapped. Sometimes, when he takes a drink of water, his hand trembles. But once again he speaks very calmly, collectedly. And he remembers. For all this after all is nothing but a matter of memories, memories more or less true, more or less ugly, more or less forgotten.

THE STORY OF A LIFE

137. Ruvin Shtein, son of Israil Ruvinovich and Rakhil Mikhailovna Shtein,[101] was born on 15 January 1926 in Koziatyn, a city in the Vinnytsia *oblast* founded some fifty years before his birth. His memory, when he speaks of

it, is clear and detailed, and he recounts with precision the many details of his childhood about his parents, the people around him, his teachers. Israil Ruvinovich, a butcher, had fought during the civil war and suffered from consequences that affected his health for the rest of his life. Even in the 1990s, claims Ruvin, the people of Koziatyn still remembered his father as having the best, most tender meat in town. He and his family were all very devout, far more than his wife and her family, who came from Baku in Azerbaijan and were better educated, and he observed Shabbat and the major religious holidays. In 1930, the family moves to Kyiv, first to Podil, a mostly Jewish neighbourhood at the time, then to Yaroslavska Street. In 1933, at the height of the Holodomor, Stalin's planned famine which exterminated over four million Ukrainian peasants, Israil Shtein brings his wife and son to Baku, to his in-laws; there, he finds work in the kolkhoz of Kuba among the Tat or Mountain Jews, a strange Persian-speaking Caucasian tribe, much closer in their customs and way of life to their Muslim mountaineer neighbours than to the Ashkenazi Jews of the plains and the cities. In 1935, the family returns to settle in Kyiv, first on Kurenivka Street, very close to Babyn Yar, then on Frunze Street, now Kyrylivska. In June his little sister Mariya is born. Then, the following year, Ruvin's father finds work in a *Dom Invalidov*, a rest home for invalids outside the city in Kytaiv, and the entire family moves there. In 1937, in a pioneer camp, Ruvin meets Spanish children evacuated because of the civil war, and becomes friendly with little Pedro González, who was the same age as him and whom he still remembers raising his fist as he cried out '*No Pasarán!*'. 'That was the first time I heard about those forces that annihilate people, that don't let people live in peace.' That same year, after a serious illness, his father dies. Ruvin is eleven, and becomes the man of the family.

138. In the years that follow, Ruvin begins to work, to earn a salary. He often goes to the cinema, and discovers fascism in films that show how the Germans are oppressing the Jews. One day, he decides to go to Kyiv, to see his grandmother in Podil, but curiously on that day the buses aren't running, so he decides to make the journey on foot. On the way, he hears sustained gunfire, he sees planes circling high above the city, and he thinks, *Those aren't manoeuvres, but enemy planes, something's happening.* He reaches the central square, sirens begin wailing, policemen push people into basements. Then, near the *Avtovokzal*, the bus station, he hears the official announcement from the radio on a loudspeaker. The Nazis have invaded the USSR, and he is fifteen years old. Back home he urges his mother to evacuate, to go to Baku, but she resists: 'It's impossible, how could we? We don't have any train tickets, any provisions, nothing.' When the Germans draw close to Kyiv he again tries to leave, with the retreating soldiers, but in vain. In the meantime the family has returned to live in the city, in a room allocated by the municipality in an administrative building near an airplane factory on Melnikova, the street now called Yurii Illienko. On 19 September Kyiv falls, and the population loots the shops; Ruvin joins them and steals some food from a bread factory. One last time, he tries to persuade his mother to take their things and hide in a village, but again she refuses: 'Winter is coming. We aren't going anywhere.' On 28 September, the Nazis post announcements in Russian and Ukrainian all over the city ordering, under penalty of death, all Jews to go the next morning to the crossroads where Antoine and I had gotten out of the

taxi. The Jews start talking amongst themselves: 'Where are they going to send us?' Almost no one thinks the Germans will harm or kill them, they only speak of the destination: 'To a ghetto? A camp in Germany? A camp in Ukraine? Or to Palestine?' Some people do realize it is the end. But they say nothing. 'Those who said "They're going to shoot us" were looked on as if they were enemies. Authority is authority. And the Jews are the kind of people who are always ready to obey.'

139. On 29 September, thousands of people, 'as if for a demonstration', mass with all their things – their best clothes, their suitcases, their provisions – in front of Ruvin Shtein's building on Melnikova. Ruvin and his family come out at around 11 a.m., with warm clothing, their family photos and letters, and their identity papers. They take some food, some *salo*, smoked pork rind, not very kosher. 'My mother had nothing, no valuables except my sister and me. She said: "This is probably the last time we'll walk on this street." She must have felt something.' In the column, people are talking, always the same thing: 'Where are we going, ghettos near the border, no one will shoot us,' and so on. As for Ruvin, he is mostly paying attention to the many pretty young women. The column advances in fits and starts, a few minutes walking, then a pause, then they start up again. From this point on, Ruvin's story is the same as the one he'd told me when we sat on the park bench, six years after his filmed interview, the same story I remembered with both a great deal of precision and a great deal of errors. The column approaches the Jewish cemetery on their right, turns to the left, then again to the right; the *shlakhaum*, in this story, is not mentioned. Already they have lost sight of the column in front of them. And after the second turn, when

they reach the military cemetery, it becomes clear that they aren't going anywhere, that they are staying here. Germans wearing different kinds of uniforms check their documents, then throw them into drums to burn them. They take his mother's ring and put it in a box full of jewellery. A little further on people are being forced to undress, but Ruvin and his sister Mariya only take off their coats, their mother also keeps her clothes on. His mother and sister are made to climb into a truck. Ruvin is placed in a group of men, young and old, dressed and undressed. Rakhil, in the truck, shouts at him to join her, but the soldiers won't let him go. She screams: '*Vsio, sinok, vsio. Nas ubiut.* It's over, my boy, it's over. They're going to kill us.' And the truck leaves. Around him, people are crying and shouting; the Germans are efficient, busy, officious; no one beats them, there is no need. Then they are made to walk, on Mototsikleta between the Lukyanivske cemetery and the military cemetery. It is a beautiful day, the sun is shining. Ruvin doesn't talk with the people around him and thinks of nothing but how to escape, at any cost. Their group is escorted by three patrols, but they are spaced out from each other; motorcycles and trucks pass them regularly, heading in the opposite direction. After the military cemetery, where the great metal television tower now stands, Ruvin sees a duct under the road, and he slips into it. It must have been noon, scarcely an hour has passed since they'd left home. This pipe for rainwater runoff is the detail I remembered best, even if I got a number of other things wrong. At the end of the VHS cassettes from the USC Shoah Foundation, we follow Ruvin to the places themselves, showing Alla Klepikova, the woman interviewing him, both cemeteries, the 'death march' street, the site of the pipe. On 29 September, he will spend the entire day in this duct, too frightened to try to flee; every five or ten minutes, another column walks over him. Finally, when it is already night and he can't hear anyone, he emerges from the drainpipe and slips over the fence – wooden at the time, today the outer wall is made of red brick – of the Lukyanivske cemetery. He crosses the cemetery, turns left onto Dehtyarivska Street, and goes home. He had kept the key, and he stays there for a week without going out, nibbling on a few provisions forgotten under the bed, shitting onto newspaper and then burning the excrement in the furnace. And all this time, he says, they were taking people away to Babyn Yar, the invalids, the sick people who had stayed home, those who had been hiding.

140. One day, he hears a key in the door, and he rushes out to the balcony and shimmies down a pipe. He starts wandering through the city, looking for someone he knows. He is hungry, he can't find anyone. Here, for the first time, Ruvin Shtein pauses; lost in his memories, he licks his lips, hesitates. Finally he says: 'And I no longer had any hope, in anything.' But he is determined to survive. He digs up some potatoes which he exchanges for bread, hides in an attic, and finally, after a long week, he finds a friend who takes him to his house. His friend's mother agrees to help him, but she doesn't want to take any risks; he sleeps in a little cave on a hill and only sometimes sneaks over to their house. The weather is getting colder. But finally his friend, by chance, runs into a classmate whose father was the head of their school, and this classmate steals another student's identity papers for him. This is how Ruvin Israilovich Shtein becomes Vladimir Sergeevich Medvedenko, a name he would keep for many years. He wants to leave Kyiv, to go to the front and if possible join Soviet forces to fight, but for that he has

to cross the Dnipro, and the bridges are closely watched by the Germans. So he finds work as a rail cleaner for the ZhD, the railway company. Thanks to this job, he obtains an *ausweis* which allows him to pass German checkpoints for work purposes, and thus to cross the river. It is now November 1941, it is snowing, and Ruvin starts walking from village to village. About sixty kilometres from Kyiv, he meets a Ukrainian prisoner of war released by the Germans as part of their ephemeral pro-Ukrainian policy and thus also provided with papers, and they decide to travel together. But many villages are burned down, they can't find any food; they leave the main motorway to look for intact villages, heading to the northeast. It is difficult to find a place to sleep, people are afraid, they are forced to go find the *starost* and show their papers; when he is questioned, he says his parents were killed during a bombardment, and that he is trying to rejoin a relative. Sometimes also they are lucky enough to come across good people, women wash their shirts and let them scrub themselves in a *banya*. In January 1942 he reaches Briansk *oblast*, in Russia; the released prisoner, it seems, is no longer with him. And somewhere near Kursk he falls asleep in the snow and freezes. But a collective farm worker saves him: his horse stops on the road, he gets down to see what's happening, finds Ruvin under the snow, puts him in his wagon and brings him home. Ruvin spends a week at the home of this *Dyada* Mitya, then goes to work at the kolkhoz *kontor*. 'And that's how I was saved from cold and hunger.'

141. In March 1942, as spring approaches, he is sent to lodge with a village woman whose husband is at the front, Agafya Evdokimovna Martinets. She already has four daughters, between the ages of two and eleven, but

she needs a man to help her. Mistrustful at first, she ends up accepting him and teaches him farm work; little by little, he begins living there as a member of the family. He is sixteen, and dreams only of joining the partisans roaming throughout the region of Briansk. But Agafya Evdokimovna refuses to help him, she wants to keep him. And so the year ends and 1943 begins, 'life in fear'. Finally, in the summer of 1943, they see Germans passing through their village, heading west. Soon afterwards comes liberation: '*Nashi zdes*, our own are here.' Mad with joy, Ruvin/Vladimir escapes the surveillance of Agafya Evdokimovna, and when the Soviet troops leave the village, he follows them for twenty kilometres, begging them to take him with them as a volunteer. But at the next halt he is interrogated by the Smerch, the special 'death to spies' department, and is abruptly put in his place: he is too young to join the Red Army, his age group hasn't been called up yet. He must go home and wait till December. And so, with a heavy heart, he returns to Agafya Evdokimovna, who scolds him roughly before taking him back. Barely six months later, however, he celebrates his eighteenth birthday, or rather Vladimir Medvedenko's, and receives his summons: this time, Agafya Evdokimovna bids him farewell ceremoniously and he leaves for training in Riazan. This is the period when the first photo of himself he still has was taken, very young and thin, in a uniform with his forage cap tilted on his head, a photo he holds up in front of the camera of the USC Shoah Foundation. In July 1944 he is sent to the front in Estonia, in an artillery unit where he joins military intelligence, in charge of adjusting the fire of a battery of 120mm mortars. He thus takes part in the 'liberation' of Estonia and Latvia, first conquered by the USSR in 1939 and then reclaimed until 1991. In Latvia, near Tukums, Ruvin is seriously wounded in the head during the major battle known as the 'Courland Pocket', during which the remains of the German Army Group North, surrounded, resist the Soviet forces until the end of the war. Unconscious, he is transported to a field hospital where shrapnel is removed from his head. His war was over: 9 May 1945 – the day the Soviets regard as that of the German surrender – finds him in an HQ deep within a forest, well to the rear of the front. That same month he is sent off to the Far East, for the war that Stalin is preparing against Japan. He only arrives there in August, and is posted to the construction of a railroad. But Japan capitulates on 3 September; Ruvin is sent back to Komsomolsk-na-Amure to guard a warehouse full of war trophies and to convoy some *zek*, former Soviet prisoners of war or deserters, still to be tried but automatically sent to camps.

142. His two years of service over, he is demobilized in December 1946. He leaves for Baku to live with his mother's family, and begins working in a foundry where he learns how to pour metal. He also passes his secondary school diploma. But he still remained Medvedenko: it is hard for him, in fact, to prove that he is Ruvin Shtein; he will take some time to recover his real name. In 1950 he begins studying at an institute for physical education. Then he contemplates becoming an officer and goes to Odessa to take the exams; but he soon realizes that this career is not for him, and returns to Baku to resume his physical education studies. Finally, in 1951, he decides it is time to return to Kyiv. His friends are there, along with his mother's and his sister's grave, at Babyn Yar. He marries a classmate from before the war, and in 1952 he starts working at his old school as a physical education

teacher. He will keep this job until 1996, a few months before this interview, when at the age of seventy he would finally retire. In the meantime, he and his wife have had three children: Edvard and Ina in 1952 and 1954, and then another daughter late in life, in 1966, Yana. It is actually when he introduces Yana to the camera that he cries for the only time in the interview: 'I told her everything,' he explains, 'the murder of her grandmother, of my...', and at that moment he bursts into tears, his hand twisting his mouth. 'I've known everything since I was little,' Yana says. 'Pápa told us everything.' The interview ends with a few family photos: 'All our photos were burned in Babyn Yar. But later on, I recovered the ones I could from our relatives.' The camera shows us a sepia photo of his mother, taken at the age of twenty in 1923, then one of his father and mother after their wedding in 1925. The interview took place on 15 November 1996; I met him on 20 August 2002; I don't know when he died.

THE GRAVES OF NOBODY

143. The place that Ruvin Shtein indicates in the film as the site of the tables where the Nazis took the Jews' keys and valuables, and separated the men from the women and children, is located at the corner of Dorohozhytska and Simia Khokhlovykh Streets, in front of the wall of the military cemetery. So that is where Antoine and I headed at first. At the designated spot, there was just a strip of dirt with cars parked haphazardly. We continued a little further on and entered the military cemetery. Of all the cemeteries in the zone, the ones still here or the ones that are gone, this is the only one that's at all ecumenical. Right after the gate, on the right next to the guards' container

with its barred windows, lay the section for the dead of the Donbas war, a forest of marble graves decorated with laser-engraved hyper-realistic images, surrounded with Ukrainian flags and flowers, mostly dead ones. All of them followed more or less the same model: on the front, a portrait of the dead man, in uniform or civilian clothes, with his name and dates; on the back of the grave, a photograph engraved with the combatant's *pozyvnyy* or call sign: 'Advokat', 'Tourist', 'Kozak', 'Vidmak', 'Belaz', 'Kuzmych', 'Zurab', 'Tsink'. The photos often showed the hero in action, armed from head to toe, like the photo of Leonid Mikhailovich Provodenko, killed in December 2016, posing with his sniper rifle, or of Oleksei Volodymyrovych Marchenko, standing in front of the ruins of the Donetsk airport where he probably died. Others were more suggestive, like the one showing a deserted motorway with a destroyed truck in the foreground and a tank in the background: the place and sad circumstances of the death of the man lying there, perhaps. The engraved slogans, in either Ukrainian or Russian, followed a similar pattern: NO ONE BUT US, often repeated, EVEN DEATH WILL NOT CONQUER THE MEMORY OF THE TRUE WAR! But beyond this entirely natural glorification, some details revealed all the sadness, pointlessness and terrible cost of this filthy little imperialist war, a dress rehearsal for the actual invasion. The grave for example of a father and his son, the son, Vyacheslav Vasylovych Kutsmai, killed almost one year to the day before his father Vasyl Rostyslavovych: had they fought together? Did the father sign up after his son died? And what could the mother have thought of all this? It's true that in this war not all women stayed home, there were many at the front and not just in auxiliary positions, and so they were in the cemetery as well, like Mariya Zakharovna Shcherbachenko, killed at the age of twenty-four. In this section there were also some astonishingly old men: Air Force Major-General Volodymyr Hryhorovych Pristromko, who died in 2015 at the age of eighty-five, or Vladimir Gavrilovich Vorontsov, born in 1929 and dead in 2017, whose more recent portrait, with his entire chest covered in medals, stood next to a medallion of his wife and himself in a uniform clearly dating from the era of Stalin: if these men, whose career should logically have ended soon after independence, and who could have just about fought at the very end of the Second War if they had lied about their age, died a quiet death, what were they doing here, among the heroes of Donbas? Or had they hastily come out of retirement during the first disastrous days of the war, when the Ukrainian army, neither prepared, trained or equipped, threatened to collapse all at once? Did they also die at the front, commanding troops one last time? As we moved away from the Donbas section, the graves became simpler. Those of the Afghanistan dead, many of them women, and those of the veterans of what the Soviets still call the 'VOV', the Great Patriotic War, still had a simple engraved portrait; the graves of those who fell at the front between 1941 and 1945 were much more sober stelae, with just a name and a date; to the rear of the cemetery stood rows of collective obelisks, officers killed with their soldiers, all named together. Since the beginning of the current war, I haven't had the time to return to this military cemetery. Thus I do not know if they have started burying the more recently killed soldiers there. There wasn't much space left, near the ones from Donbas, and now there are many more dead. I'll have to go see.

144. Since we were there, we also went across the street to have a quick look at the Lukyanivske cemetery, even

though it didn't have much to do with our story, aside from its location. It's true that its wall, or rather its old fence, saw the Jews walking to Babyn Yar. And that's where the young Ruvin Shtein had hidden at night, when he finally came out of his drainpipe. It would have made for a lovely spring stroll, with its pretty, rectilinear, wooded lanes, its imposing nineteenth-century tombs, the little pink-walled museum decorated with photocopies of old postcards and portraits of famous dead people, and the stinking latrines. But we still had a lot of things to see, and meetings later in the day. I just lingered there for a few minutes, proffering my fingers to be sniffed by the cats gambolling in the front yard, meowing quietly in the hope of a treat. Then we went back out and continued on Dorohozhytska, walking alongside the red brick wall of the cemetery.

145. To look at the old Jewish cemetery, next to which the Jews of Kyiv had been ordered to gather in September 1941, we would have had to detour and walk back up towards Illienko Street. But there was no point, nothing remains of it, aside from the old administrative building at the entrance, under renovation and surrounded by scaffolding, and a few gravestones a little further up, in a little triangle nestled behind the television offices, just after the Menorah. We had come across it by chance at the end of our first stroll, when we emerged from the Repyakhiv Yar to the rear of the big new apartment buildings at the edge of the forest, near the older neighbourhood between Herzen Street and Akademik Romodanov Street. Instead of continuing on that way to join the main street and call a taxi, we had come back towards the park, passing children, young women, older women, all quietly coming and going. The path, here, followed the outer

wall at the rear of the television headquarters; we could see the antennae and satellite dishes above the wall, and that's where we discovered the graves. I was surprised, I thought nothing was left of the Jewish cemetery, aside from the gravestones that had been recovered and lined up further down, along the alley descending from the Menorah to Illienko Street. But that was indeed what the plaque indicated. The long triangular plot was defined by a very low concrete border and contained a dozen graves, all erased except one, almost indecipherable, with a few words in Hebrew and the others in rather archaic Cyrillic characters, calling to mind the Tsarist era rather than the only legible date, 1935. Like so many other things here, the destruction of the Jewish cemetery had been a German-Soviet coproduction. The Germans had started by using the gravestones in the summer of 1943 to build the giant furnaces where the corpses of the Jews dug up by the *Sonderkommando* were burned; later on, in 1962, the municipal authorities decided to liquidate what was left to build a sports complex, 'Avanhard', and later still the headquarters of Ukrainian television. When the huge television tower, on the other side of Melnikova/Illienko Street, was erected on part of the old military cemetery, the descendants were invited to come and move the graves. But this was not the case for the Jews, most of whose descendants were in any case also dead: 'these "nobodies' graves" were bulldozered into the ground', as the Ukrainian historian Vladyslav Hrynevych writes.[102]

146. Even if we had turned towards the Jewish cemetery rather than staying under the poplars on Dorohozhytska, we wouldn't have been able to escape the sight of the immense tower standing there. It seemed almost logical to me that there, where the earth was full of bodies,

triumphant Sovietism would soar skywards. It must be said that the structure is remarkable, a masterpiece of 60s Futurism, all metal tubes painted white or already faded red, dominating the entire territory of Babyn Yar. When I consulted Wikipedia, I learned that it's the tallest self-supporting construction in the world, that no rivets were used in building it, but that 'every joint, pipe, and fixture is attached by welding.'[103] The tower was in fact designed for Moscow, but in the end was rejected in favour of the project for the Ostankino Tower, deemed more solid. Adopted by Kyiv, it had to be lowered from the 540 metres initially planned to 385 metres, for political reasons, obviously: even in 1968, under a Ukrainian First Secretary, the USSR couldn't allow Kyiv to equal Moscow. The way it was built was truly astounding: since no crane could reach that height, all the elements were built on the ground, top first, then lifted with four giant hydraulic jacks to insert the next segment below it, one after the other, until 3,000 tonnes of metal had been hoisted skywards before being stabilized by immense lateral concrete pillars. The construction turned out to be remarkably solid: when a Russian cruise missile struck the tower head-on on 1 March 2022, it took the blow with just a few vibrations. Wikipedia also said the tower was not open to the public. That was true, but we were a little more successful than we had been with the psychiatric prison, and were finally granted access. The appointment was for that afternoon, we still had some time.

NOTES FROM THE HOUSE OF THE DEAD

147. At the corner of Dorohozhytska and Oranzhereina Streets, the cemetery wall turned left and we followed it,

leaving the tower behind us. A little further up, we cut across the street towards a long, three-storey building, its façade decorated with yellow, brick-red and bottle-green tiles, dilapidated, shabby, slowly crumbling. There was no one on the front porch. I walked up the steps to read the plaques placed next to the main door: MAIN OFFICE OF MEDICAL-LEGAL EXPERTISE OF THE MINISTRY OF HEALTH OF UKRAINE. Also known as Morgue No. 1, the main morgue for the right bank is located, as if by chance, in Babyn Yar, at No. 9 Oranzhereina Street. 'Is this it?' Antoine, who had joined me on the steps, asked me as he got out his e-cigarette, sniffing the air mistrustfully. 'This is it.' While he puffed with a sharp whistling noise on his cigarette, I knocked repeatedly on the door's glass panel. Finally a figure appeared in the dark lobby and peered around the door. 'Yes?' 'We're here to see Oleksandr Viktorovych.' 'He's not here.' *Oi, blin.* I explained to this man that we'd made an arrangement with Oleksandr Myzailenko, the director, to visit his establishment. 'Yes, I know.' I had to get out my notebook quickly because this doctor, Mykola Viktorovych – no one here gave his surname, this place remained firmly 'old school' – immediately started, still standing on the porch, to tell us about his morgue. This was where all the unidentified corpses in the city were brought, along with all those who died under suspicious circumstances. The year before, they'd received 5,700; that year, 2,940 already. He himself had carried out 47 autopsies in one month. 'To give you an idea, a forensic pathologist in France or Germany will do two, three at most. But please, come in.' Despite the masks which we hastily pulled on the smell struck us in the face as soon as we came through the door. The year after that, with the war, we'd soon become used to it, but at that time it was still rather new to me. It invaded our mucous membranes, stuck to our skin, to our clothes; I hadn't expected it to be so *material*, like a thing occupying the air and partly taking its place. As for Mykola Viktorovych, he didn't even wear a mask. He led us through the lobby to the left. In the first autopsy room lay two naked male corpses, each on its metal table, the first one obese, with legs purplish with varicose veins, the second one old and thin, marbled with yellow and red, with the handmade tattoos of a former prisoner. The skulls had been sawed open and emptied, the skin on their faces peeled back, their brains placed next to them, in pools of fresh blood. Across the hallway, in another room, lay a completely putrefied corpse, black, green, yellow, hardened, wizened, which had been found in an apartment. A doctor was opening his head with a hand saw; noticing us, he angrily threw us out, but the door didn't close well and through the gap I could still see him sawing, cutting, carving as if into old rotten meat. A loud metallic noise behind me made me turn my head: the freight elevator was clattering open and some attendants were pulling out two stretchers with bodies that they placed alongside the wall; one of them, naked, its head wrapped in a blanket, its yellowish skin covered with thick black hair, had already been stitched back up, a label attached to his wrist gave his name and address. Along with Mykola Viktorovych, we took the place of the stretchers in the freight elevator and went down, the corpse visible in the opening slowly disappearing above while the concrete surface between the floors went by and then blocked everything from sight. Downstairs, we emerged into a long, gloomy, cold corridor, lit by neon tubes and full of debris, of pipes and of rolls of flypaper covered in fat black insects. A little embarrassed, Mykola Viktorovych apologized for the state of the building: 'We rent it, you understand, we don't have the right to make

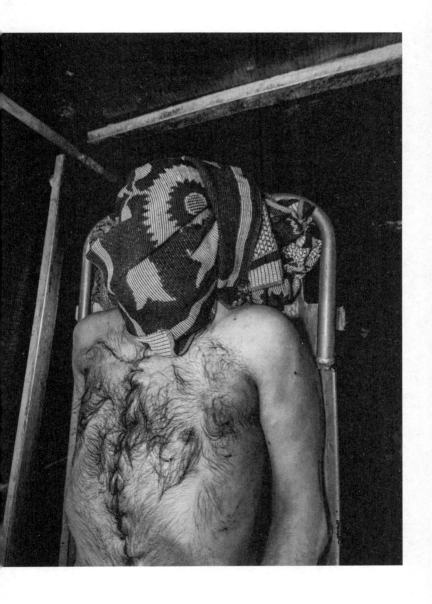

any major renovations.' Under the pale fluorescent light, as we passed the doors of fridges he refused to open for us, he rattled off a list of all the dead they received: 'Accidents, suicides, poisonings, murders, diseases, fights, drownings, car accidents, train accidents, plane accidents, unexplained deaths.' At the end of the hallway, a door opened onto an ancient, shaky piece of machinery that rose to the backyard of the building, and that the ambulance drivers used to send the bodies down. Mykola Viktorovych, who had been rather tense and nervous at the start of the visit, seemed relaxed and almost affable as he accompanied us to the exit. We stayed on the porch for a long moment, smoking to try to mask the stench stuck in our throats.

148. We were finally getting ready to leave when a little car pulled up and parked in front of the building. A massive, smiling man emerged from it and walked towards us. This was Myzailenko, the morgue's head doctor. So we started smoking again while we talked, and I asked him why he'd chosen this profession. '*Pochemu, potomu shto.* Why? Because. For me it would be much worse to work in a cancer or a burn ward. Here, at least, when they arrive, they're not suffering anymore.' The expert, he went on, must reconstruct the where and the how; he has the results in front of him, and must reconstitute the story starting from the end, must set off from the trace to arrive at the facts. The why is up to the police. 'And Babyn Yar?' He shook his head: 'No, we've never had any bones from there.' But in the 1980s, during perestroika, they had carried out investigations in a wood on the left bank southeast of Kyiv, in a place where some 40,000 people killed by the NKVD in the 1930s were buried. As we smoked and talked, we tried to convince him to show us the fridges,

and little by little his unwillingness gave way. 'If you want to see them, OK. But no photos.' Antoine protested, showing him the abstract images generated by his thermal camera: 'See? You can only see shapes.' 'Alright, alright.' We plunged back into the stench and went back downstairs. As soon as he opened the first fridge I understood why they hadn't wanted to show them to us. The corpses, frozen, almost all naked, were stacked on top of each other like cords of firewood, some on shelves, others, because of the lack of space, on rickety, rusted stretchers. A very young boy, about 11, his eyes closed, a little dried blood on his nostrils, naked and stitched up from his genitals to his neck, lay head-to-foot on top of the corpse of an equally naked man; a young guy in a green T-shirt and jeans, his body twisted, one sneaker removed so that a label could be attached to a toe, lay on top of a man whose face was covered in blood; other bodies were rolled up in blankets, in dirty sheets. Antoine attempted a few images with the thermal camera, but it obviously didn't work, cold on cold there was no contrast for the camera to read. Oleksandr Viktorovych, warming up to the idea of our visit, also showed us the room where the bodies are prepared for the families, shabby with tables covered with makeup and brushes, and a corpse under a white sheet; next to this stood an empty room with a long marble block on which the paltry coffin provided by the morgue to deliver bodies to their families was placed: it was a little cleaner than the rest, but just as foul-smelling, and poor, and sad. Behind the building lay a quiet back yard. Families were sitting patiently under a flowering arbour, next to wreaths of artificial flowers for sale, placed on steps. A cat was threading its way through the cars parked there; a black and white magpie jumped onto an open rubbish bin, nicked a clear plastic bag full of candy, carried it a little further away and started pecking at it to get at the sticky sweets.

149. The following year, at the beginning of the war, Antoine went back to see Oleksandr Viktorovych: as I wrote earlier, he served him tea and denied him access. In September, while visiting Kyiv, it was my turn to stop by to say hello to him. I found him on the porch, talking on his phone, and I waited while he finished his call. The building had suffered, most of its windows, especially to the right of the entrance, had plastic sheeting stretched over them in place of glass, dozens of tiles had come off the wall, leaving empty rectangles in the faience patterns; the front door had lost its glass panels as well. The shockwave of the missile that had struck the TV tower had shattered them all. 'The building was full of people,' Oleksandr Viktorovych told me after we'd exchanged greetings. 'Our employees, policemen, soldiers. I sent everyone down to the basement. You know the place. The entire hallway was full of dead bodies piled up along the walls. After the 24th we were the only morgue still functioning in Kyiv, and more bodies came every day. It became a second wall on each side, the whole length. And so all the living were lined up in rows between the dead. There was a colonel, he was looking at all that, on one side and then on the other, and he said to me: "Interesting, your air raid shelter."' I gently scolded him for not letting Antoine in. 'I would have loved to! I have no problem with Antoine, he's a good, serious guy. But you understand, everyone was falling all over me, all these *New York Times,* CNN, BBC, everyone. I had to say no to everyone, otherwise we'd have gone mad. But come back with Antoine whenever you like. I'll show you whatever you want.'

150. On that day, I didn't enter the morgue, there was no need: the contents of Oleksandr Viktorovych's smartphone was more than enough. Recently, after an exchange of bodies with Russia, he had received over 120 corpses of combatants from the Azov battalion killed in Azovstal, in May during the last stand of Mariupol. He'd had to identify them all. 'With the tattoos, it's pretty easy, it's faster than with the DNA.' He showed me some messages on WhatsApp in which families sent him photos of the tattoos of their missing relatives; he just had to compare them to the images of the dead bodies, also on his phone. Symbols from Nordic or Egyptian myths, patriotic slogans or symbols, even jokes (one corpse with a shaved head, quickly identified, had tattooed on the back of the neck PRIVIET PARIKHMAKER, 'hello barber'). The problem came from the fact that many of the families were so disturbed, psychologically, that they refused to accept the bodies, even when everything corresponded, the tattoos, the rings, the DNA. 'They tell me no, it's someone else, one of his friends copied his tattoo, someone stole his ring, who knows. Some of them finally face the facts, but others don't.' In that case he could only return the body to Azov, which gave it a military funeral, without the family.

RABBITS AND BOAS

151. After taking my leave of Oleksandr Viktorovych, I walked up Oranzhereina Street towards the park. The television tower dominated the sky whitened by the cold autumn light, its support pillars on the western side still blackened, deformed, and in some places pitted by the missile fired in March. In the park, to the right of the big ravine-shaped depression surrounding the immense

bronze pile of the Soviet monument to Babyn Yar, a long complex of trenches had been dug parallel to the street and the outer wall of the tower complex, with a little command post covered with a reinforced roof, shooting positions protected by gutted sand bags, palettes and boards carefully placed at the bottom of the trenches, and lain over everything handmade camouflage netting with mismatched pieces of cloth rolled and then braided into large plastic nets. Everything was gradually beginning to collapse, these positions must have been abandoned months ago, ever since the Russian retreat probably. Below, sitting in the sun on the grass of the fake ravine, a few young people were chatting, looking at their phones, painting watercolours; on the sandy bed in front of the monument, another teenager in a tracksuit was forming loops on his scooter. Further on, towards Olena Teliha Street, opposite a long building belonging to Ukrenergo, the national electricity company, another little trench drew a gash in the grass, also surrounded with little partially collapsed walls of earth and sand bags; a dozen metres further on, Tetiana Markus, a Jewish partisan tortured and shot by the Gestapo in January 1943, stood contemplating the scene with her implacable bronze face, fists clenched against all this relentlessly renewed injustice. At the intersection of Dorohozhytska and Olena Teliha Streets, all the cafés we used to go to before the war were closed; the windows of Banka, our favourite cafeteria, were still covered with boards. The entrance of the *perekhid* allowing you to cross the avenue was protected by a baffle of white sand bags; at the corners of the pavement, antitank obstacles of all sizes, made of welded train tracks and pipes, were quietly rusting as they waited to be redeployed.

152. The previous year, Antoine and I had followed almost the same path from the morgue to head straight towards the Soviet monument. 'More than once,' reports the writer Anatoliy Kuznetsov, 'I heard the Kiev Communists saying things like this: "Which Babi Yar? Where they shot the Yids? And for what should we build a monument to some insignificant filth?"'[104] His colleague Viktor Nekrassov also heard similar words, showing how widespread they must have been at the time: 'What monument? To whom? Monuments are erected to heroes. But these people went voluntarily, like rabbits into the jaws of a boa constrictor.'[105] *Nad Babim Yarom pamiatnikov niet.*[106]

153. No monuments, no ravine, nothing. A smooth and flat place. For a long time. But why? In 1945, the sculptor Yosyf Kruhlov and the chief architect of Kyiv, Oleksandr Vlasov, had swiftly proposed a monument be built; in 1949, their project was included in the general plan of the city's reconstruction, but never came to fruition; in a city so ravaged by war, there were other priorities.[107] The decision to fill in Babyn Yar, made by the 1950 municipal commission (at least half of whose members were Jewish), was also based on a logic of urban development: in the minds of the city planners, it would allow the city's expansion – hindered till then by the topography – with the creation of a new modern neighbourhood on the levelled terrain, and also the opening of major motorways which would link the industrial neighbourhood of Petrivka, at the time very isolated above Podil, to the city centre. Rational choices, in short. But practical considerations were not the only ones taken into account.

154. For Stalin, in fact, and for all of the USSR after him, what we call 'the Holocaust' or 'the Shoah' did not exist, had never existed, must never exist. There were reasons for this. Timothy Snyder shows how Stalin was obsessed by the ideological response the USSR had to bring to German anti-Semitism:

> From a Stalinist perspective, it was not the killings of Jews that mattered but the possibilities for its political interpretation.... In November 1941 Stalin was thus preparing an ideological as well as a military defence of the Soviet Union. The Soviet Union was not a state of the Jews, as the Nazis claimed; it was a state of the Soviet peoples, first amongst whom were the Russians.... [Thus,] Stalin's answer to Hitler's propaganda shaped the history of the Soviet Union for as long as it existed: all the victims of German killing policies were 'Soviet citizens.'[108]

This interpretation had the advantage of glossing over bothersome facts, such as the massive collaboration with the occupying forces by a portion of said Soviet citizens, and their participation, if not always enthusiastic, in any case compliant, in the massacres of the Jews. What's more, 'the murder of the Jews was not only an undesirable memory in and of itself; it called forth other undesirable memories'[109] – memories, obviously, of the colossal Stalinist killings of the 1930s, of which the peoples in the territories occupied by the Germans in 1941, especially the Poles and the Ukrainians, were the main victims.

155. During the war, however, Stalin assiduously paid court to what he perceived as the American 'Jewish lobby'. He authorized the creation (or rather the reopening) of a Jewish Anti-Fascist Committee (EAK in Russian),

led by the famous actor and director of the Moscow State Jewish Theatre Solomon Mikhoels, and sent Mikhoels and other members of the EAK abroad to plead the cause of the USSR and raise funds from the great Jewish solidarity organizations such as the 'Joint'.[110] In December 1942, the USSR signed a common declaration with its allies denouncing the extermination of the Jews; on 19 December that same year, *Pravda* published a declaration from the Information Bureau of the NKID (the People's Commissariat for Foreign Affairs) condemning the 'special plan for the total extermination of the Jewish population in the occupied territory of Europe' – the last document, notes the historian Hennadii Kostyrchenko, 'in which the Soviet leadership assessed the Nazi's crime against the Jews in historically adequate terms.'[111] A year later, in December 1943, the Soviet authorities had several groups of foreign correspondents based in Moscow visit Babyn Yar, including Bill Downs from *Newsweek* and Bill Lawrence from the *New York Times*. These men, sceptical of the amplitude of the massacres being described to them, were authorized to interview three survivors of the *Sonderkommando* formed by the Germans to burn the corpses of Babyn Yar, Efim Vilkis, Leonid Ostrovky and Vladimir Davidov, and published long articles in their respective journals.[112]

156. But already the official line was solidifying, and Russian and Ukrainian anti-Semitism, repressed before the war, making an open return. In 1943, during a meeting of the Ukrainian Union of Soviet Writers called to discuss the dismissal of its Jewish president, Natan Ribak, the great Ukrainian filmmaker Oleksandr Dovzhenko made a speech: 'Jews have poisoned Ukrainian culture. They have hated us, they hate us now, and will always

hate us. They try to crawl in everywhere and take over everything.'[113] When David Hofshtein, a Soviet Jewish poet, tried to organize a memorial gathering in Babyn Yar, the local authorities refused to grant him permission, declaring it to be 'an expression of Jewish chauvinism that could provoke anti-Semitic demonstrations.'[114] In January 1944, the ChGK[115] drafted a report on the fate of the Jews of Kyiv; when the report was published a month later, it bore no mention of the Jews, only 'thousands of innocent Soviet citizens'.[116] Solzhenitsyn tells how Nikita Khrushchev, 'then the First Secretary of the Communist Party and President of the Sovnarkom of Ukraine, [when confronted with] the old Jewish Communist Ruzha-Godès, who had survived the entire Hitlerian occupation by passing as a Pole from Chełmno, and who with the long-desired arrival of the Communists couldn't find any work because she was Jewish, with his usual frankness explained things to her directly: "In the past, the Jews committed quite a few sins towards the Ukrainian people. The people hate them because of that. In our Ukraine we don't need Jews.... It would be better for them not to return here. It would be better for them to go to Birobidzhan... This is Ukraine here. And we are not interested in seeing the Ukrainian people interpret the return of Soviet power as the return of the Jews."'[117]

157. The Soviet Jews, obviously, saw things from a different perspective. Visiting Kyiv in September 1945, Mikhoels – then one of the most famous and respected artists in the USSR – was invited to speak at the Kyiv State Jewish Theatre. He appeared at the podium with a crystal vase filled not with flowers but with a 'yellow and black substance'. Mikhoels addressed the audience in Yiddish: 'Before I came, some friends from the Moscow

211

Theatre and I went to a shop to buy this crystal vase. We then went directly to Babi Yar and filled this vase with earth.' Lifting the vase, Mikhoels went on: 'Look at this. You will see laces from a child's shoes, tied by little Sara who fell with her mother. Look carefully and you will see the tears of an old Jewish woman.... Look closely and you will see your fathers who are crying "*Sh'ma Israël*" and looking with beseeching eyes to heaven, hoping for an angel to rescue them.... I have brought you a little earth from Babi Yar. Throw into it some of your flowers so they will grow symbolically for our people.... Despite our enemies, we shall live.'[118] Mikhoels, alas, was mistaken. On 12 January 1948, he was assassinated in Minsk by the MGB (Ministry of State Security), on Stalin's orders surely; too popular to be openly executed, his death was made to look as if he'd been run over by a truck. This was the start of a virulent campaign of persecution against the Soviet Jews. A significant number of the leaders of the Jewish Anti-Fascist Committee, less well known than Mikhoels, were arrested, tried and executed; only the writers Vasily Grossman and Ilya Ehrenburg, both immensely popular with soldiers at the front for their war articles, were spared. In 1951, for sinister reasons linked to in-house politics, a department of the MGB created the 'doctors' plot', in which Jewish doctors were accused of conspiring to assassinate Soviet leaders under cover of medical care. Although there is no concrete proof to demonstrate it, many historians think the arrests and indictments of nine doctors, in January 1953, were the prelude to a vast anti-Jewish campaign of persecution, perhaps even of a mass deportation of Soviet Jews. But on 5 March 1953, Stalin died. Very quickly, the collective leadership that replaced him denounced this manipulation, and Lavrentiy Beria, who had just been named Minister of Internal Affairs, cleared the doctors in a decree dated 31 March, while also arranging the execution of his rival Mikhail Ryumin, the deputy minister of State Security and the author of the 'conspiracy'. Things, on the surface at least, quickly calmed down. But state anti-Semitism was there to stay, and the resolutely pro-Western orientation of the new Jewish state of Israel, the creation of which had originally been supported by Stalin, didn't make things any better. A permanent suspicion would henceforth weigh over the Jews of the USSR, giving a new form and a pretext to the historical and visceral anti-Semitism: 'cosmopolitanism', 'fifth column', 'bourgeois nationalism' was the politically correct aspect this anti-Semitism would henceforth take in *Pravda* articles and the speeches of Party officials.

158. And so the monument project of 1945-1949 was filed away once and for all. But Yevtushenko's poem, followed by demonstrations in Babyn Yar organized by a new generation of young Soviet Jews, made for a new state of affairs. Despite the attempts at repression by the KGB, the agency that succeeded the MGB, young activists continued to talk publicly about the massacre and to demand a worthy commemoration. In 1965, finally giving in to pressure, the authorities announced a contest for the creation of a monument to the victims of fascism in Kyiv. Hundreds of projects, some of them designed by famous artists and architects, were submitted, but none were accepted, officially because of their 'poor artistic quality'.[119] In September 1966, for the 25th anniversary of the massacre, Jewish activists, reacting to this decision and of course without any official authorization, organized the largest demonstration up to that point. 'Babyn Yar began to be perceived ... as a place [for] Soviet Jews protesting against government persecution.'[120] Taking a step

214

back, the authorities erected a granite obelisk bearing the inscription: 'A monument to the Soviet people will be erected here – to the victims of the atrocities of fascism during the temporary occupation of Kyiv in 1941-1943.'[121] But 1970 and 1971 saw an intensification of the repression aimed at 'the Zionist Internationale'. The Communist Party's Central Committee passed several decrees handing over more authority on the matter to the KGB. 'In [these] circumstances,' Hrynevych writes, 'Babyn Yar was objectively transformed into an arena of conflict.'[122]

BRONZE VICTIMS

159. The long-awaited monument was inaugurated on 2 July 1976. What can be said of it? Standing in front of this bronze pile, I suggested to Antoine that he might try to photograph it: 'Sheer torture,' was his only comment after several attempts. That didn't surprise me much. 'According to the architect Anatolii Ihnashchenko, the work was marred by Politburo intervention, which censored the original project and repeatedly introduced ideological adjustments to the submitted proposals.'[123] At the last minute, the authorities saw a Star of David in the six branches of the pseudo-ravine dug around the monument, and sent for 600,000 square metres of earth to fill in three of the branches.[124] But what scandalized the Jewish community of Kyiv more than anything else was the plaque in Ukrainian placed at the foot of the monument: HERE, IN 1941-1943, THE GERMAN-FASCIST INVADER SHOT OVER 100,000 CITIZENS OF THE CITY OF KYIV AND PRISONERS OF WAR. Of the Jews as such, not a word. The situation lasted until perestroika, in 1989, when the authorities, finally giving in to pressure from the various activist

215

organizations, added two plaques bearing the same text, one in Russian, the other in Yiddish, an 'absolutely surrealistic ... "nod" to the Jews'[125] –'Recognizing without recognizing,' as says Moshe Reuven Asman, the rabbi of the Brodskyy synagogue in Kyiv.[126]

160. For lack of photographs, we'll describe it. From Dorohozhytska, at the edge of the park, a sandy double lane had brought us to the monument, the work of the sculptors M.H. Lysenko, V.V. Sukhenko and O.P. Vitryk, as well as the architects M.K. Ivanchenko, V.M. Ivanchenkov and A. Ihnashchenko. It rises above a wide pink granite triangle in the shape of an uneven staircase at the top of which, at the foot of the sculpture, are lined up the three verdigris-covered bronze plaques, Ukrainian in the centre, Russian on the left and Yiddish (written in Hebrew characters) on the right, the language of nobody except for some of the victims. The interlocked figures of the mass of weathered bronze, backlit in front of the blue sky, resolutely turn their backs to the actual site of Babyn Yar, further on beyond Illienko Street. The first character, the one that dominates the central ensemble, is an older man in an open coat brandishing his right fist, his determined and stoic face barred with a moustache, his trousers, torn at the ankle, floating over partly untied boots. On his left a young sailor, his back turned (to the invisible rifles and machine guns the whole setup is meant to conjure), also raises his fist; he is hiding an old woman held in his right arm, whose tearful eyes under a scarf are the only things to appear over his virile shoulder and neck, raised to protect her from the bullets; next to him, a woman in a slip dress twists in anguish, her face invisible beneath her raised arms thrown backwards. To the right of the man with the moustache, another, older man, almost bald,

bare-chested, also triumphantly brandishes his fists: the fists, as much as the faces, spell out a major part of the social-realist grammar at work here. Seated above them all, on a bronze spiral in the shape of a cloud or a rocky peak (we'll go with the second interpretation, unless one of the sculptors had secret religious inclinations, clandestinely coded into the monument, the way dissidents slipped encrypted messages meant for imprisoned friends or for the 'happy few' into their endnotes[127]), a woman whose billowing blouse reveals her generous curves leans over to try to kiss her naked baby sprawled on her lap, dying or already dead; you have to walk around the bottom of the monument to the left, and lift your head towards the television tower, to see that this woman has her wrists tied behind her back with leather straps, and is struggling with her bonds, her arms in a triangle raised to the sky, to give her child this last kiss. It's also only from behind and below that you can see the other figures, the ones that, already mown down, are either tumbling or on the verge of tumbling into the ravine. On the left, a naked young man leaning to the side, a twist of cloth opportunely floating in front of his crotch, bends his knees and rests on his left hand, struggling till the last moment not to fall to the ground, his right fist clenched in the throes of death; from the front of the monument, his head is hidden behind the other figures, as if he were trying not to be noticed; it's only when seen from below that he finally looks like a man who has been shot and, eyes closed, is slowly slipping to the ground, exposing his muscular buttocks. On the right, a kneeling young woman in a thin dress weeps into her left hand over the almost naked corpse of another young man with unconvincing feet. On this side of the monument, the face, eyes closed, of the young woman in the slip dress and her long, thick hair twisting in the wind are

217

visible; just when I was contemplating it from this angle, thin rays from the partly hidden sun were touching her left ankle, the bottom of her slip, her left armpit, and her upper lip. In the back, finally, on a rocky hillock, a final figure of a naked man, his crotch also hidden by some cloth, is sprawled with his head on his crossed arms, his right foot, with massive toes, stretched over the void. This magnificent, deformed, almost Baconian foot is the finest piece of the whole monument. I took an excellent photo of it. This foot is almost a masterpiece.

ELEPHANT

161. Antoine had wandered off while I was finishing up my notes. I joined him and we headed towards Illienko Street and the metro, cutting diagonally across that part of the park. There was another monument I wanted to see on the way, I knew it was somewhere nearby, and found it easily enough. A grey marble cross, sober, unmarked, stood before a half-circle of little cypresses; at the foot of the cross a marble plaque bore the following inscription: **1941-1943 IN OCCUPIED KYIV DURING THE STRUGGLE FOR AN INDEPENDENT UKRAINIAN STATE, 621 MEMBERS OF THE ANTI-NAZI UNDERGROUND OF THE ORGANIZATION OF UKRAINIAN NATIONALISTS FELL, AMONG THEM THE POETESS OLENA TELI-HA. BABYN YAR BECAME THEIR COMMON GRAVE. GLORY TO THE HEROES!** Two other plaques bore a list of names, I recognized a few of them, Teliha of course, Bahazii, Rohach. It was curious. Especially here, in Babyn Yar.

162. The OUN, the Organization of Ukrainian Nationalists, is the elephant in the room of the memory of contemporary Ukraine, the one that smashes the china

but that everyone pretends to ignore.[128] Even a historian as scrupulous as Serhii Plokhy, in his remarkable history of Ukraine, skims quickly over the OUN's collaboration with the Germans, and doesn't mention their role in the 1941 pogroms or their participation in the Shoah at all.[129] There's a problem there, something that puts everyone in an awkward position. The Russians, obviously, run with the ball, repeating all the clichés of Soviet propaganda about the OUN and creating new ones in order – moving blithely from the particular to the universal – to call all the Ukrainian people, as well as their democratically elected government and their Jewish president, fascists and Nazis. It must be said that if things hadn't been so complicated, these past thirty years, it would have been easier to reply to them. In the Soviet era, it was anti-Semitism that made Babyn Yar so inconvenient. But if the place, after 1991, has remained covered with such a strange, embarrassed half-silence, has remained such a chaotic non-place, it is indeed because of Ukrainian integral nationalism, or rather the ambiguous relationship contemporary Ukraine has had with it. As Renan wrote so aptly, 'Forgetting, and I would even say historical error, are an essential factor in the creation of a nation.'[130]

163. Impossible to sketch this forgetting without talking about what is forgotten. But it is not simple. Nonetheless, the history of the *Orhanizatsiya Ukrainskykh Natsionalistiv* is well known, and the facts are indisputable. The OUN was founded in Poland in 1929 by Galician veterans of the Polish-Ukrainian war of 1919, at first essentially to contest the annexation by Poland of former Ukrainian provinces of the Austro-Hungarian Empire, Galicia and Podolia as well as Tsarist Volhynia. It was, as Timothy Snyder writes,

'an illegal, conspiratorial, and terrorist organization bound to destroy the status quo.' Racist, anti-Semitic and soon fascistic, 'its goal was an independent Ukraine to include all Ukrainian territories (widely understood) but only Ukrainian people (narrowly understood).'[131] It was also an entirely minority movement, which would have counted for nothing in the Polish political landscape if not for its recourse to violence, under the form of attacks perpetrated against government officials and Ukrainians regarded by the OUN as 'collaborators'. The rise of Hitler's Germany would quickly reshuffle the cards for an OUN weakened by the imprisonment of its most radical activists. Its leader, Colonel Yevhen Konovalets, had opened negotiations with the Abwehr not long before being assassinated by the NKVD in May 1938; his replacement, another former colonel from the Austro-Hungarian army named Andrii Melnyk, continued this rapprochement, which was perfectly logical from the perspective of an organization that saw its principal enemies as Poland and the Soviet Union. When Germany invaded the USSR in June 1941, two Ukrainian Abwehr battalions, Nachtigall ('Nightingale') and Roland, as well as several OUN militias, entered Lviv at the side of the Nazi forces.

164. The leaders of the OUN, dazzled by the experience of Ante Pavelić's Croatian Ustashis, to whom Hitler had the year before offered an independent Croatia carved out of the rubble of Yugoslavia, imagined that collaboration would make their dream of a reunified, independent Ukraine come true. On 30 June 1941, Yaroslav Stetsko proclaimed the independence of Ukraine from the balcony of the Lviv town hall. This declaration was accompanied by violent pogroms against the Jews, secretly incited by the Germans, but led by Ukrainian nationalists,

which rapidly extended to all of Galicia and claimed about 20,000 victims.[132] Even today, the question of the direct participation of the OUN in these killings – which affected, it should be noted, only the Polish territories occupied by the USSR in 1939, and not the previously Soviet territories further to the east – remains open. Did the OUN militias encourage or incite them? Did their members take part in an organized way or only on an individual basis? It seems to depend on the place. There were no trials after the war for these pogroms, and no one can be identified.[133] But as the historian John-Paul Himka demonstrates, the OUN militias also helped the Germans round up a large number of Jews whom the *Einsatzgrüppen* executed in the first days of the occupation, often on the pretext of 'reprisals' for the massacres of thousands of Ukrainian detainees by the NKVD just before the Soviet retreat.[134] This was the first phase of the Shoah, and the OUN took part in it without any qualms. In a long passage in *Bloodlands*, Timothy Snyder tries to pinpoint the ambiguous (to say the least) motivations of the pogromists:

> Political calculation and local suffering do not entirely explain the participation in these pogroms. Violence against Jews served to bring the Germans and elements of the local non-Jewish population closer together.... [And] the idea that only Jews served communists was convenient not just for the occupiers but for some of the occupied as well.
>
> Yet this psychic Nazification would have been much more difficult without the palpable evidence of Soviet atrocities. The pogroms took place where the Soviets had recently arrived and where Soviet power was recently installed.... They were a joint production, a Nazi edition of a Soviet text.[135]

165. Even before the war, the OUN had split into two factions, which clashed more and more openly after the invasion of the USSR. It was essentially a generational divide. The older militants, often veterans of Ukrainian battalions of the Austro-Hungarian army, remained faithful to Andrii Melnyk. But the younger generation raised in the Galician *gymnasiums*, radical intellectuals fascinated by the figure of the *Provodnik* or Führer, and the peasant youth that followed them, turned towards Stepan Bandera, a young Galician activist imprisoned in 1934 for the assassination of the Polish Minister of the Interior Bronisław Pieracki, and freed by the Abwehr after the invasion of Poland in 1939. It was he who precipitated the slightly premature declaration of independence of Stetsko, his right-hand man. But the OUN-B hadn't understood that the Yugoslav option was not conceivable for Hitler, Göring and Himmler, who were planning a slave-state colonization for the Ukrainian territories entirely centred around the needs of the Reich. The Banderist dream of an independent Ukraine was short-lived: On 9 July, the Germans shut the game down, arresting Bandera, Stetsko and their entire entourage, and shooting hundreds of their men.[136]

166. Melnyk, prudently, had rejected the 30 June declaration, and his men continued to collaborate with the Germans, at the risk of being occasionally murdered by Banderist extremists. When the Germans took Kyiv, most of the Ukrainians appointed to important positions, like the *Bürgermeister* Volodymyr Bahazii, came from the ranks of the OUN-M. The most bitterly debated question is evidently that of the participation of the Melnykist militants in the Babyn Yar massacre. The debate mainly centres on the presence in Kyiv on 29 September of an

auxiliary police unit, the *Bukovinskyy Kurin*, which had already taken part in massacres of Jews in Chernivtsi, Zhytomyr and Bila Tserkva; according to Yurii Radchenko, a Ukrainian specialist of the OUN-M, it is possible that certain units of the *Bukovinskyy Kurin* were already in the city, but not the bulk of the troops.[137] What is certain is that some Ukrainian *Polizei* recruited by the OUN-M served in the first cordon that screened the Jews, at the *shlakbaum*. Raisa Meystrenko, another survivor who was three years old at the time and whom I interviewed in 2002, had confirmed this to me: when confronted with the *Polizei*, her grandmother had taken her in her arms and made the sign of the cross, shouting that she was Russian; one of the *Polizei* had then tried to bash in the little girl's head with the butt of his rifle; the grandmother had turned away and taken the blow on her shoulder, fracturing her clavicle, then in the confusion had managed to escape, but without her daughter, Raisa's mother, who was executed. Several other survivors, who were around the same age as Raisa, nonetheless testified after the war that some Ukrainian *Polizei*, either because they knew their parents, or out of sheer humanity, had agreed to take them and carry them away, without the Germans interfering. Some witnesses claim they saw Volodymyr Bahazii in Babyn Yar, along with his bodyguard; these testimonies are debated, but Radchenko confirmed to me that they appeared credible to him. Finally, Melnykist elements were put in charge of the Jewish goods accumulated during the massacre, some of which they stole, including gold teeth collected from the corpses. On 1 October, 'Orlyk,' the Melnykist commander of the Kyiv police, issued an order demanding that all *dvirnyky* in the city hand over Jews, Communists and NKVD cadres to the Germans.[138]

167. Be that as it may, the honeymoon between the OUN-M and the Germans wouldn't last much longer than that of the OUN-B. In January 1942, the Gestapo arrested Bahazii and his son Ihor; the following month, it was the turn of over 200 journalists from *Ukrainske Slovo*, the city's main collaborationist newspaper, and other activists from the OUN-M. Most were swiftly executed and the survivors scattered, joining the German civil service or the police while refraining from any political activity, or else going underground. It is these executions that justify, in principle, the monument in Babyn Yar. But the aforementioned poses a number of problems. First of all, the appropriation of the place: according to Yurii Radchenko, it was only around 1973-1974 that the Melnykists of the American diaspora started identifying Babyn Yar as the place where Olena Teliha and the others died. In reality, no one can say where or how they died. Oleh Shtul, one of the OUN-M leaders, wrote about Teliha's death in 1946, in a letter preserved in the organization's archives: '... we, of course, know nothing about her death itself. The walls of the NKVD prison at 33 Korolenko Street, where the Gestapo was located, are very thick. And Babyn Yar and the other graves are silent. And that's why we don't know much...'[139] It is even possible, according to the historian Andrii Usach, that Olena Teliha committed suicide in prison. What became of the corpses is equally vague: were they burned? Buried in the Lukyanivske cemetery? Or even thrown into one of the mass graves filling the ravines of Babyn Yar? Impossible to say. Next, the number – 621 – which according to Usach and Radchenko is grossly exaggerated. The two plaques on each side of the main inscription bear 62 names or aliases in all; however, Radchenko states, 'This list is not good quality, it hasn't been verified. Many people who are

on it were killed neither in Kyiv nor by the Germans.'[140] Sozontii Pynduliak, for example, a soldier from the *Bukovinskyy Kurin* who then joined the 115th Battalion of the Security Police (SIPO) before becoming a member of the Security Service of the OUN under the *nom de guerre* Bukovinets, ended up hanged by the Soviets in 1944; Roman Fodchuk, a well-known OUN-M activist who had enlisted as a translator for the Wehrmacht, was killed at the front, in Donbas on 5 March 1942.[141]

168. Finally, there is the cause of their death. The reasons for the liquidation of the Kyiv cadres of the OUN-M are not very clear; the takeover of *Reichskommissariat* Ukraine by the *gauleiter* Erich Koch, appointed by Hitler on 20 August 1941 and known for declaring 'If I find a Ukrainian worthy of sitting at the same table as me, I'll have to have him shot,' could have played a role. In any case it was not a question of resistance. According to Radchenko, Bahazii and his son were arrested and then executed for corruption and embezzlement of stolen Jewish goods and apartments, behaviour the Nazis did not take lightly (speaking to the SS leaders about the extermination of the Jews in his famous Posen speech in 1943, Heinrich Himmler recalled an order he'd given at the beginning of the Final Solution: 'He who takes even one mark of [Jewish property], that's his death'[142]). Many of the other victims belonged, as I've said, to the editorial board of *Ukrainske Slovo*: Ivan Rohach, his sister Hanna and especially Olena Teliha, a well-known poetess who had also founded *Litavre*, the literary supplement of *Ukrainske Slovo*. Despite the denials of the nationalists, from the diaspora to the present day,[143] *Ukrainske Slovo* and *Litavre* were purely organs of pro-Nazi propaganda, advocating collaboration and publishing violently anti-

Semitic articles: 'The Jews are trying in every way to avoid their just punishment. They pretend to be Armenians, Azerbaijanis, Bulgarians, but the Ukrainian patriots will not allow them to do so.'[144] Teliha, an ardent admirer of Mussolini and Hitler, also wrote anti-Semitic articles, such as 'The Fraternity of the People' published on 12 October, just before she arrived in Kyiv, in another collaborationist newspaper in Rivne called *Volyn*: 'The eternal enemy turned into a friend, the revolver in his hand blurred, became invisible, and the clenched fist appeared as an open fraternal palm ... And then the brothers from Moscow and the Yid-brothers came and stripped the Ukrainian brothers to the last thread.'[145] None of this prevented their liquidation; the fact that it took place at the hands of the Nazis was enough to make them into heroes. This is what has led the city of Kyiv to give Teliha's name to the street formerly named after Demyan Korotchenko, a head of government of the Ukrainian RSS in the 1930s and the 1950s; and allowed Vitalii Klichko, the mayor of Kyiv – who happens to be deeply involved in the projects of the BYHMC, where his brother Volodymyr sits on the Supervisory board – to inaugurate another monument in 2017, this one near the metro station, to the glory of Olena Teliha and her comrades (without any mention of the OUN, however). 'It's our schizophrenia,' the historian Sofia Dyak said to me one day in Lviv. 'I wonder what they're smoking.' Indeed, the blurring of Ukrainian memory means that no one, among the authorities, seems to see the contradiction, any more than they can see the irony of the fact that the only street in Kyiv that honours a victim of 'Babyn Yar', one that passes just above the very site of the massacre, bears the name of a fascistic, anti-Semitic collaborator.

COLLABORATIONS

169. This ambiguity in contemporary Ukraine's relationship to the memory of the OUN is understandable.
Ukraine sees itself as a Western country, turned towards
Europe and democracy; but as Per Rudling notes, 'In
Ukraine, two cultures of memory, the cult of Nationalist
heroes and the western European memory culture in
which the Holocaust plays a central role, are mutual-
ly exclusive.'[146] Yet the Ukrainian government has no
choice but to forge a common discourse, one capable of
speaking to the entirety of this country composed of such
different memories. I discussed this with Serhii Plokhy a
few months before the war: 'They can't handle the dirty
ride of the history of the OUN. Not for now, in any case.'
And the way Russian propaganda constantly adds fuel to
the fire doesn't make matters any easier. The essentialist
arguments of Vladimir Putin and his sycophants – 'the'
Ukrainians collaborated, so 'the' Ukrainians are Nazis, so
'they' must all be de-Nazified – demand that things be put
into perspective. First of all, unlike for instance French
collaboration, which involved the highest levels of the
State (it was the French police that rounded up the Jews,
the French State that handed them over to the Germans to
be transported to Auschwitz), the leaders and the activists
of the OUN, an ultra-minority among the Ukrainian people, represented only themselves. Its members amounted
to tens of thousands, possibly 200,000 at its peak in 1944,
whereas seven million Ukrainians fought Nazism in the
Red Army. Russia, supposedly at the forefront of the
anti-fascist fight, also had its hundreds of thousands of
collaborators, not just poor guys pressed into service
locally, but an entire army, led by one of Stalin's best gen-
erals, Andrei Vlasov. Stalin himself openly collaborated

with Hitler when he thought it opportune, at first by allowing the Wehrmacht to train in the USSR to avoid the restrictions of the Treaty of Versailles in exchange for the transfer of technology and know-how, then by signing the famous non-aggression pact in August 1939 that allowed the Nazis to start the Second World War. He even went so far as to hand over to the Gestapo the anti-fascist German activists imprisoned in his Gulag. Like the OUN, Stalin had his reasons, his justifications. We can read them in *The Falsifiers of History*, a book published in 1948 which he is supposed to have personally edited and partially re-written:

> No forgers will ever succeed in wiping from history ... the decisive fact that under these conditions, the Soviet Union faced the alternative: either to accept, for purposes of self defence, Germany's proposal to conclude a non-aggression pact and thereby to ensure to the Soviet Union the prolongation of peace for a certain period of time, which might be used by the Soviet State better to prepare its forces for resistance to a possible attack on the part of an aggressor; or to reject Germany's proposal ... and thereby to permit war provocateurs from the camp of the Western Powers immediately to involve the Soviet Union in armed conflict with Germany at a time when the situation was utterly unfavourable to the Soviet Union and when it was completely isolated. In this situation, the Soviet Government found itself compelled to make its choice.[147]

This book obviously does not mention the secret protocols of the Ribbentrop-Molotov pact, by which Nazi Germany and the USSR split Eastern Europe between themselves, with the USSR being granted the three Baltic countries, the east of Poland up to the Bug River (including western Ukraine) and Romanian Bessarabia. Today, discussing these facts in Russia is regarded as 'historical revisionism', and can lead to prosecution.

ON THE INVENTION OF ETHNIC CLEANSING

170. The monument to the OUN in Babyn Yar could give rise to another question, one which is no mere detail. While all the commemorated dead belonged to the Melnykist faction, which was *de facto* a separate organization from the Banderist faction, why does the monument only mention OUN without any additional information? This is clearly linked to the divergent fates of the two factions, which became particularly obvious as of 1943. In early August 1942, Galicia, until then under the control of the *Reichskommissariat* Ukraine, was transferred, at Hitler's orders, to the General Government, the name the Nazis gave to occupied Poland. This decision created powerful tensions within the two OUNs, which strongly hesitated about how to react, and provoked mutinies among the Nachtigall and Roland battalions. Nonetheless, the two factions encouraged their members to volunteer for the German police battalions; at least, they reasoned, they'd be armed and trained for whatever was to come. This decision had fatal consequences: these tens of thousands of young men in German uniform, supporting a few thousand German policemen, provided the bulk of the manpower for the extermination by bullets of the Jews of the occupied Ukrainian RSS as well as of large parts of Poland. Historians are unanimous on this subject: without the support of the Ukrainian volunteers, the Germans would never have been able to carry out their

extermination programme; many Jews would have been killed, of course, but by themselves, the Germans didn't have the necessary manpower to cause all traces of Jewish life to disappear from these vast regions.[148] These massacres, committed 'for a cause that was not even their own',[149] had profound consequences on the men involved, consequences Snyder very rightly emphasizes: 'The Final Solution had already taught them that the mass murder of civilian populations may be achieved by way of precise organization and the timely presence of men willing to shoot men, women and children.'[150] The lesson was learned, and would soon be directly applied.

171. The German debacle in Stalingrad at the end of January 1943 had major consequences for Ukrainian nationalist groups. They immediately understood what Hitler and his chiefs of staff had long refused to contemplate: the war was lost, the Soviets were coming back, and it was only a matter of time. But the two branches of the OUN drew diametrically opposite conclusions from this. Despite the elimination of his cadres in Kyiv and elsewhere, Andrii Melnyk renewed his collaboration with the Germans, who suddenly expressed their readiness to arm Ukrainians *en masse*. In April 1944, Melnyk supported the creation of a Ukrainian SS division, the 14th *Waffen-Grenadier-Division der SS 'Galizien'*, which was first deployed against Polish partisans before being sent to be annihilated in Brody by the Soviets that July. The *SS-Galizien* committed a significant number of atrocities during its operations in Poland, but cannot be accused of taking part in the Shoah, which, as Snyder points out, was already over when the division was formed.[151] The path followed by the OUN-B, however, was much more circuitous. Ever since the debacle of the declaration of

independence, Bandera and Stetsko had been incarcerated in Germany, in Berlin at first and then, from January 1942 onwards, in the 'VIP' section of KL Sachsenhausen; but their cadres, who had gone underground during the July 1941 crackdown, chose after Stalingrad to definitively break with Germany. On orders from their leaders, thousands of Ukrainian *Polizei* who had taken part in the Final Solution deserted *en masse*, taking their weapons with them and coming to swell the ranks of the OUN-B.[152] Numerous officers and soldiers who had fought in the ranks of the Wehrmacht also deserted, including Roman Shukhevych, an old OUN activist who quickly took on a pivotal role in the organization. In the spring of 1943, Shukhevych and his colleague Dmytro Klyachkivskyy, known as 'Klym Savur', turned on another Ukrainian nationalist group, the *Ukrainska Povstanska Armiya* (UPA, the Ukrainian Insurgent Army) of Taras Bulba-Borovets, killing most of its cadres and taking it over by force, transforming the UPA into the military branch of the OUN-B.[153] The leaders of the new UPA knew they still had months, even a year or more, before having to directly confront the Soviet steamroller: they had to take advantage of this time to arm and prepare themselves, and especially to settle all unresolved problems, including the historic problem of the OUN, the Polish problem. In April 1943, Mykola Lebed, the first leader of the new UPA, proposed they 'cleanse the entire revolutionary territory of the Polish population'.[154] This initiative put a definitive end to centuries of Polish-Ukrainian cohabitation in these regions. 'Liquidate all Polish traces', orders a UPA directive sent out in early 1944. 'Destroy all walls in the Catholic Church and other Polish prayer houses. Destroy orchards and trees in the courtyards so that there will be no sign that someone lived there. Destroy

233

all Polish huts in which Poles once lived.... Keep in mind the fact that if anything Polish remains, then the Poles will have claims to our land.'[155] Between 1943 and 1944, the UPA put this plan into action with stunning ferocity. Dozens of Polish villages in Volhynia were razed to the ground, their inhabitants killed with axes, pitchforks and cudgels, or else burned alive in their churches, especially during attacks that coincided with the major Catholic feast days. 'The retreat of the Germans had left a clear field for the Banderas,' writes Henry Friedman, a Jewish survivor of the Shoah in Galicia.... [They] seemed to have gone berserk, killing every Pole they got their hands on.'[156] In total, historians estimate that the UPA murdered between forty and sixty thousand Poles in Volhynia, and forced out tens of thousands of others.[157] In January 1944, the UPA extended its campaign to Galicia, where they killed another twenty-five thousand Poles in an equally atrocious way. By inventing what would decades later come to be called 'ethnic cleansing', the UPA had broken new ground, but others soon would imitate them: the UPA slaughters provoked equally massive Polish atrocities in retaliation, in the region of Lublin especially, led by the *Armia Krajowa* (the Army of the Interior), by self-defence groups constituted to try to protect Polish villages, and by Poles serving in German police forces, often replacing Ukrainian deserters, leading to what Snyder unhesitatingly calls a 'Ukrainian-Polish civil war'.[158] For the Germans, it was yet another problem they could well have done without.

172. The UPA didn't only attack Poles: they also systematically killed all the Jews they found, the last survivors of the Shoah gone to ground deep in the forests in makeshift shelters or else hidden by Polish or Ukrainian peasants.

234

Once again, these weren't individual initiatives of anti-Semitic militiamen, but a clear policy of the UPA and the OUN-B: orders enjoined the UPA's fighters to 'liquidate without delay communists and Jews' (11 March 1944, signed by 'Berkut'),[159] or to 'destroy NKVD personnel, informers, Jews, and Poles.'[160] The number of Jews killed in this way remains relatively low, a few thousand probably, but in some regions could reach 85% of the Jews who had survived the Nazi cleansing.[161] Above all – unlike the Nazis, who were content to 'coldly' exterminate the Jews with bullets or gas, or to send them to die of exhaustion in a camp – the men of the UPA often sought to kill those they captured in medieval, almost unimaginable tortures. Berl Lieblein, a Jew who survived by being hidden by a Ukrainian, writes: 'The bandit Suslynets [probably Dmytro Suslynets, the commander of a *sotnia* of the UPA in the Hoverla military district] ... got in his clutches two Jewish girls, whom he hanged on a branch upside down. Under them he placed a pile of branches which he set on fire and thus burned both victims.'[162] According to another survivor, Hilary Kenigsberg, 'The Banderites' ... terror in the woods was so great that the Jews were actually fleeing from the woods to the Germans for protection.'[163] The UPA, finally, also killed a large number of Ukrainians, almost as many, Snyder thinks, as Poles, even though the subject has never been studied in detail.[164] Supporters of Bulba-Borovets and Melnyk, collaborators with the Germans or with Soviet partisans, peasants who refused to support anyone, all were pitilessly hunted down and massacred. A particularly atrocious fate was reserved for the many Ukrainians who hid Poles or Jews, either for money, or out of personal sympathy, or out of simple humanity: most often, they ended up the same way as those they had tried to save, beaten or tortured to death with

their entire family. Once again, it was an explicit policy of the leaders of the UPA: 'For hiding Jews or Poles, everyone will be shot,' states the notebook of an agent of the OUN security service.[165]

173. At the beginning of 1944, Soviet forces reoccupied Volhynia; from then on, the Ukrainian nationalists gradually directed all their efforts towards the fight against Stalin. In any case, as far as the Poles were concerned, the problem had been taken care of, and their hands were free, at least in Volhynia. The UPA took advantage of the German retreat to seize huge numbers of weapons, including heavy artillery. In October 1944, by the time the Soviets had occupied half of Poland and all of Romania and Bulgaria, and were advancing towards Budapest, the Germans finally freed Bandera and Stetsko, sending them to take direct control of forces now entirely behind enemy lines. The fighting between the UPA on one hand and the NKVD and the Red Army on the other lasted years after the end of the war, slowly winding down in the early 50s. Stalin tried to settle the problem with his usual brutality: not only UPA fighters but also thousands of sympathizers in Western Ukraine were summarily executed, and hundreds of thousands of civilians of dubious loyalty were deported to Siberia and Central Asia, where decades later large Ukrainian populations could still be found. Klyachkivskyy was killed in January 1945 in a NKVD ambush near Rivne; Shukhevych, apparently, killed himself in May 1950 when the MGB surrounded the house where he was hiding in a suburb of Lviv. Bandera, Stetsko and Lebed all managed to flee to the West when the UPA finally collapsed. Lebed, who quickly forged a new political career for himself by reinventing himself as a democrat and collaborating with the CIA,

238

long headed pro-UPA publishing houses in exile; Stetsko presided over the Anti-Bolshevik Bloc of Nations until his death in 1986; as for Bandera, the Soviets finally caught up with him in Munich in October 1959, having him assassinated on his doorstep by a certain Bohdan Stashinskyy, a Ukrainian nationalist turned by the KGB, with a pistol that sprayed cyanide gas.

EMPTY SIGN

174. For many ordinary Ukrainians today, these men are heroes, and the cult of Bandera and the UPA endures in Ukraine. One reason is that, as Per Rudling writes, 'Here, in a new, weak state, divided by language, religion, and historical experience, the leadership has put considerable effort into producing historical myths of political utility, a significant part of which stand in direct opposition to contemporary sources and current scholarship.'[166] The first Ukrainian president to openly rehabilitate the symbols of the nationalist movements of the Second World War was Viktor Yushchenko, elected in 2005 after the 'Orange Revolution', the country's first clear break with Putin's Russia.[167] He 'started a purposeful promotion of a distinctly apologetic and even hagiographic memory of the OUN-UPA and its leaders by the Ukrainian state',[168] making it state policy by creating the UINP, the Ukrainian Institute of National Memory, and appointing as its leader Volodymyr Vyatrovych, a historian who would later be accused of having tried to 'purify' the Ukrainian archives of evidence of pogroms and other nationalist crimes.[169] During his time in office, at the same time as the Shoah was finally being recognized as a central historical fact, the Ukrainian post office issued stamps bearing

Bandera's portrait, and monuments to the OUN were erected on several sites where Jews were massacred, including Babyn Yar. Yushchenko, having failed to make it past the first round during the January 2010 presidential elections, played his trump card in an attempt to have his despised Prime Minister, Yulia Tymoshenko, defeated by the pro-Russian Yanukovych: knowing it would drive Russian-speaking electors in the south and east of the country mad with rage, he awarded Bandera the title of 'Hero of Ukraine', the highest distinction in the country (Yanukovych, elected in the second round, hurried to have this distinction annulled).[170] But nationalist symbols became especially widespread during the Maidan demonstrations: red and black UPA flags, portraits of Bandera, OUN songs and the call 'Slava Ukraina! Heroyam slava!' ('Glory to Ukraine! Glory to the heroes!', the slogan of the UPA, taken up and given new meaning by the entire population in the wake of the Russian invasion). Given the strong presence of extreme right-wing thugs on the square, this was not surprising; but a large number of ordinary demonstrators also adopted these symbols. And after the Russian invasion of Crimea and Donbas, 'Bandera' quickly became the all-purpose symbol for resistance to Russia. In July 2016, not long before the trip to Warsaw of the new president Petro Poroshenko during which he knelt before a monument to Polish victims of the massacres in Volhynia, the city of Kyiv gave the name of Bandera to the motorway continuing Olena Teliha Street (in Lviv, such an avenue had already existed since 1992, perpendicular to the Street of the Heroes of the UPA). On New Year's Day 2022, not long before the Russian invasion, I was strolling through the Christmas fair on St. Sophia Square, in front of the cathedral: beneath a giant illuminated fir tree, a happy crowd was ambling around to the sound of the corniest American Christmas carols, taking selfies, drinking *blintvein*, snacking on sausages, and watching their children ice-skating on the little rink set up between the kiosks; further down, on Khreshchatyk, under the New Year fairy lights, nationalist groups, brandishing flags and portraits, marched as they do every year in honour of Bandera's birthday, unsurprisingly providing a field day for Russian television.

175. But it is precisely the fact that Russian propaganda is against it that renders it good in the eyes of the Ukrainians. 'If the Russians say we're Banderists,' the leftist activist Anna Shtiken-Shnaider said to me one day, '*pust*, let us be Banderists.' It's a fact that aside from the most motivated ultranationalists, the great majority of Ukrainians are completely unfamiliar with the history of Bandera and his organization. It was never taught during the Soviet era, and is only partly taught today; as the journalist Nataliya Humenyuk pointed out to me, the only history books in Ukraine in 1991 were Soviet, and the government at the time ordered new ones from Canada, written by the diaspora formed by the survivors of the OUN-UPA, thus directly importing their prejudices and narratives. Anton Drobovych, the current director of the UINP, adds that no serious historical biographies of Bandera, Melnyk, Bulba-Borovets or Shukhevych exist in Ukraine: 'It's a symptom.'[171] For many people, the image they have of Bandera or the UPA comes from revisionist films like *The Undefeated*, financed in part by the diaspora.[172] 'Today's Banderists have no relation to the historical Banderists,' Anna Shtiken-Shnaider added at the end of our conversation. 'It's like in the United States, with the Democratic party and slavery. Even the gays and lesbians carry UPA flags to Pride marches. It's

an anti-Russian symbol.' The most paradoxical example of this cult completely detached from reality is the phenomenon of the '*Zhydobanderivtsi*', the 'Yid-Banderists' who appeared during the Maidan revolution; even Ihor Kolomoiskyy, one of the most controversial oligarchs in Ukraine, a Jew who in 2014 financed battalions of extreme right-wing volunteers to counter the Russian occupation of Donbas, was seen wearing a T-shirt with this meme. For Drobovych, it signified the union, during the Maidan revolution, of the middle classes, many of whom were Jewish, with the nationalists. 'Bandera is not a historical person, he's a simulacrum. He's a *pustoy znak*, an empty sign.'[173]

176. This identitarian bricolage, half-fanciful, half-self-referential, made of a potent mixture of ignorance, humour, sarcasm and a couldn't-care-less attitude, is no doubt the most characteristic feature of Ukraine. It's deeply problematic, of course, when you want to memorialize a place like Babyn Yar, when you want to seriously tackle important questions about the past, with its truckloads of dead and all its pain and suffering. But for now, this fragmented memory and its reverberations might be what is saving the country, what has allowed people with such different memories and identities as those from Lviv, Odesa, Kherson, Dnipro and Kharkiv to unify into one solid, compact block, determined to resist the Russian steamroller. Is it that necessary to know who Bandera and Shukhevych really were? To really know who actually did what to whom all over these lands? Maybe installing an IKEA kitchen, dancing in nightclubs and even heading to the forest on the weekend to train in weapon-handling is just as important. 'The Banderists want a simple history,' Timothy Snyder told me one day. 'But it's not a problem if

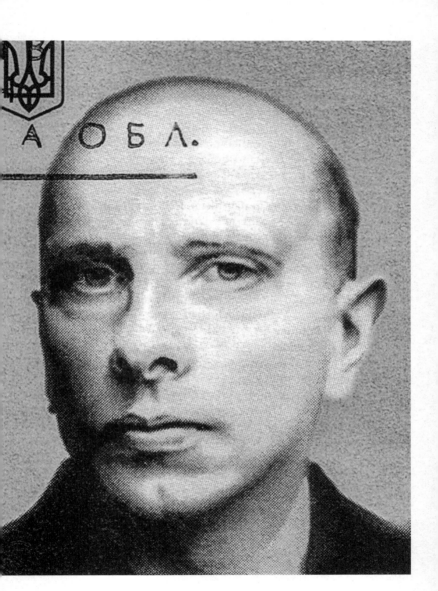

Ukraine isn't following the old nineteenth-century model of nationalist identitarian politics. Can Ukraine function without a simple history? Why not?' And can Ukraine function with a patchwork identity? I asked him in return. 'Why not?'

177. Nonetheless, many people in good faith find it difficult to understand how the integral nationalism and terrorism of the 1940s can be invoked for a just cause, how you can go risk your neck against a fascist and increasingly totalitarian dictatorship under the banner of racist, anti-Semitic murderers. The fact is that today's Ukrainians, after forty-five years of Sovietism and thirty years of ruthless capitalism paired with an ill-formed but robust democracy, don't really have anything to do with the 'Ukrainians' of Stalin and Hitler's era. Włodzimierz Odojewski, whose work is haunted by the memory of the killings in Volhynia, has the narrator (a Pole addressing his Ukrainian lover) of his final novel *Oksana* say: 'What you've told me [about the atrocities of the UPA] is the sin, the mortal sin, of a single generation. Which is neither mine nor yours, even if I was already in the world then.'[174] I can still remember my father's utter confusion, one day in the garden of his house in the Lot valley, it must have been in 1992 after the Vukovar massacres, in any case before I left for Bosnia in 1993: 'My whole life, I learned that the Croats were fascist bastards, and that the Serbs were heroes who had fought the Nazis. Now I don't understand anything anymore. Nothing at all.' Similarly, today, it's the supposedly 'fascist' Ukraine that dreams of Europe, democracy and freedom, while Poland, the great victim of the Second War, is regressing on all fronts towards authoritarianism, narrow-minded nationalism and religious bigotry, and Russia, wrapping itself in the cloak

244

of the conquerors of historic Nazism, is sinking into a deadening, apocalyptic and nearly genocidal vision, unleashing onto Europe the demons everyone thought they'd seen the last of in 1945. What does all this mean for our relationship with the past? That it is anything but frozen in time, that it doesn't always necessarily determine the present, and that the children of yesterday's killers can turn out to be the heroes or victims of today, just as the victims of yesterday – and this isn't only true of the Russians – can just as easily become the killers of today.

178. And what of the far right, then? In the same way that Vichy and collaboration, and then torture in Algeria and the OAS, have left deep marks in the French body politic, the OUN and the UPA, with Stalin's repression and Soviet anti-Semitism, have spread their metastases throughout the Ukrainian body politic, constantly mutating on the way. In 1991, at independence, some former members of the OUN came back to Ukraine to attempt a return to politics they imagined would be triumphant: they were quickly swept aside by new forces, macerated in the cauldron of declining Sovietism. For Serhii Plokhy, 'Contemporary radicals consider the Banderist diaspora, people like Stetsko, as too moderate. Starting in the 90s, they were marginalized. The new radical right is *made in Ukraine*. And they're no longer just Galicians, western Ukrainians: now, it's a pan-Ukrainian phenomenon. There are many Russian speakers among them.'[175] Let us again put things into perspective. Like the Rassemblement national, the Alternative für Deutschland and the Russian extremists such as Zakhar Prilepin or Aleksandr Dugin, the nationalist right in Ukraine is loud, visible, provocative, manipulative and aggressive; but unlike them, it is politically insignificant.

After an electoral peak at the beginning of the 2010s, their support began to collapse following Maidan, despite the engagement of a great many nationalist volunteers on the Donbas front and their heroic feats of arms. At the last elections in 2019, which brought Zelenskyy to power with an overwhelming majority, all the far-right parties in the country, after (God knows how) managing to negotiate a joint list of candidates for the parliamentary elections, failed to get a single MP elected to the Rada. Compare that to the 89 MPs from the Rassemblement national in France, or to the 'postfascist' party now in power in Italy, before talking about Ukrainian 'Nazis'. 'Why is the right so weak?' Serhii Plokhy had rhetorically asked me. 'Why are there so few of them in a country at war?' Replying to his own question, he quoted Andrew Wilson: 'Unlike Polish nationalism, [radical] Ukrainian nationalism is a minority faith.'

ANOTHER LIFE

179. And what do the nationalists themselves think of all this? A friend from the BYHMC had organized an interview for me with Artiom Skoropadskyy, the press attaché for Pravyy Sektor ('Right Sector' or 'Right-Wing Sector', a radical nationalist organization, deeply involved in Maidan and then in the Donbas fighting); at the last minute, he cancelled the meeting, he was ill, cancer I think, he wasn't well at all.[176] This same friend had also spoken to me about a former ultra-nationalist who had become a progressive, rather well-known for his public denunciations of his ex-comrades, a certain Dmytro Reznichenko. He instantly agreed to speak with me. Since we had some time before our meeting at the television tower, I had

247

suggested he come meet me in Babyn Yar on that day. It was almost time, and as Antoine and I left the monument to the OUN, we headed towards the metro, talking about all these stories as we reached the monument to Olena Teliha and the Teliha Street intersection. We crossed the *perekhid* to go wait in front of Aroma Kava where we each ordered our tea and coffee, sipping them slowly while contemplating the *bomzh* and the people walking in the park. Finally Antoine left me to go take some photos a little further on, near the synagogue and the little ravine; we had agreed to meet up later. Reznichenko arrived soon after, right on time, and shook my hand with curiously deformed fingers while the sun reflected off his small wire-rimmed glasses, which clashed with his craggy features and his crewcut of a former right-wing thug. It obviously wasn't by chance that I had asked him to meet me in this place, but he foiled my feeble attempt with surprising frankness: 'You know this place, then?' 'Obviously. I even brought my daughters here recently, to show them around. There's a good app for that now, it explains everything, it's very well done.' I offered him a coffee but he refused, and we went out into the park, pausing on the way in front of one of the four large pink granite stones erected by the BYHMC to peer, through a small optical device embedded at eye-level in the rock, at one of Johannes Hähle's colour pictures, positioned at the very place he had taken it on 1 October 1941. 'This is the quarry where they had the Jews undress. See there, the Germans sorting through the clothes?' 'Yes, I know. We saw all that with my daughters. It's a nice idea, these stones.' 'In Auschwitz, they put glass steles with photos pretty much everywhere, placed like this exactly where the photos were taken. It's very impressive.' 'I've never been to Auschwitz. I'd like to go.' We continued on into

248

the park, talking as we walked along the wide central lane. 'Can we sit?' I finally asked him, pointing to a bench. 'I'd like to take some notes, it's not easy while we're walking.' And so it was on a bench in Babyn Yar that Reznichenko told me his curious story for the first time. I saw him several times again afterwards, to flesh out some details and also to talk; we quickly grew to appreciate each other and gradually developed a good relationship; despite our almost diametrically opposite paths, from a political point of view, I felt as if we understood each other. But he'd already told me most of it on the first day.

180. Reznichenko – 'Like our current president,' as he immediately pointed out – was born in 1982 in Kryvyy Rih, 'the Twisted Horn', an industrial city in the centre of Ukraine decimated by the collapse of the USSR and left poor, dilapidated, sad, glum, a city with no future. His father, who died in 2016, spoke Ukrainian; as for his mother, she was a Russian speaker, like most people in Kryvyy Rih, and at home Dmytro spoke Russian. 'Even today, my mother supports the enemy. All her life, she commanded my father, and destroyed him as a man. That must have been my first unconscious motivation for fascism. In any case, for me, the idea of a free Ukraine is a family idea.' Apart from that, his childhood was normal, for Kryvyy Rih: gang violence. Reznichenko left to study journalism in Dnipro, Dnipropetrovsk at the time, another immense industrial city situated at the bend in the river, closed to foreigners during the Soviet era because of its concentration of military and space industries. The Orange Revolution in 2004, the first uprising against Yanukovych, found him there, and he gladly took part. The demonstrators in Dnipro were mainly liberals (in the American sense of the term), but some nationalists also

took part, and that's where Reznichenko heard for the first time about the UPA, the OUN, the history of Western Ukraine. 'A guy from Lviv had brought a red and black flag, and I carried it in the demonstrations. It was the only one in Dnipro. I felt very *krutoi*, very cool.' After the revolution, he joined the few nationalists in Dnipro, who had their headquarters in an office above the Biloknyzhnyk bookshop, the only one in the city at the time to sell books in Ukrainian. 'In the 1990s, the 2000s, the police were a gang of racketeers, and the army a band of pensioners who had no intention of fighting. So for a normal guy, with strength and honour, it would have been shameful to join them. Now it's different, obviously.' He continued hanging out with the nationalists after getting his diploma in 2005, and in 2006 he moved to Kyiv where he started working as a journalist. A fan of Chuck Palahniuk's novel, he decided to found a 'fight club' where he could fight and let off steam. A chance meeting led him to join his first far-right party, Bratstvo 'Fraternity'), a Christian party led by Dmytro Korchynskyy, who baptized him and became his godfather. 'Korchynskyy is talented, but has no honour. Now we're perfect enemies.' And he added, with a burst of laughter: 'It was my war with the father.' He left the party with his future wife and a little later met some skinheads, members of what would become S14, but which didn't yet have a name. Reznichenko liked to fight, and these guys fought; he would organize fights with them in courtyards or parks. But all this violence wasn't gratuitous. The Orange Revolution had taught young people that they could do something, that civil society mattered. Reznichenko joined a group of the new generation that regarded traditional nationalist parties as 'old nostalgic idiots'; they were involved in local social activism and city politics, they fought against drugs and

250

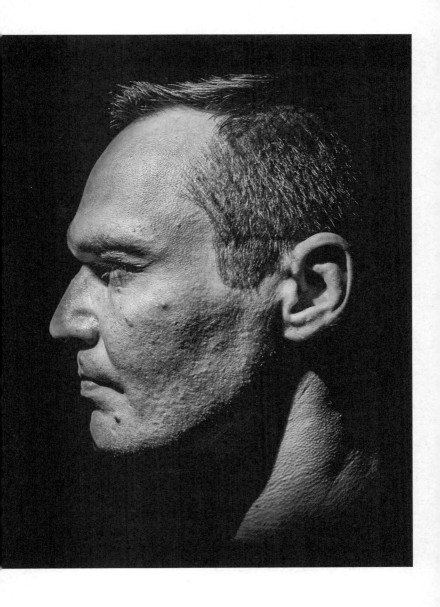

against illegal construction projects, one of the plagues of Kyiv. 'If you're an activist and you fight for local causes, usually they send some *titushky* [strongmen, thugs] against you. So, to defend themselves, the activists would come to see the young nationalists, and asked us for help.'

181. These 'young nationalists' were neo-Nazis, Reznichenko stated unequivocally: 'There was no difference.' It was almost a fashion, a subculture imported from Europe and Russia, with its music, its logos, its slogans, its violence. Around 2010, the ultranationalist party Svoboda encouraged some of these young people to form a movement that adopted the name S14, a reference at once to the Cossack Sich (the Cyrillic, *C14*, looks like 'січ') and the famous '14 words' of David Lane, an American terrorist and white supremacist who died in prison in 2007: 'We must secure the existence of our people and a future for white children.' 'S14 had no theoretical concept. They were for Ukraine, for the race, for the nation, that's all. Everyone wrote his own political programme, then we fought for different programmes that no one gave a fuck about. It was just force, hardcore youth. We spent our time in the gym, practising combat sports. We fought against other groups, leftists, pro-Russians, anyone. The Gypsies, then, weren't fashionable. We didn't have pity for anyone, including ourselves. As Hitler said: "Words separate, action unites."' Little by little, S14 became involved in most of the street protests against the regime of Viktor Yanukovych, the despised pro-Russian president. In 2012, Yanukovych asked the Rada, which he controlled, to repeal the law making the teaching of Ukrainian compulsory in all schools, which would have caused the Ukrainian language to disappear from entire parts of the country. This decision provoked massive

demonstrations in which the skinheads took part; when the police attacked the demonstrators, S14 went to fight. In one of these street battles, Reznichenko, who already had a broken finger, was photographed spraying a policeman in the face with a can of teargas, for which he ended up in court, but managed to avoid prison. 'Even though I speak Russian, I fought for the Ukrainian language. It's pretty funny. But it's my father's language. I fought for the father.'

182. When Maidan began, S14, like Pravyy Sektor, came to the square to control access and defend the demonstrators. 'At the beginning of Maidan, all the activists in the street were nationalists. There were no leftists. The whole *silovoi blok*, the block of force, was right-wing.' But on 18 February 2014, when the crisis reached its peak and the police started killing demonstrators, S14 slipped away. 'Our leader, Karas, was actually in the pay of the security services. On the 18th, the SBU called him to tell him to pull back his guys, and he did it, the bitch. Two hundred guys. We all left and took cover in the Canadian consulate, which looks out onto the Maidan. It was the same for Pravyy Sektor. The SBU controlled all the groups and made them get out. Outside they were fighting, but we weren't there, we were hiding. The next morning, I heard some noise outside, and I went out, alone. That's when there was the charge up Instytutska, when all the guys were killed by the Berkut snipers. I went up with them. They were all individual activists, who went there of their own free will, without orders and without leaders. All the nationalist groups fled.' A few days later, the 'polite green men'[177] from Russia took Crimea without firing a shot. Reznichenko set off there right away, hoping to find an opposition group he could join. But everything had been so well prepared that there was no opposition.

Reznichenko quickly realized that despite his press card he could be arrested. 'On the beach in Feodosiya, I emptied a bottle of wine, threw it into the sea, said goodbye and left.' In Kyiv, in the meantime, S14 had occupied the offices of the Ukrainian Communist Party, a large building in Podil that soon became a nationalist-revolutionary hub, a centre for the entire hard right of Ukraine and Europe. But the adventure came to an abrupt end: the Communists were protected by Svoboda, who forced S14 to vacate the site; furious, the youths set fire to the building as they left. In any case, the Donbas events had begun, and already by May it was clear where things were heading. Reznichenko left to sign up with a volunteer unit, the Donbas battalion.

183. Very quickly, the war opened a rift in the mind of Reznichenko, the committed fascist. 'The master idea of the right is the cult of violence, the cult of force. War is the greatest test of human existence: if you are killed, your memory will live forever. It turned out that was a load of bullshit.' The first incident that forced him to reflect took place in the summer. A soldier from his unit had captured a separatist and had brought him to the abandoned village where they had their quarters. Their officer, a Russian who had fought in Chechnya, declared: 'I saw what happens when you let a Chechen live: they come to Moscow, fuck our wives, act as if they owned the place... You should have killed him right away. You brought him back, you kill him.' While the soldier was hesitating, another intervened: 'No, we should give him to the SBU so they can interrogate him.' 'The SBU can go fuck itself,' the officer barked. 'Kill him.' When the first soldier finally raised his gun, the second one struck him in the face. Immediately all the men rushed at each other, staggering

in the muddy street, shouting and grunting, while the prisoner stood there, awaiting his fate. Faced with this scene, Reznichenko was overcome with an uncontrollable rage. He started firing volleys into the air, over the heads of the men fighting in the mud, but no one paid any attention. Beside himself, he howled: 'Right, you can all fuck off! If that's how it is, I'll take him out myself.' He grabbed the prisoner, dragged him behind the corner of a ruined house, shoved him violently against the wall and aimed his gun. *It should be easy*, he thought. *A light pressure on the trigger, a few marks on his chest, he falls and it's over.* But he hesitated. He lowered his rifle, then forced himself to raise it again. At that instant an automatic sprinkler, blocked for a long time, came unstuck, or else its timer went off, and a fine spray of water lashed his face. Stunned, he turned to where he could hear the mechanism's delicate *tchik-tchik*, and saw the iridescent sunlight in the jerky spray, the rainbow forming in the droplets. And he realized he could not kill this man. So he brought him back into the street where the other soldiers, sitting quietly, were smoking or cleaning the mud from their uniforms, having already almost forgotten the incident. The prisoner was handed over to the SBU. Later, in the barracks, Reznichenko thought for a long time about the scene, imagining several scenarios, some in which he fired his gun, others in which he didn't. He finally realized it wasn't the miraculous sprinkler that had kept him from killing the man, but that even before it went off he had already unconsciously made up his mind. Unconsciously, he had realized that if he killed the prisoner, this act would bring him to another side of his life, a different side in spite of all the violence he had already been living in, one that he would never return from. And he remembered Dostoyevsky, and Raskolnikov's phrase: '*Tvar li ya*

drozhashchaya, ili pravo umeyu?' Am I a trembling creature,
or have I the right?

184. 'On another day, I was in an abandoned house, in a
little girl's bedroom, and I found her portrait. I held it in
my fingers and I thought: Where is this little girl now?
Why am I here in her room, with my dirty boots, my cut-
off gloves and an assault rifle?' Then at the end of August
came Ilovaisk, one of the war's worst battles, a national
trauma. Along with the Donbas battalion, Reznichenko
found himself trapped in the pocket while the Russian
noose was tightening around them. Every day, his comrades were dying under intensive shelling. 'When you're
cornered like that, you start thinking about why you're
there. I thought about my girls, whom I wanted to see
again, not about the pure race or the nation, all that bullshit. I had always believed that death was the ultimate
meaning of life. And there I said to myself: To die for
an idea is a stupid idea. My whole life had led me to this
place. I had come on my own two legs, of my own free
will. I couldn't even understand my motivations. All of us,
we hated ourselves, we hated everyone else, and we put
all this hatred into action. Politics was just a rationali-
zation of our hatred. If I hadn't been who I was, I would
never have listened to all those *vozhdi*, those leaders.'
This illumination transformed him. And he got lucky:
On 20 August, a piece of shrapnel wounded his hand,
and he was evacuated. Between the 24th and the 26th, the
Russian forces completed the encirclement; the battalion
was annihilated, over six hundred of his comrades were
killed, the others taken prisoner. After he recovered,
Reznichenko returned to the front, and continued fighting until 2016. But it was out of a sense of duty, his heart
wasn't in it anymore; the fact that his wife was cheating

on him with his commander and ended up leaving him added to his despondency.

185. One evening, after sharing a drink with Reznichenko, I went to dinner with my old friend Oleksandr Glyadyelov, a well-known Ukrainian photographer who, despite being 65, has been working on the Donbas front without respite since 2014. I mentioned Reznichenko to him and Sasha started laughing: 'Dima? I know him well. We were wounded together, we got out together from the pocket.' I knew that Sasha had been wounded in the leg in Donbas, but I didn't know it was during the Ilovaisk encirclement, and the coincidence astonished me. Sasha turned on his computer and showed me two grainy black-and-white images (no matter the conditions, Sasha only photographs on film stock, with an old Leica). The first one showed a bloodied soldier dying on the floor of a tiled room in front of a helpless military nurse; in the fore-ground are two legs stretched out, one of them covered in blood: Sasha's, waiting his turn to be treated. 'The foot on the right there, that's Dima.' The second one, taken in-side the armoured vehicle that evacuated them together, shows Reznichenko smoking, his gaze lost in the void be-hind his little intellectual's glasses. I love these moments when the divergent paths of people's lives, veering almost randomly in every direction, suddenly fold back and in-tersect, in a knot that signifies nothing but that suddenly reveals the thick texture, the pure density of the human network we live in.

186. Back in civilian life, Reznichenko quickly found him-self at odds with his old comrades. At nationalist rallies, he would hear leaders who hadn't spent a second at the front bawling '*Ukraina ponad usé*, Ukraine above all', and

it was starting to get to him. He began asking questions in public: 'Our artillery bombed Pervomaika, civilians were killed. Whose fault is that?' 'The occupiers, of course, the Russians.' 'No, that answer isn't good enough.' 'Our people are always right.' 'No, that's not good enough.' *When you've shed blood,* he thought, *you have the right to ask questions. You're not just forced to listen to the* Vozhd, *the* Provodnik, *the Führer.* And also things had changed. 'Under Yanukovych, any patriot who loved Ukraine had to join a nationalist group. But after Maidan, you didn't have to be a nationalist anymore to love Ukraine. When your president [Petro Poroshenko, 2014-2019] cries out "Army, Language, Faith", you don't need Nazi mythology anymore. Today, the nationalist groups are completely marginal, they're just people who have nowhere else to go. The only reason there are so many groups, the only difference between them, is the egos and the ambitions, everyone wants to be the *Vozhd.* It's more criminal than political. In any case half of them take money from the Russians, Svoboda first and foremost, everyone knows it.'[178] Gradually his relations with the S14 activists deteriorated, violently. There were fights, weapons were drawn, Reznichenko was beaten. In December 2017, his former buddies threw *zelionka* (a green antiseptic, often used in the ex-USSR for political attacks) in his eyes; when he recovered, he took a hand grenade, gathered some friends and barged into an S14 meeting. Everyone went out into the street, the S14 guys brandished some pistols, Reznichenko pulled the pin from his grenade and the others took flight. That was the end of his problems with his ex-comrades, who never bothered him again. 'And now?' I asked him there on the bench in Babyn Yar. 'Now? They leave me alone, otherwise...' A large knife, already open, appeared as if by magic in his hand. 'Have you had to use it?' 'No, they're cowards. In any case, after the business with the grenade, I went to the Carpathians to lie low. I said to myself, all these weapons, these grenades, I'll end up inside, that's for sure. After that we never saw each other again.'

187. In the spring of 2017, even before the final conflict with S14, Reznichenko knew he had lost everything. He had beaten up his commander, the one who had taken his wife, and because of that he'd lost his war comrades. Fascism seemed ridiculous to him, and all his former friends, grotesque. Then he fell in love with a left-wing feminist activist. She taught him a lot of things, about toxic masculinity, LGBT people, tolerance, and then she left him, in the beginning of 2018, because the arthritis he had developed standing for so many long, cold nights on Maidan and then at the front was starting to make him an invalid. This was when he seriously began to think of the reasons that had led him to follow this path, this evil path. He returned to Kyiv, enrolled in a psychology institute, studied Freud, Fromm, Reich, met his new wife, brought his daughters to live with him, and started living again. He raised his daughters, taught them useful things, took them to Pride. He had been the first person, in the spring of 2018, to wave the red and black flag of the UPA at a Pride: 'I had a close friend in the army, *Frantsuz* ["the Frenchman"], Viktor Pylypenko is his real name. We were in the war together, and at the time of the grenade incident he fought with me and supported me. So, when he came out – the very first man to do so in the army – I decided it was my turn to support him, and I went to Pride with him. I took the UPA flag because I knew a lot of these right-wing guys were secretly gay, and also because this flag is sacred to the nationalists. I did it on purpose to spit on those bitches. Afterwards, they all swore I was a dead man.

Of course they didn't do anything.' Once a year he spoke to his mother, she granted him an hour on the phone, in Russian: 'It's my birthday present.'

ANOTHER LIFE (FINAL INSTALLMENT)

188. At the time I first met him, in Babyn Yar, Dmytro was finishing his thesis and just starting to work as a psychologist. When I saw him again in January 2022, we spoke for a long time about the Russian threat at the border. He was the first to insist to me that if Russia invaded, things wouldn't happen the way Putin, the West and the media thought: 'Everyone thinks we'll get wiped out and that it'll be over in three days. But our army isn't the same as in 2014. We have hundreds of thousands of guys who have experience at the front and who will come back right away. We have weapons, artillery, and we know how to use them now. We even have missiles we make ourselves. The Russians will have a nice surprise.' We'd stopped by his house to pick something up before joining Antoine for a portrait, and he opened some ammunition boxes piled up in his living room under a portrait of Ernst Jünger: inside, along with the collection of nationalist flags he kept as a souvenir, were his Kalashnikov, his helmet, his bulletproof vest and his uniform, which he had bought himself in 2014, like all the volunteers. 'Even if I am an invalid,' he said calmly, raising his arthritis-ridden hands in front of me, 'if they attack Kyiv, I'm joining up. But only to defend Kyiv.' On 26 February, two days after the invasion, I wrote to him to ask how he was. I didn't receive any sign of life until 11 March: *Hi Jonathan! Sorry, there wasn't any time to answer you. A lot has happened. I remember, you had asked me to tell you how my studies were*

going – well, I had time to pass all my exams, the final one too. All that was left was to finish writing my thesis and defend it. Can you believe, I finished writing it exactly on 23 February, and sent it to the reviewer. And on the morning of the 24th the war started. My thesis defence was supposed to be on 4 March, but the institutors fled, and I was left without a diploma. It's all so stupid and symbolic, the Russians didn't let me finish my studies. The first day of the war, I gathered into the car all my women – my daughters and wives (former and future) – and brought them to Lvov, in a huge flood of refugees. There, in Lvov, I set them up so they could live and I returned alone by train to Kiev. I signed up for the army, I'm serving. For now we're guarding one of the airports. At the same time he sent me a selfie showing him under the snow in his helmet and uniform, smiling in his delicate glasses, in front of two of his comrades, also smiling, a slightly hesitant young man and an older guy in a cap making the V for victory. We wrote to each other again a week later, when Antoine was passing through Kyiv and wanted to meet him. Things had changed already. *I left the Territorial Defence. As it turned out, it was just a complete shitshow, idleness, lots of people. And Covid. Since it's all my stuff – the weapons, the equipment, the cartridges – I decided it was better to wait for the Russians at home. It makes more sense. At the same time I'm getting over the Covid that I caught there. Sitting there with their automatic rifles, waiting and eating lots of food from volunteers, they can do that without me. I'm at home now, writing my book. Outside the window, the sirens are wailing, something explodes from time to time. It's romantic... Yes, I already told you, I would only take part in the war in case of absolute necessity. As it turned out, the absolute necessity hasn't happened yet, the Russians were stopped short outside of Kiev. You remember, I told you that Ukraine had a strong army and it would fight? Well, they're fighting, like animals.*

264

189. I finally saw Reznichenko again in May, when I returned to Kyiv with Antoine. We met on the terrace of the Osteria Pantagruel, an Italian restaurant next to the Golden Gate. Dima was pretty dejected. His ex-wife, after he'd left her with their daughters in Lviv, had run away with them to Europe without any papers, taking advantage of the refugee status they were given. Then, rather quickly after leaving the TO, he had spent a month in prison. During this time, his ex had turned the two girls against him, and he no longer had any contact with them; of course, he couldn't leave the country to go looking for them: 'I couldn't do anything, I was ready to hang myself,' he told me. The prison story was complex and sordid. His upstairs neighbour was a schizophrenic who had convinced himself that Reznichenko had set up a machine to send him radioactive waves. Over the years they'd had several arguments, Dima had even broken his nose once, then the year before he had brought him into his apartment to show him there was no machine. Things had calmed down a little, and Dima thought that was the end of it. But one day after he'd returned from the TO he found the leather covering of the door to his apartment cut up with a knife. Furious, he went upstairs and knocked on his neighbour's door. For once, the door opened: 'Suddenly, he appears and he has a pistol. He aims this pistol right in my face and starts shooting at me. Point-blank. When I saw the gun, I thought, *That's it, I'm fucked*. He shoots and I'm still standing. I remember the pistol in my face, the gunshots, then I realize I'm alive. Beyond that it's like a fog. And then the fog dissipates, I'm standing over him, the pistol in my hand.' The neighbour was lying on the floor, covered in bruises, several ribs broken. His gun was very small calibre, and Dima thought he wasn't wounded. He called the police, who

wrote a report and put the pistol under seal. But when the prosecutor summoned him, he was placed in custody. His partner Olha hired a lawyer, and the prosecutor then summoned her to tell her: If instead of spending that money on a lawyer you'd brought it to us, Dima would already be free. In prison, conditions were harsh, but while the other inmates were taking drugs and smoking, Reznichenko read neurobiology textbooks. Then he had a stroke of luck: one of the criminal authorities of the prison, a convert to Islam who called himself Mansur, found out someone wanted to kill him and obtained a transfer to a small cell. Dima was sent to keep him company. The conditions were much better, but his case wasn't getting anywhere. One day, lying on his cot, he rubbed his chin and felt a lump under his skin. His lawyer managed to get them to give him an X-ray, which revealed that tiny bullets from the pistol had remained stuck in his jaw. In Ukraine, if someone with a bullet in his body is imprisoned without medical assistance, it's considered an act of torture. His lawyer filed a complaint. After a month, he appeared before a judge, and there he understood that neither his neighbour's mental illness, nor the pistol, nor the gunshots, nor the bullets appeared in the criminal proceedings: officially, he'd just gone upstairs to his neighbour's apartment and beaten him up, for nothing. The judge set his bail at 100,000 hryvnias, which Olha raised by borrowing from friends, and they set him free. The lawyer had now brought a suit against the prosecutor and the policemen responsible.

190. At one point we went back to talking about the war. Ten days earlier, the last defenders of Mariupol, fighters from the nationalist Azov battalion, had finally surrendered to the besiegers, and Kremlin propaganda

rhapsodized about the surrender of these 'Nazis', as if they alone justified the invasion. 'You know, Jonathan, the truth is that that's how we were at the time.' Dima was looking for his words, trying to explain his idea precisely. 'For us, before... you understand... When you have a sort of idea, a sort of... not an understanding of the world, but a *feeling* of the world, you have to dress it up in certain ideological forms, in certain words, because it can't be transmitted at the level of feeling. And in this country, you couldn't find material for it anywhere, unless you went searching in the past to find all these symbols, the red and black flag and all that.' The previous year, in a far-right demonstration, I had met a fighter from Azov, and I had stayed in touch with him. I took out my smartphone and showed Dima the guy's profile photo on Telegram, his body completely tattooed with runes and macabre symbols. 'Listen, if you show that to a European, he'll understand immediately this is a criminal and, very likely, a neo-Nazi. But when I was in the ultra-right, I knew that every member of the movement had a Jewish friend or a black friend, it was normal. It's as if we were all just putting on a performance. As if we weren't real fascists, but just wanted to look like real fascists. Especially with anti-Semitism. I don't remember the subject of anti-Semitism ever being brought up in one way or another, ever being treated seriously by anyone. Except by some half-mad idiots no one paid any attention to. On the contrary, the Jews were rather respected. Nonetheless we still wore swastikas.'

191. He thought some more. 'Now... there's a kind of strange substitution, which still has to be named. The Russians catch the Azovs, take photos of their tattoos and clamour: "So, there's no fascism in Ukraine?" But I recently realized that tattoos have nothing to do with

fascism. Fascism is when opposition is forbidden in the country, when there's no freedom of expression, when gay marches are broken up... Totalitarian state, leader, all that bullshit, fascism is *there*, in Russia. Azov isn't fascism, it's a subculture, with signs that don't even signify what they represent. It's like what Baudrillard said: a simulacrum. It's like playing with Vikings, Walhalla, a child's dream, like my dreams when I was twenty-five.' He paused. 'Now, the Russians are preparing these trials [for the Azov fighters]. They need them, to look as if they're fighting against fascism. But it's so strange: in Mariupol, the real fascists defeated people who want to look like fascists. It's a kind of new set of meanings that don't fit into the old ways of understanding. Because according to the old way, the Russians are the anti-fascists and Azov are the fascists. But in fact it's the opposite. The only thing is, the Russian government hasn't adopted the Nazi aesthetic, like us. Their aesthetic is Soviet. But their ideology is Nazi.' We started talking about other things. But a little later, he continued: 'In *Mein Kampf*, my favourite quote is when Hitler says: "Nothing annoyed me more in my youth than the fact that the era of great heroic actions is already over. And before us lies only the peaceful coexistence of peoples." Hitler was angry about that. In the 2000s we were just as angry, we had the same feeling that the wars were over, that there wouldn't be any wars anymore. That there wouldn't be any great historic achievements. That we'd always live in a boring Eastern European country that influences nothing and decides nothing. *Fight Club* talks about the same thing: the guy was suffocating in his work, he didn't think it was possible to make his own happiness, and he only found a way out when he started fighting. Then he finally felt it: This is it, yes, finally, here it is, real life. It's not a simulation, it's a real experience. Me, I started with fight clubs, like him. And now, the war is real, just as I wanted it to be. When I was young I dreamed there would be a war, that men in military uniforms would march through the streets, that there would be many of us and we'd have tank battalions, that we'd fight the empire and defeat it. And that people would finally understand Ukrainian nationalism in the right way, would understand that we were good guys. That was my childhood dream. But I don't want that anymore. They say: Be afraid of your desires. Now I'm horrified by what I dreamed about, because it came true, and I'm an unwell and unhappy person, and I don't want to wage war anymore. I joined the army when they were fighting for Kyiv, but I didn't take part in the fighting. And I realized: Good Lord, I don't even want to! I don't want it to be this way. I'd rather see a calm, peaceful Ukraine again. But no. Be afraid of your desires. They say: Now they've come true – you can rejoice in that. But I'm not rejoicing.'

AN ORDINARY NEIGHBOURHOOD

192. The year before, in June after our first conversation on the bench in Babyn Yar, I had walked with Reznichenko back to the *perekhid*. We'd left each other in front of the metro's heavy swinging doors, and I'd continued on, crossing Teliha to join Antoine at the Banka, on the corner of Dorohozhytska where the Syrets neighbourhood starts. He was waiting for me on the terrace and we ordered chicken salad with mayonnaise, pork chops two fingers thick and some beer. We still had quite a bit of time before the meeting at the television tower and we thought we'd take a little stroll through the neighbourhood, which we hadn't yet really explored. The Banka sat

against the side of one of the long red-brick *khrushchiovki* lined up along Teliha Street, and instead of braving the crowd and the noise of traffic we decided to cut behind it. I've already used this word *khrushchiovki* several times: it's what they call the apartment blocks, all built to almost identical plans, from the construction boom enacted by Khrushchev in the 1950s to reduce overcrowding in the *kommunalki*, the communal apartments where an entire family had one room at most, and to improve the lives of people a little after decades under Stalin when all the country's resources were reserved for weaponry and heavy industry. For the first time since the Revolution, the wellbeing of the people became important, and you could feel this the minute you left the street, with its garishly coloured plastic kiosks and its fruit and vegetable stands under canvas roofs, to pass under one of the high arches leading to the inner courtyards with their simple elegance reflecting the confident Sovietism of the 60s. A profusion of greenery, trees and flowers masked the banal ugliness of the buildings themselves; we strolled from courtyard to courtyard, between the children's play areas painted red, blue and yellow, the little sheet-metal garages, the entrances to the *pogreba* that residents had dug without permission next to the asphalt paths, and the meticulously maintained flowerbeds. The paths were swarming with people walking their dogs, watching their children, or smoking a cigarette on a bench. Every time we looked up, we could see over the roofs the tall rectangle of the building under construction on Teliha Street that we could also see from the park, a mass of bare cinderblocks, brick balconies and rickety platforms hanging alongside the façades between still-gaping windows and those where glass still covered in stickers had already been set. Making our way diagonally between

272

the *khrushchiovki*, we entered a half-shaded dirt path that snaked under little low trees, then ran alongside a flaking concrete wall covered in graffiti, through the cracks of which we could see a little stadium. All around us rose the balconies of the apartment buildings, all different, personalized, little handmade nests along these identical units, some open, others closed with wooden or aluminium and PVC structures, others still covered in a whimsy of scrap iron like a Soviet Facteur Cheval Palace. The lane emerged onto two rows of little private garages, rusty and dilapidated, and then the back of an abandoned cinema. We walked over to the fire escape, littered with syringes scattered amongst fragments of brick and marble; at the top of the steps, a gate with twisted bars, the collapsed floor, the buzzing of thousands of flies and a rank stench kept us from exploring the rubble of the dark auditorium any further. Further on, on the side of the cinema, a girl crouching on a concrete block was smoking next to her friend, who was sitting and swinging her legs, two young guys were chatting in an isolated shaded corner, a father was walking with his daughter. I felt as if nothing had changed here in thirty years, as if the outdated poetry of declining Sovietism still lingered in these places, unchanged.

193. We crossed Shchusiev Street, weaving between the cars to avoid making a long detour, and continued on between the apartment blocks. A few months later I returned to the one to our right to visit Lera and Nadia, two friends who work for the BYHMC and had helped us a lot with our investigations. That evening Nadia had gone out to walk her dog Dzhia, and Lera was alone bustling about the apartment they rented together on the fourth floor, at the level of the treetops turning red in the soft

autumn light. She poured me some tea and we sipped it sitting opposite each other across a little tiled table placed against the kitchen wall while she talked to me about her life in the neighbourhood. When she had caught Covid, she had spent sixteen days isolated in the apartment; all she could do was go to Babyn Yar and lose herself there. It was mid-April, the beginning of spring, there were flowers everywhere, leaves were starting to appear on the branches. 'The world was beautiful. But I didn't feel I could rest in that place. It was tense, this forest is not a place where you can relax, not me at least. Because you know.' So why had they come to live here? 'That's a good question.' She and Nadia had been looking for an apartment for a long time, in Kyiv it's hard, the apartments are shitty and too expensive. Finally a girl had called them and said: I have an apartment for you. They had visited, it matched what they were looking for. 'But Babyn Yar... well, at least we'd be close to work! We joked it could be the headquarters for the 80th anniversary ceremonies...' For most people, it was a pretty good place to live, with these woods in the middle of the city, it was just a park, nothing more. But in the beginning Lera had trouble sleeping there. 'Maybe just because it was a new place? It's always like that. The first three or four weeks, I had terrible nightmares, I'd wake up, I couldn't remember my dreams but I was so anxious. I wondered if it was coming from my mind or from the energy of the place.' She wasn't alone, in any case. There were a lot of miserable people in the neighbourhood, not in the economic sense, but just unhappy, people who did a lot of drugs, of alcohol. Once, during lockdown, Lera went for a walk around midnight, and she'd passed a completely wasted guy who was shooting up, running around, howling. 'Maybe it's because of the family origins of the people in the neighbourhood,

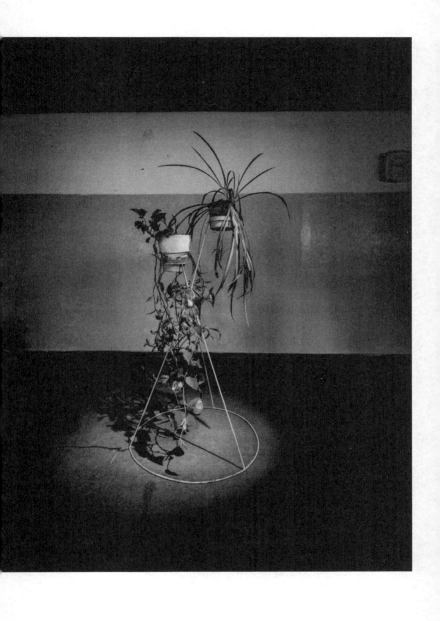

who are mostly descendants of Soviet workers? You know, I come from Troieshchyna, on the left bank. It's a neighbourhood with a bad reputation, full of *titushky*, guys from Azov, dealers, alcoholics. But it's still better than Syrets. It's not that I've had any problems, I'm just always a little on edge here.'

194. Anton Drobovych, the new director of the UINP, had grown up with his grandmother in the neighbourhood, or rather just past it, in a little Tsarist-era suburb nestled in the large forest that borders Syrets to the west, beyond the eponymous stream and Tirasposlka Street. At that time it was still the end of the city, a little-known suburb, closed in on itself. During the war, the people who lived there had never given up their Jews; a neighbourhood *Polizei*, who had gone off with the Germans in 1943, had discreetly returned there a few years later, and they hadn't denounced him either. 'That kind of people, you know,' Drobovych had said to me. His family had Polish ancestry; his grandfather had served in the *Ludowe Wojsko*, the Polish People's Army set up by Stalin to counter the pro-Western Poles. The father of that grandfather had been arrested in the 1930s during the fierce anti-Polish repressions. Twenty years later, during the Khrushchev period, his widow, Drobovych's great-grandmother, had written to find out what had become of him; the reply stated that he had been illegally executed, but that the Soviet State was rehabilitating him and she could receive 200 rubles for the suit he was wearing at the time of his arrest. On Drobovych's grandmother's side, two brothers had fought in the Red Army and had both been killed. When after the occupation she started studying at the Institute for International Relations, this grandmother had to walk several kilometres every day through the forest, then

through Babyn Yar, to reach the first tramway stop. 'She always felt strange, crossing the *yar*. At the time, with the beginning of state anti-Semitism, it was obviously forbidden to talk about what had happened there. And my grandmother was a Soviet teacher who respected the law. But still she felt so strongly about it that she told her family, that's how this little story has been miraculously preserved.'

195. As we walked, I explained to Antoine that the neighbourhood covered not just the filled-in ravine but also the large concentration camp adjoining it, KL Syrets. The camp had been opened in the spring of 1942, on the site of Tsarist and then Soviet military training camps, to take the place of the temporary camp on Kerosyna Street (now Sholudenko Street) where the prisoners of war were held whom Johannes Hähle had photographed in the process of flattening the earth poured into the ravine the day after the massacre. In July 1942, KL Syrets was attached as an 'external camp' to KL Sachsenhausen, one of the mother camps of the German concentration camp system, the one Bandera and Stetsko had been transferred to a few months earlier. The death toll there was terrible, as it was everywhere; but a certain number of Jewish artisans who plied trades useful to the Germans – tailors, shoemakers, furriers, bookbinders and other professions – remained alive there almost until the end of the occupation. It's probably from these artisans that the Germans recruited the members of the *Sonderkommando* charged with digging up and burning the corpses in Babyn Yar, so few of whom survived the uprising of September 1943. After liberation, the Soviets used the camp to keep German prisoners of war, many of whom were buried there, not far from a symbolic cemetery built in 1999 by

the German government. The camp was only completely shut down in 1946. Unlike what many local residents
believe, it wasn't located at the spot of the present Syrets
park, with its lovely little children's train that runs all
day through the woods, the lanes, the playgrounds, the
ravines and the refreshment stands, and which is actually a real train used to train new recruits for the national
railroad company, Ukrazaliznytsia. Thanks to wartime
aerial reconnaissance photos, the BYHMC team identified the site with certainty: the camp was situated north
of the Syrets park, west of Babyn Yar, occupying half the
area of the *khrushchiovki* from Olena Teliha Street to the
Syrets metro station on one side, and from Ryzka Street
to Volodymyr Salskyy Street on the other.

FAITH AND MEMORY

196. We were approaching what had been the northern
boundary of the camp. Emerging between a nursery and
a building taller and more recent than the others, we
found ourselves in a large open area, half vacant lot, half
garden, with a row of poplars running down the middle.
The buildings here were mostly concrete, developments
from the 80s assembled from prefabricated elements,
grey and ugly; to our right stood the large high-rise under
construction, dominating all the other buildings. Behind
the poplars nestled a little church, and we decided to
visit it. It was quite pretty for a neighbourhood church,
made from wooden logs with steep green roofs, raised in
the centre with a golden dome mounted by an Orthodox
cross. A woman in a headscarf was weeding the flowerbeds at the entrance and I asked her if the priest was there.
'*Otets* Ioann?' she asked as she stood up, her hand full of

weeds. 'No, not today. You'll have to come back.' Which I did, several times, quickly taking a liking to this affable priest who was also so intense, so human, the opposite of Father Sergey who ran the church in the park. We'd sit on a bench in the church, or a woman would serve us tea, and he'd talk to me not just about the spiritual but also about the psychological lives of the neighbourhood people, about his own as well. His grandfather, Petro Tranko, had been a rather well-known historian, and he had clearly inherited from him an interest in the things of the past; his father-in-law, who lived in Kassel in Germany, was Jewish, and the oldest of his seven children, who was twenty-two, wanted to go to Israel to study. 'And you, are you a believer?' he asked me one day, listening with curiosity to my negative reply. The church had been built very light, so that the foundations could be as shallow as possible, eighty centimetres deep and barely twenty centimetres wide; yet they had still found, when they dug the foundations, many human remains that they had re-buried under the church, beneath the altar. In the old days, in the catacombs, the liturgy was performed over the bones of the deceased priests; for Father Ioann, it was a continuation of this tradition, with the bones of the victims of Nazism.

197. The question, clearly, had been bothering him for a long time, and in a completely different way from Father Sergey. Before he came to found this church, in 2006, he also officiated at St. Cyril's church in the psychiatric asylum. He had known an old man there, one of the few Jewish survivors of Babyn Yar, who, as a very young boy, had fallen under the bodies and then crawled out at nightfall to flee. 'His spirit was broken. All his life. He howled all the time, that's why he'd been committed there.' Lully's

282

March for the Turkish Ceremony interrupted us; he smiled as he pulled his phone from his pocket to mute it: 'Sorry, sorry!' He turned to an icon on the right of the iconostasis, a Virgin with a serene, absolutely calm face, with seven arrows aimed at her heart. 'You see this icon? It's the one I chose to dedicate the church to. It's the icon of the Mother of God "who softens cruel hearts". In my youth, during perestroika, it was my favorite icon.' The one hanging near us was by Serhii Vandalovskyy, a very well known icon-painter from Kyiv. 'This image is close to us because... how can I say it? She is not pierced by the arrows, but she is ready to accept it.' It had been a long struggle to establish the church; twice, people had tried to burn it down, a company wanted to get hold of the land. 'But thanks to God, we have remained. This neighbourhood is difficult, really difficult. You can't imagine. There's a terrible suicide rate, the worst in the city.' He thought it was because the tragedy of Babyn Yar hadn't been digested. In post-Soviet Ukraine, there hasn't been any in-depth work on memory, as there had been in Germany after the war. They had tried to put up information panels around the church, but the inhabitants had refused, they didn't want to accept any monument, any act of memory. There was also the problem of the participation of the Ukrainian *Polizei* in the murder of the Jews, which no one wanted to talk about. 'It's not honest. For me, as a priest, it's one of the most burning questions. People don't want to talk about their mistakes. No one really wants to carry out de-Sovietization all the way.' Twenty years earlier, around 2002 or 2003, the city wanted to transform the Kino Gagarin, the cinema now in ruins a few streets further on, into a museum of the Syrets camp; there were huge protests, and the administration of the local market had sued and won: the market stayed, and the cinema was abandoned.

'You can hardly imagine the cultural and spiritual level of the people in the neighbourhood. People didn't want this church because it bothered them when they walked their dogs. Others wanted a car park, or a stadium. Now, the only reason they tolerate us is that we're preventing the construction of another high-rise like that one over there. Even the neighbourhood Jews aren't interested in the memory of Babyn Yar.'

198. What all these people – Lera, Drobovych, Father Ioann – were talking about were phantoms, ghosts haunting the neighbourhood's wooded lanes and its beautiful park, the stairwells of the dilapidated apartment buildings, the rubble mixed with syringes of the abandoned cinema, the construction sites of the new buildings, the schools and nurseries. Mournful and tenacious ghosts, stubbornly spoiling the little pleasures of the residents just as much as their most ambitious projects, constantly dragging this rather cheerful and pleasant place to live down to something gloomy, mournful, heavy. Ghosts swarming as if at their nests or burrows around the countless monuments and memorial projects scattered all over the area, strewn every which way by the associations, the foundations, the churches and the government. Ghosts that took all innocence away from the most innocent things in life.

199. I returned to the Syrets church with Antoine in early 2022, for the evening Mass on 6 January, the eve of Orthodox Christmas. Aside from Father Ioann and the old woman who runs the shop for religious books and icons, I had always seen the church empty, but that night there was a small crowd, and people from the neighbourhood were flowing in. Father Ioann was officiating with one of his colleagues, Father Roman; the two priests were

in grey, the faithful were still wearing their coats and parkas, the women in headscarves, the men with bare heads, everyone wearing masks, as Covid dictated, and everyone standing. On the little balcony over the room, a man and woman were intoning the opening liturgy; Father Ioann embraced people as they entered, then, as the little room filled up, leaned over a corner prie-dieu to hear confessions, in front of everyone as it is done here. Behind the iconostasis, other acolytes were bustling about, joined by a third priest, Father Oleksandr, a lanky, balding man who had rushed in in his street clothes, and who now was changing into his priestly vestments. His emergence, in his golden, high-collared cape, announced the beginning of the Mass: censor in hand, he walked slowly around the church, blessing each corner with incense while the audience turned round to follow him with their gaze. On the balcony, while the woman continued to chant, the choir gathered around the only score, chatting quietly, only to abruptly start singing *S nami Bog*, 'God with us', as the woman continued reciting, four female voices and a beautiful masculine bass filling the space. In the room, there was a constant murmur of chattering, whispering, muttering, coats rustling, footsteps on the wooden floor. A penitent finished her confession and bent down to touch the Bible open on the prie-dieu with her forehead; Father Ioann covered her head with his gilt stole, placed one hand on it and murmured the words of forgiveness. Father Oleksandr placed a tray of little cakes, *bulochky*, on a small stand in the middle of the room surrounded by three candles. The ambiance was completely different from that of a Catholic Mass, where everyone, priest and participants, is focused on one thing at a time, prayer or song or blessing; here, there was a bustling feeling, many religious affairs happening at once, overlapping one another without getting in the way, each person absorbed in their own particular task.

200. We went to see Father Ioann one last time in May 2022, after the Russian attack on Kyiv. He had asked us to meet him at his house, in a northern suburb, instead of at the church, and we went there by car. Leaving Kyiv, just after the little Sviatoshyn Airfield, the motorway entered a vast pine forest stretching as far as the eye can see on both sides. In the middle of the woods, at a crossroads in front of a completely destroyed gas station, the army had set up a massive checkpoint with trucks overturned on the side to block part of the road. It was easy to pass on the way out, but the line heading back, in the direction of the city, stretched out for hundreds of metres, each vehicle was checked. Afterwards, we rolled straight through the forest, glimpsing defensive positions here and there on the slopes; behind the trees on our right, invisible from this road, stretched the fashionable neighbourhood of Pushcha-Vodytsya, with its sanatoria and government dachas. Horenka started just beyond that, nestled between the forest and the fluvial plain of the Irpin river the Ukrainians had built their defence of Kyiv on. The Russian forces had never managed to establish a foothold in Horenka, but the fighting had been intense and the entrance to the town was ravaged: the church overlooking the motorway was in ruins, with only a disfigured plaster Christ still standing; a little further on, in the middle of the bombed houses, their blackened walls covered in the silicone globules used to maintain the panes of insulating polystyrene ripped off and carbonized by the explosions, stood the remains of a Fora supermarket, and then the monument to the dead of 1941-1945, the words NO ONE IS FORGOTTEN still legible on the marble pockmarked with

shrapnel and bullet impacts, with, in the centre, a bare-headed, kneeling bronze soldier, completely riddled, his cheek open as if by a scar, pensive. This was where we had to turn to reach Father Ioann's house. The long street that cut through the hamlet was torn open by the impacts of shells; we wove back and forth and jolted along, passing apartment buildings, warehouses and shopping centres, all of them badly damaged by the shelling. The priest lived a little further on, in the *pryvatnyy sektor* in the middle of houses surrounded by fences as in Bucha; his was nestled at the end of a little lane behind a red fence riddled with shrapnel, its roof pierced by a small mortar shell.

201. We knocked for a long time at the metal gate and the priest finally came to open: 'Sorry, I was in the back, I didn't hear,' he said as he welcomed us warmly. He'd been very lucky: not only had the mortar shell not set fire to the house, but a Grad rocket had exploded in his garden, churning up the earth and sending a shower of shrapnel flying but sparing his house. He showed us the remains of the missile: 'Two metres further, and I wouldn't have a house anymore.' Along the fence stood a shipping container with windows, his little family chapel. The inside was covered in smooth, lacquered wood, and there were several icons on the back wall: a Virgin with child with a piece of shrapnel stuck in Mary's chin, an adult Christ with a gouge in his halo; the wooden cross, the gift of a friend, came from Tbilisi, in Georgia; the broken windows were covered in plastic. The main icon came from Mount Athos, a Mother of God 'swift to listen'. It was thanks to this chapel, Father Ioann believed, that his house as well as that of his immediate neighbours had survived: 'Further down, the houses were completely destroyed. And next door, over there where a large family

with six children lived, everything in their house burned, they have nothing left to come back to. I'm very grateful to God for protecting us, it's a miracle.'

202. Inside, the priest made us tea, and we all squeezed in around the little kitchen table to drink it. The first day of the war had found Father Ioann at home with his family. On 26 February the electricity had been cut off; the Ukrainians had set up artillery nearby, SAU self-propelled howitzers probably, and every time they fired, the house would shake. His children weren't afraid, and there hadn't been any return fire, but in the beginning of March some planes started dropping bombs on Irpin, one and a half kilometres away. 'I didn't want to leave, I didn't think it would be so tragic, that it would be on such a scale. But then I saw with my own eyes that they were using phosphorous munitions. And I said *vsio*, that's enough. I put my whole family into the car and drove them to Munich.' As the father of a large family, he had been able to obtain a permit to exit the country, but he came back quite quickly and stayed in Kyiv, celebrating Masses in his church in Syrets and offering food to the people who came there to pray, and also working as a volunteer to deliver gas, propane and food to the Territorial Defence fighters defending Horenka.

203. While he was speaking, half in shadow, Antoine was trying to photograph him, leaning back as much as possible. But the priest wasn't paying attention. He had taken his phone out and was playing me the voice messages he'd sent by WhatsApp to some Russian friends when the war broke out: *May God save us. Because Kyiv is being bombed...* Then: *They say that tomorrow they'll bomb us again, the historic centre too. Because Kharkiv... was bombed very hard and...*

no one imagined that could happen. 'That was on 2 March.' Then he played another one for me: *Planes, bombs... Right now.* [A loud noise can be heard on the recording.] *That was a Russian plane, Natasha. And now we're going to hide in the shelter.* At the start of the war, he had spoken for a long time with this Russian friend, Natasha. 'She even heard an explosion, not far, the same plane as that one.' But her reactions had been strange. 'She had several different reactions, she was clearly experiencing a cognitive dissonance... In the beginning she was angry, she cried. Then she became aggressive: "You're fooling me, none of that's true. It's not us." And then she hid in conspiracy theories. Then... "Evil is everywhere. Evil is in America and in Russia, everywhere, so everyone is guilty." Afterwards she stuck to that.' One of his parishioners had told him that her daughter had called her father in Russia, to tell him she was in an air-raid shelter. And the father had replied: 'You're lying, they told you to say that.' But the most common reaction was silence, absolute silence. Many people complained about this; they said their relatives and friends in Russia hadn't phoned a single time during this period, not even to ask how they were. Father Ioann gently shook his head. 'No one thought there would be a war. No one believed it. Myself, I tried to convince everyone it was impossible, that in the twenty-first century it was absurd. But there is a reason it happened: the countries of the Soviet Union haven't gone through repentance, the way Germany did. Consequently, sooner or later, it had to blow up. It's like a tumour that hasn't been removed... it metastasized. The West wanted to paint an image of Russia as a democratic country that perhaps just had a few problems, corruption, governance, a transition that had yet to be completed. But that was just the outer shell. Inside, there was a completely different meaning.

292

Another sense. The Russians for example didn't notice when Putin banned access to the archives, in the 2000s. They let it go by without realizing. For if the archives are closed, it means for instance that a neighbour in a communal apartment, who denounced someone in '37 under Stalin to free up a room, will never be discovered. You understand? His act will never be revealed.'

204. From time to time I'd translate bits for Antoine. Father Ioann took a deep breath and went on. One day, he had heard the confession of an old woman, a parishioner who was over ninety years old. She had died since then, and he didn't tell me her name, thus he could tell me her story. He had decided to question her in detail: 'What could have happened, really, for God not to allow you into his monastery, after you die? What could there be?' She had reflected, and had said: 'Well, maybe the first husband.' 'And what happened with the first husband?' 'Well, we lived together, and I suspected him of cheating. So I wrote a denunciation against him. And a few days later he was taken away, and I never saw him again.' This was before the Great Patriotic War, he didn't know exactly when she was born, 1920 maybe, or 1917. When she had gotten married she was a little over twenty. 'But what she did is not the main issue. The main issue is something else: When she told me that, I took a moment to get over it. She'd told it to me in an ordinary tone of voice. Just like... like a memory. She felt no emotion about it. Me, I was shocked, I was... I was silent for half a minute, and then I asked her if she repented of it. Did she ask God for forgiveness for it? She shrugged and said: "Well, lots of people did that." You understand? She'd been a practising Christian for many years. But she didn't see any crime in her action, or anything terrible. Maybe she'd justified

it to herself by saying to herself that she'd simply done her civic duty, because he'd spoken against the Soviet regime. And imagine, over sixty years have gone by since that time. She'd remarried, had several children, went to church all the time. And until the moment she departed this world, she didn't feel any repentance. In Greek they say *metanoia*: etymologically, it means "a change of mind and of heart". And she never had that. Nothing, not the church, not society, not history – the war, the Soviet years, Gorbachev, perestroika, children, age – was able to bring her to the realization that it was a terrible crime, which she should mourn all her life. You understand?'

205. This lack of repentance, of rehabilitation, he thought, was due to the fact that the Soviet government had continued to exist. It hadn't been destroyed like the Third Reich, and so there was no equivalent of denazification, defascisation. And Russia had kept a large part of the inheritance of the Soviet Union for itself; not just in its ideology, but in its methods, its approaches. 'Have you heard of "the grandmother with the red flag"? In some village somewhere, an old grandmother came out to welcome the Russian troops with a Soviet flag. It was in Kyiv *oblast*, I think. Or Kharkiv, I'm not sure. She was photographed, interviewed, the Russians even built a monument to her. You can see her image painted on their tanks. This grandmother is alive, she was found...'[179] He started to laugh. 'She thought she was welcoming her liberators, probably.' 'Where is she now?' 'She was evacuated. To the Ukrainian side. But that's not the issue. That red flag isn't just in people's hands. That red flag, despite all the horrors, all the historic turning points, continues to veil eyes and hearts.' He became pensive. 'It continues to veil eyes and hearts. And the people who look at everything

else through this red, they don't see the blood anymore, and they don't smell it. You understand? The mind isn't purified, the heart isn't purified. There's no change.' Now it was my turn to laugh: 'You know, Antoine is colour-blind. He can't see red either.'

206. The tea had long grown cold, and it was too dark now to photograph. The priest had started talking again, and the conversation was taking on a more philosophical turn. I had asked him if Russia might someday follow the path of Germany. 'Russia... I don't see the necessary steps taking place. Before it was denazified, before it repented, Germany was invaded. But neither Ukraine nor Europe is going to invade Russia to change the political system. Today, Russia is so far from that that I can't imagine it being possible.' At every stage of its history, he went on, Russia had never been ready to renounce this form of power, this model of autocracy inherited from the Byzantine Empire. It was something natural, and if it rejected it, it would lose itself as Russia, as a State. 'Do you understand what I mean? What would have to happen to Russia for it to repent for its Nazism, for modern Russian Nazism? I can't begin to imagine it. And Ukraine, somewhere, has a similar problem: how to stop the aggressor, but at the same time make it so that Ukraine is still able to join Europe? What answer can Ukraine offer to this test, to the formation of a new Ukrainian mentality? Of a new social identity? Here too, repentance is indispensable. Has Ukraine repented for the fact that Ukrainian citizens took part in the massacres of the Holocaust? Have there been any public apologies? Ukraine has the same disease as Russia, Ukraine is sick too. And this de-Sovietization will be much more difficult than just renaming the streets.'

TOPOGRAPHIES

207. Let's return to our walk in June, the summer before the war. After taking our leave of the lady who was gardening, Antoine and I had walked around the church to head between the two buildings framing it in a V, built precisely on the line of the eastern boundary of KL Syrets. Behind them stood the solitary high-rise, still unfinished then, a mixture of white, brown, pale yellow, dark red, surrounded by a green metal fence. During our brief exchange, the lady at the church had told me that when the construction of this building had begun, the workers there too removed a huge number of bones from the ground. 'I forget when it was. They stopped building so often before starting up again...' She thought it had been the site of an NKVD camp, but she was wrong: this twenty-five storey monolith, located at No. 25 Olena Teliha Street, was planted right above the western spur of Babyn Yar, the little branch of the ravine where the Germans had perpetrated their massacre before filling it in. For a long time, after the massive reorganization of the zone and the construction programmes of the 1950s and 60s, no one remembered exactly where the ravine was situated anymore, and no one really cared. When they built the big bronze monument, in 1976, it was over five hundred metres from there; the Menorah wasn't placed in the right spot either. Everyone who studied this question had their own hypothesis, but the arguments, often contradictory, remain shaky. The question wasn't definitively settled until 2019, when the BYHMC took it on. A young architect, Maksym Rokmaniko, with his colleagues from the Centre for Spatial Technologies, deployed high-end computer technology inspired by the work developed by Eyal Weizman and Forensic Architecture to analyze

war crime sites. All the available materials, aerial photos from 1941-1943 showing the ravine at Babyn Yar, old topographical maps, and of course the photos of Johannes Hähle, were scanned and rendered in 3D. For the photos, software made it possible to determine the lens' focal length and thus to determine the distortions of the perspective, and then, from the shadows, the time of day, as well as the position of the sun and therefore the orientation of the image; the position of certain trees or hills, distinguishable from one photo to the next, could also be superimposed over that of the crests or trees visible in aerial photos. This data allowed Rokmaniko and his team to create a perfectly oriented 3D model of Babyn Yar, and then to superimpose it to the nearest metre over a 3D model of the contemporary topography. The result was crystal clear. The quarry where the Jews were stripped was situated under the park and the entrance to the metro *perekhid*; the Jews were then led, through an opening dynamited into the flank of the quarry, to a spur of the ravine which began in the heart of the present park, continued beneath Teliha Street, passed directly under the tower under construction at No. 25, and curved to the left below the *khrushchiovki* to end between what is now Nos. 12 and 16 Shchusiev Street, right next to the Shevchenko District Technical Lyceum.[180]

208. Locally, it seems that all this wasn't completely forgotten; while the *khrushchiovki* along Teliha Street are lined up one after the other, with just an alleyway between them, the space between the current Nos. 23 and 27, just above the spur of the ravine, remained empty for decades, occupied only by a refreshment stand without foundations. I don't think this was entirely by chance, although it might have been. If it is a case of administrative

memory, it slowly disappeared with the functionaries who bore it, and at independence property developers rushed onto this lucrative lot. The first building project, the one the church gardener had told me about, began in the early 2000s, but it was halted in 2008, for lack of funds no doubt, and the stump of the unfinished building remained there, abandoned until 2019 when a company named Uno City House bought the land from the Polish bank that had seized it, razed the five floors that had already been built and reconstructed the building on the basis of the same plans but with a different cladding. The BYHMC attempted to discuss the problem of its location with the investors, but they hadn't wanted to hear anything about it; Rokmaniko and his colleagues infiltrated their discussion group on Telegram and discovered openly denialist comments there, casting doubt not only on the identification of the site but on the massacre's reality itself. The BYHMC had then launched an intense campaign at the town hall against the developers, and just before the war was planning an advertising campaign aimed at potential buyers. If you wanted to visit the building, it was best not to go through the developers. But a few days earlier we had managed to secure a visit by asking a friend, Oleh, to call them and pass himself off as a real estate agent tasked with showing property to a French investor interested in acquiring several units in this promising neighbourhood. And so on the appointed day I presented myself in a linen suit and a Panama hat, accompanied by Oleh and Antoine, whom we described as my personal photographer, documenting my visits for my wife in France. I pretended I couldn't speak Russian, and Oleh translated for Viktoriya, the frosty agent who received us and who didn't speak a word of English. She had us put on some hard hats and took us first to the fifth

floor, where the hallways had been finished with a hideous orange paint and poor-quality steel security doors. Then we went up to the twenty-fourth floor to see some duplexes. The walls were bare cinder block: the apartments were sold as is, with just the windows, the door and the electricity and water inlets, nothing else, not even a staircase to climb up to the upper part of the duplex. 'It's a *comfort class* building,' Viktoriya explained, 'not *business class*. And this way, each owner can decorate the apartment as they like, it's simpler.' The price was 35,000 hryvnias per square metre, or around 120,000 euros for a hundred-square-metre apartment. For Kyiv, it's by no means cheap, but the view was incredible, the entire park and the Kyrylivskyy Hai stretching out at our feet. The visit continued, more modest apartments, little shared balconies for smokers. Finally we went back downstairs, passing on the way the most gorgeous construction worker I'd ever seen, a young man with diaphanous skin and soft, feminine features, standing just outside the front door, hands on hips, his lips in a sceptical pout. Before ending the visit I asked to see the underground car park.

209. It was only a car park and there was nothing to see, aside from the concrete and cinder block walls that should never have been built on this ground. The Soviet writer Anatoliy Kuznetsov had grown up not far from here, in the Kurenivka neighbourhood just behind. At the age of twelve he had seen the Jews marching on Kyrylivska Street towards Babyn Yar, and during the two long years that followed he heard almost every day the hammering of machine guns, carried by the wind. Several of his Jewish friends were swallowed up by the ravine. After the liberation, he came up with a friend to see the place. He writes:

It was an enormous, you could even say a majestic ravine – deep and wide, like a mountain gorge. Shout from one side, you can barely hear it from the other.

... In the bottom there always ran a very friendly and clean little stream. The cliffs were sheer, steep, sometimes even overhanging, and landslides were frequent in Babiy Yar. In fact it was common here: the right bank of the Dniepro is completely cut up by such ravines, the main street in Kiev Kreshchatik was formed out of the Kreshchatiy Yar, there's also the Repyakhov Yar, the Syretskiy Yar and others, there are many.

On the way we saw, crossing from one side of the ravine to the other, an old man in rags with a bag. From his confident stride, we understood that he lived somewhere around here and wasn't walking this way for the first time.

'*Dyed*,' I asked, 'grandfather, did they shoot the Jews here or further on?'

The grandfather stopped, looked me up and down from head to toe, and said:

'And how many Russians lie here, and Ukrainians, and people from every nation?'

And he left.

We knew this stream like the five fingers of our hand, in our childhood we blocked it with little dams – 'gatkami' – to swim in it.

It was full of good, coarse sand, but now it was strewn for some reason with little white pebbles.

I bent down to pick one up, to study it. It was a burnt piece of bone the size of a nail, white on one side, black on the other. The stream rinsed them somewhere and carried them away. From this we concluded that the Jews, the Russians, the Ukrainians and the people from every nation had been shot further up.

And so we walked for a long while on these bits of bone, until we reached the very beginning of the ravine, and the stream disappeared; it was born here from many sources springing from under the sand bed, and from somewhere over here it rinsed the bones.

The ravine here had become narrow, divided into several branches, and in one place the sand turned grey. Suddenly we realized that we were walking on human ash.

Nearby, washed away by the rains, a layer of sand had collapsed, and from under it appeared a hewn ridge of granite and a layer of coal. The thickness of this vein of coal was about a quarter of a metre.

Goats were passing on the slope and three little shepherds, about eight years old, were diligently striking the coal with hammers and crushing it onto the granite ridge.

We went over to them. The coal was grainy, brown in colour, like for example if you'd mixed locomotive ash with wood glue.

'What are you doing?' I asked.

'Look!' One of them took out of his pocket a handful of something shiny and dirty, which he spread out on his palm.

They were half-melted gold rings, earrings, teeth.

They were mining gold.

We walked around, and found many whole bones, a fresh skull with shreds of flesh, and again pieces of black ash mixed with the grey sand.

I picked up a piece, about two kilograms in weight, took it with me and kept it. It was the ash of many people, all mixed together – international ash, so to speak.[181]

210. Kuznetsov and the little shepherds weren't the only collectors in the area. Ilya Levitas, the man I once met but don't remember, also roamed through the ravines

of Babyn Yar after he arrived in Kyiv in 1945, when he was just fourteen or fifteen, two years younger than Kuznetsov, and collected all the half-buried objects he could find there. Later, as the ravines were progressively filled in, he extended his research to the apartments of the murdered Jews, recovering many objects and souvenirs of the dead families; when he became known among the Jewish community of Kyiv, people would directly bring him the possessions of the dead, entrusting them to his care and vigilance. After independence, he founded a little museum to exhibit his collection; then, in 2014, he died. The objects were orphaned a second time. Finally the museum decided to offer them to the National Preserve of Babyn Yar, the *Zapovidnyk*. Its director, Roza Tapanova, took custody of the objects in October 2021, at the time of the commemoration of the massacre's 80th anniversary, and a few days later invited us to come see them in her office. They were heaped up haphazardly, but no one minded, you could touch and pick up what you liked. There I found: a rusted German helmet, full of old oxidized bullets and pieces of barbed wire, with an MP40 cartridge clip. A box containing coins, also oxidized, a bracelet and some broken glass. An old suitcase containing two Jewish books, a manuscript in Hebrew on vellum, an old leather-bound Bible, a Jewish prayer shawl, a Soviet forester's cap with a tefillin inside it, a pile of old, very heavy records of Jewish dances and songs released in the USSR before the war, a poster for an *estrady* contest, a bag full of papers – including a certificate, signed on 2 May 1917 by a rabbi, attesting to the birth on 24 August 1898 of Shaya, son of Yankel Angelev Levit and of Hanna Levit – a pen, a pipe, a roll of blotting paper, a shaving mug and brush. A white handbag containing metal ribbons. An empty green felt bag bearing the gilt

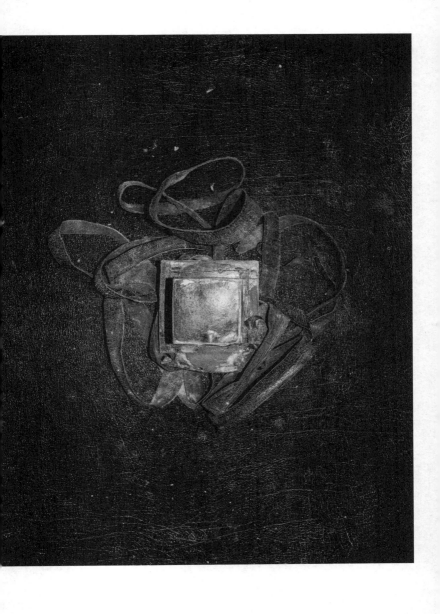

logo of Frank Meisler. Two pieces of embroidered cloth ringed with black, white and red macramé. A roll of faded red corduroy. And even more things, which I didn't note down.

211. There was one final way to get closer to the vanished *yar*. All these ravines had been carved out, over the centuries, by flowing rainwater, and a stream ran at the bottom of Babyn Yar, as Kuznetsov described. There is no clear testimony on the logistics of the massacre, on its practical disposition, but one can logically suppose that no matter which method was used the bodies ended up at the bottom, blocking the stream and reddening its waters, until everything was covered over in earth. But every year the autumn rains must have re-formed this stream, hollowing out a new little bed or seeping into the earth mingled with bones and ash to well up a little further on, where children and collectors wandered about. When the municipal authorities started filling in the ravines with the muddy discharge from the neighbourhood brick factories, or else later on, when everything had been levelled, they installed concrete pipes to channel these streams. The pipes still exist, the stream of Babyn Yar still runs: it's never the same water, but it's certainly still the same stream. The very precise Soviet-era map I found indicates that the pipe begins under the park and the first *khrushchiovki* of Syrets, a little past the Dorohozhychi metro station; follows the route of Olena Teliha Street as it curves towards the Petrivka industrial zone; crosses Kyrylivska Street (which on my map is still called Frunze Street) to follow Stepan Bandera Avenue (the former Moskovskyy Prospekt); at the corner of Tulchynska Street (which hasn't changed its name), it joins the pipe carrying the stream of the Repiakhiv Yar, which emerges

from under the psychiatric asylum; from there, the two conduits, side by side, follow the course of Verbova Street to finally empty into the Pochaina River, a little tributary of the Dnipro, about 5.4 kilometres from the point where they started.

212. In the autumn of 2021, we managed to find an urban explorer able to guide us there. This Kirill agreed to meet us in the car park of a shopping centre on Bandera Avenue, where he handed us big rubber boots taken from old hazmat suits, then led us to a little dirt path that ran alongside the Pochaina. This isn't just any river: it is here, according to one account, that Prince Volodymyr (or Valdemar) of Kyiv had himself baptized along with his court, forever converting the Slavic peoples of the East to Christianity (according to another account, this baptism took place in Chersonesus, in Crimea, where Volodymyr is said to have gone to welcome his Byzantine betrothed). Today it's nothing but a foul little greenish canal flowing between the garages and warehouses of Petrivka, channelled between crumbling concrete banks and almost completely hidden beneath vegetation and weeds. At the foot of a big maintenance station for commercial vehicles, we headed down to a little bridge, sat down to pull on our boots and attach them to our belts with loops of string intended for this purpose, and started up single-file on the concrete rim of the canal, to find a little further up the mouth of the double stream a culvert above us which emerged from the grass-covered bank. Inside, water flowed towards us at ankle-level; daylight quickly disappeared, and we turned on our flashlights. The culvert soon split into two parallel ducts and we took the one on the right, moving forwards with difficulty in the muddy sand that covered the ground, the same sand in

which Kuznetsov had played as a child. The concrete was old, grey, dirty; streams of brown mud mixed with rotten leaves sometimes oozed from cracks in the wall or from smaller pipes that discharged there. Little by little, the pipe narrowed. We had to bend forwards to keep walking, then double over; the muddy earth was treacherous, these conduits were obviously never maintained, there were holes where your foot sunk in by surprise and twisted, suddenly. The water around our ankles was flowing fairly fast, perpendicular pipes also brought in a little water; sometimes, where there was a slight rise in the ground, the water flowed on bare concrete, walking became easier for a few metres, then the muddy sand began again. Here and there the greenish, dancing light of our flashlights reflected off a frozen spider, all white, devoured by a strange underground fungus that took its shape. Further on, the beams captured a poor little bird fluttering there blindly, terrified, trapped between the water and the concrete; it sped behind us and disappeared into the dark, to follow the flow of air to the exit or else drown of exhaustion. All these underground streams were part of the urban run-off drainage system, and when it rained, Kirill told us, the duct could fill up in fifteen minutes, it came quickly, streams of rubbish first and then water that rose to the ceiling, people had died like that, trapped. At this point the pipe was less than a metre high; if we'd had the courage and the strength to continue on all fours, we could have reached the very heart of Babyn Yar, some two and a half kilometres further on. But Antoine and I were too old for that, and a little before we reached Kyrylivksa Street we gave up. On the way back, daylight finally appeared in the distance like a small, very white dot that trembled, shone, grew and finally pervaded everything, leaving us blinking our eyes by the green water of the Pochaina.

311

213. Finally, there are the images. Those in colour, so precious, made by the photographer of *Propagandakompanie* 637 Johannes Hähle, and those in black and white taken by the Soviets after the liberation of the city, showing a bare, desolate, abandoned ravine. Films from the archives as well, shot at the same time in those days as during the visit of the American journalists, some of which have been used by the Ukrainian director Sergei Loznitsa in a documentary entitled *Babi Yar. Contexte.*[182] There's even a fictional film, made in the Kyiv studios around the end of 1945, *Nepokorennye* (*The Unvanquished*), directed by Mark Donskoi and based on a book by the *Pravda* correspondent Boris Gorbatov. In this film, we see Jews led to their death and shot by the Nazis: it's actually the first fiction film ever to depict the Shoah. What's more, the Jews are presented as Jews, are shot as Jews; the supporting role, a Jewish doctor played by the Lithuanian Jewish actor Veniamin Zuskin, is shot with the others. A few years later, reality caught up with fiction: Zuskin was arrested by the MGB on his hospital bed in December 1948, and would be shot for real in August 1952. And Jews being exterminated will never again be shown in Soviet cinema, ever. The massacre scene was filmed in October 1944 in Babyn Yar itself. As Karel Berkhoff, the researcher who unearthed the history of this forgotten film, writes, 'No one expressed any concern with the on-site reenactment atop the human remains of the real victims.' Donskoi's *mise en scène* was so well done that his footage has occasionally been used as authentic archival images.[183]

214. After passing around the construction site of the building at No. 25, we had found ourselves on the pavement on Teliha Street. Antoine tried to take some photos, but without much success. In any case it was soon time for our meeting at the television tower. We crossed the street as best we could, there were no traffic lights for hundreds of metres, and we cut through the park to pass through the *perekhid* and walk down Oranzhereina. In May 2022, after the fiasco of Antoine's trip in March, we had also returned here to examine the damage caused by the bombing of the tower. On Illienko Street, just in front of the outer wall of the complex, a post wrapped in grey plastic – on which had been painted, in English, the words NO FOTO – was stuck into a crater in the pavement; the outer fence, torn open by the explosion and patched up with pieces of train tracks, also bore signs saying NO FOTO – NO VIDEO. From here, you could clearly see the marks of the impact, the support pilings were blackened and deformed in places, there were no more windows on the red control floor just above them, but the tower had held up remarkably well, the damage seemed mainly cosmetic. 'Should I try to take a photo?' Antoine asked. I looked to the right, towards a ruined building guarded by some sinister-looking soldiers; one of them had come out into the street to watch us. 'Better not,' I replied. 'What about that?' he said, pointing to the big post. 'You think that's the missile?' The object could look like one, it's true. But it was hard to say. 'I don't know. Anyway we can't photograph it. Come on, let's cross over.'

215. On the other side of Yuri Illienko Street, the large gymnasium of the Avanhard sports complex had suffered

a lot of damage; no glass was left in the twisted window frames of the façade, the inside had burned and was still full of rubble. The street had been cleaned up but there was still a collapsed electric pole with piles of cables, little burned trees and a large oak rising at the edge of the pavement, scorched, bare, charred in places, with carbonized clumps of mistletoe hanging from the branches, but apparently still alive, the first leaves were poking out at the tips of the blackened branches, seeking the sun. On the ground, there were some large, dark outlines where the bodies of the five victims of the second rocket had burned, a family with their children who must have been running towards the metro and a cameraman from Kyiv Live TV, Yevhenii Sakun, who after the first explosion had come out of the TV headquarters a little further on and had been killed filming the fire. I had seen a video of firemen spraying the burning corpses with extinguishers, and also a photograph taken by Laurent van der Stockt of the five bodies rolled up in plastic or sheets, piled on top of each other in the back of a police van. The first rocket, a 3M-54 'Kalibr' cruise missile according to analyses, was the one that had struck the tower, at 5.08 p.m. on 1 March. Several people had filmed the explosion, the huge plume of brown smoke enveloping the tower and rising up like a flower to the grey sky. The control room was empty, there hadn't been any victims, and the tower had held up. The second missile had struck eleven minutes later, at 5.19 p.m. It's not clear if it completely missed the tower, or if it struck it without exploding before rebounding and crashing in front of the gymnasium: given the dispersion of the debris and the photos showing two simultaneous explosions on both sides of Illienko Street, I would incline towards the second hypothesis.[184]

314

216. Next to the gymnasium was a little garage, the STO 'Okko'. In front, on the street side, boards and plastic covered the shattered windows of a spare parts shop, hiding the shambles inside. We went behind it: two men were busily working on a car parked in front of one of the bays; on the left, sitting in another car with the door open, a rosy-cheeked blonde woman was quietly smoking. I walked over to greet her, she worked there and her name was Iryna. 'The sirens went off five minutes before,' she told me as she drew on her cigarette. 'With my two colleagues we went into the basement. An intuition.' Iryna had waited ten minutes after the second explosion before coming out. In the street, two cars had been caught in the blast, but the passengers were alive. 'The tower was burning, vibrating. I was so afraid it was going to fall. We quickly helped the people get out of their cars and we ran towards the sports centre, the one under construction, over there in the back.' I knew the way, there was a little café where Antoine, one day, had almost as he left forgotten his camera, which he'd left on the bench outside. After the gymnasium under construction the path continued to the fenced enclosure of the 'Field of Mirrors', the first of the commemorative projects erected by the BYHMC, before the synagogue and the four stones. It was a vast circular platform with ten pillars arranged so as to form the tree of life from the Kabbala; all its surfaces, polished stainless steel riddled with bullets of the same calibre as those used during the massacre in 1941, reflected the spectators wandering over it, the trees all around, the sky, the damaged tower too. We knew the guards, we got along well with them, especially Andrii who spoke broken Spanish and whom Antoine had photographed several times, and to go to greet them in their shed we walked across the monument amid ghostly sounds filling

the space, a fluctuating background of electroacoustic synthesizer (its notes determined by an algorithm according to the principles of *gematria*, which translates into numbers the letters of the victims' Hebrew names) mixed with a confused murmur made of scraps of pre-war Yiddish songs, Christian choruses, Ukrainian and Roma memorial songs and contemporary works.[185] The guards too had been there during the strike along with some other colleagues, and had seen everything. 'Me, I didn't hear the alarm,' claimed Andrii in his hesitant Spanish as he served us little shots of homebrew. 'The tower was enveloped in a ball of fire, but it was designed to withstand explosions, it vibrated for a while and that was it. Shrapnel rained down on the Field of Mirrors, we all ran further up, towards the synagogue.' On his smartphone, he showed me a little video someone else had taken from the top of the hill: the camera was shaking, you could hear swearing, shouting; the park was covered in snow, the trees were bare; in the distance, the smoke rose in spirals, hiding the entire middle of the tower.

217. The previous June, we'd gone around the other side, up Dorohozhytska, to reach the guard post that gave access to the territory of the tower. A uniformed guard behind an armoured window had examined our passports and made a phone call; a few minutes later, a tower official, accompanied by the head of security, came to welcome us at the turnstiles and let us in. They were the ones who explained the history of the tower's construction to us as we walked across the territory, passing between two of the side pillars to reach the central tube, over four metres wide. A tiny elevator opened at its base and we all piled inside with a few workers. The interior was all metal, with a futurist design worthy of a science fiction

film of the time, and it climbed slowly upwards, making a lot of noise: 'It's like rising up to hell', Antoine calmly commented. The elevator finally stopped and the door opened. In front of us stretched a red metal footbridge completely exposed to the elements, stretching over the void to join one of the three circular walkways stacked beneath the upper section. All there was between us and the ground 180 metres below was a waist-high guardrail. With my stomach in knots, I advanced step by step, gripping both railings. I concentrated on the chipped paint, the spots of rust on the metal, the small antennae placed here and there, scarcely looking at the vast landscape stretched out all around us. There was a little wind, but I forced myself to let go so I could take a few photos of the geometries of the white and red tubes and of Antoine quietly working, his camera set on the railing in the direction of Babyn Yar. Finally I rejoined the official, whose name I unfortunately didn't note; she was waiting at the junction of the bridge leading to the elevator, chatting with the security guard. She cheerfully waved her hand towards the tubes, quite happy to be there: 'We repaint them every five years, you know? The painters work hanging from ropes. It's nothing, they're used to it, even when it's windy.'

218. On the next floor, we emerged into a lobby covered in gilded aluminium, which opened onto a little empty banquet hall, very warm from the sun beating on the closed windows, clean, sad, old-fashioned. A worker in blue overalls, his elbow resting on the white tablecloth, was sitting at the table and contemplating the view with an absent air. Further on, the technical rooms were full of new servers, modern machines in the heart of this wonderful dinosaur, aging so elegantly. There was also some

older equipment, almost archaic, electrical casings, tubes, as well as an old Soviet painting placed on the broken tiled floor behind some ventilation ducts. Grates, under my feet, opened out onto the void; the windows, covered in a dirty grey film to protect from the sun, offered a blurred landscape as far as the eye could see. I walked slowly around the room. From here, I could see everything: the immensity of the old motorcycle factory, impossible to discern from the street, in front of which had been the *shlakbaum* and the sorting tables for Jewish possessions; the two cemeteries, the military one and Lukyanivske, and between them Dorohozhytska Street along which the men and boys had set off on foot; the layout of the path and the quarry, which I could now only imagine beneath the metro *perekhid* and the huge metal tower in which I stood; and finally the expanse of the park, and No. 25 Olena Teliha Street, where once lay the western spur of Babyn Yar. Further on, towards the northeast, in the immense expanse in relief of the Kyrylivskyy Hai, a large bend was outlined through the trees with their subtly varied tones, green, metallic grey, touches of yellow: the curve of the Repiakhiv Yar, the last of the ravines, beyond which lay the buildings of the psychiatric asylum. In the distance stretched the city, clear at first and then dissolving into the early summer mist towards the new peripheries, Horenka, Hostomel, Irpin, Bucha. I spent a long moment contemplating this confused and chaotic territory, shapeless, without structure, with its run-down buildings, its bountiful vegetation, its concealed, erased wounds.

219. The Kyiv poet Leonid Kiselov, who died of leukemia at the age of twenty-two, wrote the following verse in Russian:

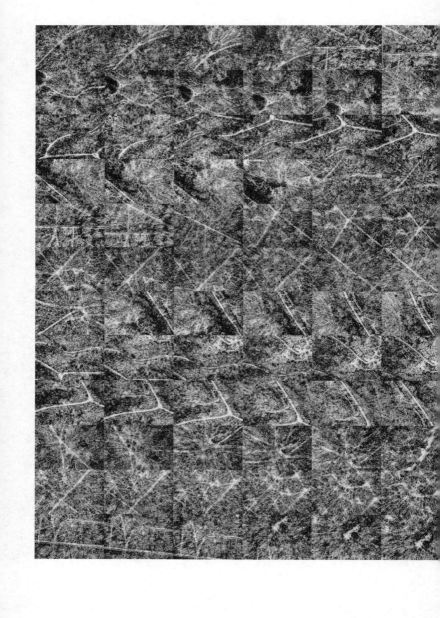

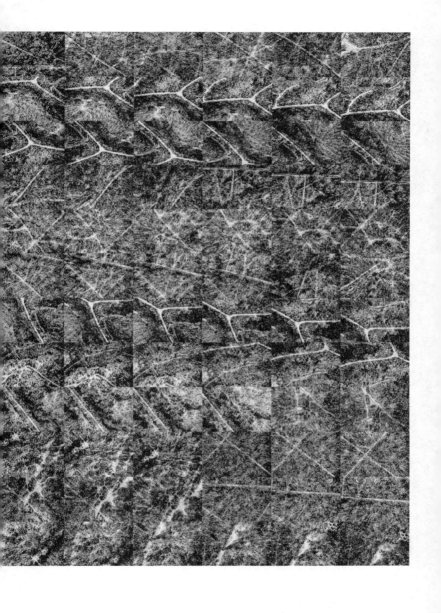

Ya postoyu u kraya bezdny
I vdrug poïmu, slomyas v toske,
Chto vsio na svete – tolko pesnya
Na ukrainskom yazyke.

I stand at the edge of the abyss
And suddenly I realize, broken by anguish,
That everything in the world is but a song
In the Ukrainian language. [186]

220. We descended from the tower, took leave of our hosts, and set off towards the metro. At the end of Oranzhereina Street we paused at the corner of the park to have a smoke. Across the way, on the other side of Illienko Street, a little bridge started at the roof of the metro station to cross over to the side of a hill, where it was closed off by a barrier. There is only one bridge in Babyn Yar, and it leads nowhere.

GIGUE

221. That summer, Antoine left Kyiv before I did. I returned one last time to Babyn Yar, alone. I was wandering along the crest of the little ravine under the synagogue when I heard the first rumblings of a summer storm. The air was heavy, oppressive, suddenly the wind started lashing the leaves. I passed the three black metal crosses lost in the vegetation along the steep slope of the old *yar*; at the edge of the cliff, two men were standing in an arbour of greenery, smoking and talking. In the woods, the rain started falling, isolated drops striking the leaves with a dull sound. Near the ruined mausoleum of the Kachkovskiy brothers, three men were filming, two others,

near a parked van, stared at me suspiciously as I walked by; a little further on I passed a man and a woman calmly walking with backpacks and hiking sticks. Again, the thunder rumbled, the rain was truly starting up. The path was becoming wet and slippery, but the thick foliage protected me a little, I sped up, the downpour was growing stronger. Through the leaves I could see the beige brick of the derelict psychiatric institute. The water was pouring down now and soaking me, here, to the top, there was no way in, you had to walk around the side of the building, on the slope I skidded in the mud, almost fell, barely regained my balance. Finally I arrived under the concrete roof of one of the entrances and entered the building, wet but completely at peace while the rain pattered down all around. I waited for a moment as I listened to the gentle rush of the water, then headed towards one of the staircases. Dirt floor, debris, rubbish, graffiti. A white light pouring in through the gaping windows. I went up. At the top it was clearer, I could see the treetops through each opening, the building under construction on the other side of the Repiakhiv Yar, the sky full of grey clouds coiled in on themselves. I thought I was alone in this immense ruin, but while I was roaming around the couple of hikers I'd passed earlier on silently appeared in an opening and crossed the big hall I was standing in behind me, without a word, ignoring me or maybe not noticing me. I set off in the other direction and crossed the width of the building, making my way at random. In one half-soaked room, leaning on a wall covered in large, colourful graffiti, a young man was quietly masturbating, his eyes closed. I turned around again and came across three kids between maybe eight and twelve, who looked at me with shock, as if they were worried to see me here. Finally I went back down another staircase. Here there was music, voices:

I peered around the corner, a little party was underway, I withdrew and continued on my way, discreetly. The shower had ended and I slipped outside the building, wading in the mud and getting soaked again by the grass and the wet leaves through which I was forcing my way. Finally I found the main path and climbed back up towards the woods. Raindrops were still pattering on the muddy ground, the moss, the leaves on the trees. Near the abandoned mausoleum I heard music, five teenagers in garish clothing, electric blue, pink, orange, fuchsia, suddenly appeared in front of me, a portable speaker blared Linkin Park, they were young, joyous, carefree, happy as they noisily headed away from me under the fine droplets of the dying rain.

CODA

222. During our very first visit to Babyn Yar, in April 2021, Vitalii, an employee at the BYHMC, had taken us on a long excursion. Antoine was already taking photos, I was looking, without noting anything down. Finally we had paused on the hill just below the Menorah. Antoine was looking through his camera at the photos he'd taken; suddenly, without a word, he handed it to me. On the back of the camera, on the little control screen, appeared two words: MEMORY FULL.

Note

Unless otherwise specified, all translations from the French are by Charlotte Mandell, and all translations from the Russian and the Ukrainian are by Jonathan Littell.

Endnotes

1   Maurice Blanchot, 'Énigme', in *Literature and the Ethical Question,* ed. Claire Nouvet, Yale French Studies, 79, 1991, 5-7. The translation notes that the French term 'me revient' can also be read as 'is my due'.

2   Maurice Blanchot, *L'écriture du désastre* (Paris: Éditions Gallimard, 1980), 24. In English: *The Writing of the Disaster*, tr. Ann Smock (Lincoln, Nebraska: University of Nebraska Press, 1995). Translation slightly modified.

3   John Steinbeck, *A Russian Journal*, with photographs by Robert Capa (London: Penguin Classics, 2000). The original edition was published by Viking Press, 1948.

4   Elie Wiesel, *Les Juifs du silence* (Paris: Seuil, 1966), 40-41, 44. In English: *The Jews of Silence*, tr. Neal Kozodoy (New York: Schocken Books, 2011).

5   Gilles Deleuze, *Leibnitz: âme et damnation* (course given in 1986-1987), Gallimard/À voix haute, 2003, audio CD, disc 2, track 8.

6   Vitaly Nakhmanovych, 'Babyn Yar: A Place of Memory in Search of a Future', in Vladyslav Hrynevych and Paul Robert Magocsi (eds.), *Babyn Yar: History and Memory* (Kyiv: Dukh i Litera, 2016), 307.

7   Kate Brown, *A Biography of No Place* (Cambridge, Massachusetts: Harvard University Press, 2004), 67.

8   Vladyslav Hrynevych, 'Babyn Yar after Babyn Yar', in Hrynevych and Magocsi, *Babyn Yar: History and Memory*, 127.

9   Vasily Grossman, '*Sikstinskaya Madonna*' ['The Sistine Madonna'], *Znamya*, No. 5, 1989. In English: 'The Sistine Madonna', tr. Robert and Elizabeth Chandler, in *The Road* (London: MacLehose Press, 2010).

10 Grossman, '*Sikstinskaya Madonna*'.

11 Vasily Grossman, *L'enfer de Treblinka*, no translator given (Grenoble and Paris: Arthaud, 1945).

12 Vasily Grossman, quoted in '*Sikstinskaya madonna*'.

13 Vasily Grossman, '*Treblinskiy ad*' ['The Hell of Treblinka'], in *Povesti, rasskazy, ocherki* (*Articles, stories, essays*) (Moscow: Voenizdat, 1958). Online without page numbers at http://lib.ru/PROZA/GROSSMAN/trebl.txt_with-big-pictures.htm. In English: 'The Hell of Treblinka', tr. Robert and Elizabeth Chandler, in *The Road*, 2010.

14   Vitaly Nakhmanovych's expression, in 'Babyn Yar: A Place of Memory', *Babyn Yar: History and Memory*, 309-310.

15   For the francophone reader interested in this mythical episode, I recommend the fine little book by Régis Genté and Nicolas Jallot, *Futbol: le ballon rond de Staline à Poutine, une arme politique* (Paris: Allary Éditions, 2018).

16   This list, modified and completed, is based on BYHMC and FORMA Architectural Studio, *Analysis of historical and contemporary context of Babyn Yar and adjacent territories*, (Kyiv: Babyn Yar Holocaust Memorial Center, 2020), 212-217.

17   Yitzhak Arad, *Belzec, Sobibor, Treblinka: The Operation Reinhard Death Camps* (Bloomington, Indiana: Indiana University Press, 1987), reprinted in paperback in 1999, 376. Arad unfortunately does not cite his source for Globocnik's boast.

18   See Nakhmanovych, 'A Place of Memory', who writes on p. 295 of the 'unprecedented activism ... demonstrated by various civic organizations, informal groups, and local authorities, who have all been working towards the goal of commemorating "their own" victims'.

19   Personal communication.

20   Nakhmanovych, 'A Place of Memory', 301. Hrynevych, in his essay 'Babyn Yar after Babyn Yar', in the same volume on p. 148, gives the date 1966, but that seems to be a mistake.

21   Hrynevych, 'Babyn Yar after Babyn Yar', 148.

22   Mykhailo Tyaglyy, '"A tragedy of guilty victims?" The memory of the Roma genocide in postwar Ukraine, part 1', translated from Ukrainian into English by Marta Olynyk and posted on the Jewish Ukrainian Encounters website on 2 October 2021 at https://ukrainianjewishencounter.org/en/a-tragedy-of-guilty-victims-the-memory-of-the-roma-genocide-in-postwar-ukraine-part-1/. See note 15 in the article for a link to a map of the sites of mass killings of Roma in Ukraine.

23   Vasily Grossman, *Za pravoe delo* [For a Just Cause] (Moscow: Eksmo, 1954), Part One, chapter 44. Online without page numbers at http://militera.lib.ru/prose/russian/grossman_vs3/05.html. In English: Vasily Grossman, *Stalingrad*, tr. Robert and Elizabeth Chandler (London: Harvill Secker, 2019), chapter 48 (this edition, based on unpublished manuscripts in Russian, has additional chapters).

24   See http://babynyar.gov.ua/en/historical-information.

25   Antoine saw this man, Misha, again, in February 2023, when he was working on a piece for the *New York Times Magazine* on soldiers being treated for PTSD at the 'Pavlovka' psychiatric hospital (see note 29 below). Every day, Misha would wedge himself into the fork of a tree and repeat this gesture until a doctor or nurse came to look for him. It calmed him down, he explained to Rita, Antoine's colleague; as for the trees, he had a special relationship with them, much closer and more

...	intense than with humans.
26	Vitaly Nakhmanovych, 'Babyn Yar: The Holocaust and Other Tragedies', in Hrynevych and Magocsi, *Babyn Yar: History and Memory*, 97-98.
27	Vitaly Nakhmanovych, 'A Place of Memory', 302.
28	Vasyl Doguzov and Svitlana Rusalovska, 'The Massacre of Mental Patients in Ukraine 1941-1943', *International Journal of Mental Health*, 36:1, Spring 2007, 105-111.
29	Ellen Barry (with Rita Burkovska), photographs by Antoine d'Agata, 'Voices from Pavlivka', *New York Times Magazine*, 19 March 2023. The publication of this report, emphasizing the massive incidence of severe trauma among Ukrainian soldiers at the front, caused the military to cancel Antoine's press card.
30	Konstantin Paustovsky, *Povest o zhizni: Daliokie Gody* [The Story of a Life: The Distant Years], chapter 18, '*Krasny Fonarik*' ['The Red Lantern'], in *Sobranie Sochineny* (*Collected Works*), vol. 4. Online without page numbers at https://librebook.me/povest_o_jizni__knigi_1_3/vol3/1. In English: 'Book One. The Faraway Years', in *The Story of a Life*, tr. Douglas Smith (New York: New York Review of Books, 2023).
31	This trial, which lasted over two years, opened wide the floodgates of Russian anti-Semitism; not only the press, but also famous writers like Maksim Gorkiy and Aleksandr Blok denounced Beilis's alleged crime.
32	Mykhailo Kalnytskyi, 'Babyn Yar in Space and Time', in Hrynevych and Magocsi, *Babyn Yar: History and Memory*, 15-17.
33	Paustovsky, *Povest o zhizni: Natchalo Nevedomogo Veka* [The Story of a Life: The Beginning of an Uncertain Age], chapter 80, '*Hetman Nash Bosiatsky*' ['Our Barefoot Hetman'], in *Sobranie Sochineny* [Collected Works], Vol. 4. Online without page numbers at https://librebook.me/povest_o_jizni__knigi_1_3/vol5/11. In English: 'Book Three. The Dawn of an Uncertain Age', in *The Story of a Life, Collected Works.*
34	'An inconvenient place': the expression is not my own, but that of the historian Vladyslav Hrynevych. See Hrynevych, 'Babyn Yar after Babyn Yar', 126.
35	Renamed – irony of fate – Fort Shevchenko by the Bolsheviks in 1939.
36	Taras Shevchenko, '*Yakby vy znaly, panchi...*' ['If you knew, young Lords...'], 1850.
37	Maurice Blanchot, '*Les deux versions de l'imaginaire*' ['The Two Versions of the Imaginary'], in *L'Espace littéraire* (Paris: Gallimard, Folio Essais, 1988), 347. In English: *The Space of Literature*, tr. Ann Smock, (Lincoln, Nebraska: University of Nebraska Press, 1982).
38	Blanchot, '*Les deux versions de l'imaginaire*', 344.
39	Steinbeck, *A Russian Journal*, 109; Capa's photograph, 110.
40	Map in Carlotta Gall, 'Bucha's Month of Terror', *New York Times*, 11 April 2022.

41   Yehor Firsov, 'I've seen the unannounced casualties of the Ukraine war', *The Washington Post,* 24 November 2022.

42   For the following section, I've supplemented what V. I. Shepitko and his nephew told me with details gleaned from Gall, 'Bucha's Month of Terror'.

43   The photo is by Daniel Berehulak, published in Carlotta Gall, '"Such Bad Guys Will Come": How One Russian Brigade Terrorized Bucha', *New York Times*, 22 May 2022.

44   Florent Marcie and Patrick Chauvel, 'Tombeau pour Oksana' ('A Grave for Oksana'), *Paris-Match*, 6-12 October 2022.

45   Carlotta Gall and Oleksandr Chubko, 'Three Women of Bucha: Their Deaths and Lives', *New York Times*, 15 October 2022.

46   Information taken from Marcie and Chauvel, 'Tombeau pour Oksana', and Gall and Chubko, 'Three Women of Bucha'.

47   This video was published the same day at 2.20 p.m. on the official Telegram channel of the State Service of Special Communications and Information Protection of Ukraine at https://t.me/dsszzi_official/1140. See also the Radio Free Europe/Radio Liberty channel on YouTube at https://www.youtube.com/watch?v=cD8K2_M83eY for a version with English subtitles, albeit censored and incomplete (the last part of the video especially is missing).

48   Yousur Al-Hlou, Masha Froliak, Evan Hill, Malachy Browne and David Botti, 'New Evidence Shows How Russian Soldiers Executed Men in Bucha', *New York Times*, 19 May 2022.

49   Daniel Boffey, '"Why did they do this to us?": Bucha's survivors come out of hiding', *The Guardian*, 4 April 2022.

50   Yousur Al-Hlou, Masha Froliak, Dmitriy Khavin, Christoph Koettl, Haley Willis, Alexander Cardia, Natalie Remeau and Malachy Browne, 'Caught on Camera, Traced by Phone: The Russian Military Unit that Killed Dozens in Bucha', *New York Times*, 22 December 2022.

51   Masha Froliak, Yousur Al-Hlou and Haley Willis, 'Their Final Moments: Victims of a Russian Atrocity in Bucha', *New York Times*, 21 December 2022.

52   Kim Vinnell, Zohra Bensemra, Mike Collett-White and Guy Faulconbridge, 'Special anniversary episode: the Ukraine war', automated transcription of a podcast, *Reuters,* 24 February 2023.

53   Curiously, sources give the same surname for the father-in-law and the son-in-law.

54   Mari Saito, 'Love letter, ID card point to Russian unit that terrorized Bucha', *Reuters*, 5 May 2022.

55   Human Rights Watch, 'Ukraine: Russian Forces' Trail of Death in Bucha', 21 April 2022.

56   Human Rights Watch, 'Ukraine', and Saito, 'Love letter'.

57   Human Rights Watch, 'Ukraine'.

58   Al-Hlou et al., 'Caught on Camera'.

59   Al-Hlou et al., 'Caught on Camera'.

60   Gall, 'Bucha's Month of Terror'.

61   Al-Hlou et al., 'Caught on Camera'.

62   Photo published in Gall, 'Bucha's Month of Terror'.

63   Al-Hlou et al., 'Caught on Camera'.

64   Froliak et al., 'Their Final Moments'.

65   See especially Al-Hlou et al., 'Caught on Camera'.

66   Testimony of Ivan Skyba, in the documentary by Tom Jennings, Annie Wong and Erika Kinetz, 'Putin's Attack on Ukraine: Documenting War Crimes', PBS/AP and Frontline, 25 October 2022.

67   He wasn't killed, and was put on trial for treason by the Ukrainian authorities; as far as I know, his name has not been made public.

68   See especially Al-Hlou et al., 'New Evidence'.

69   This information comes from phone calls intercepted by the Ukrainian intelligence services, studied by the *New York Times* in Al-Hlou et al., 'Caught on Camera'.

70   Video in Al-Hlou et al., 'New Evidence'.

71   Saito, 'Love letter'.

72   Saito, 'Love letter'.

73   Personal communication with Malachy Browne.

74   Al-Hlou et al., 'Caught on Camera'.

75   Max Bearak et Louisa Loveluck, 'In Bucha, the scope of Russian barbarity is coming into focus', *The Washington Post*, 7 April 2022. See also Froliak *et al.*, 'Final Moments'.

76   This number is quoted in Thomas d'Istria, '"*Nous ne pardonnerons jamais": à Boutcha, ville martyre d'Ukraine, la population commémore la libération*' ['"We Will Never Forgive": In Bucha, the Martyred City of Ukraine, the Population Commemorates its Liberation'], *Le Monde*, 1 April 2023. In December 2022, the number quoted by the *NYT* was still 485 residents of the city killed; see Carlotta Gall, 'In Bucha, A Final Rampage Served as a Coda to a Month of Atrocities', *New York Times*, 31 December 2022.

77   This list was drawn up based on a number of articles, notably from *Le Monde*, the *Guardian,* the *New York Times, The Washington Post* and *Reuters*.

78   Emma Graham-Harrison, Isobel Koshiw and Lorenzo Tondo, 'How the barbaric lessons learned in Syria came to haunt one small Ukrainian village', *Guardian*, 30 April 2022.

79   Lorenzo Tondo, Isobel Koshiw, Emma Graham-Harrison and Pjotr Sauer, 'Alleged Wagner Group Fighters Accused of Murdering Civilians in Ukraine', *Guardian*, 25 May 2022.

80   Steinbeck, *A Russian Journal*, 89.

81   Erika Kinetz, 'Russian Violence in Ukraine was Strategic', *Associated Press*, 27 October 2022.

82   In English on the website of the Office of the President of Russia,

...   '64th Detached Motor Rifle Brigade receives honourary Guards title,' 18 April 2022, at http://en.kremlin.ru/events/president/news/68235, and 'Greetings to command and staff of 64th Guards Detached Motor Rifle Brigade', 18 April 2022, at http://en.kremlin.ru/events/president/news/68238.

83   Gall, 'A Final Rampage'.

84   The Russian original is available online at https://t.me/nevzoro-vtv/4540.

85   Paul Celan, '*Todesfuge*'.

86   Yousur Al-Hlou, Masha Froliak and Evan Hill, '"Putin is a Fool": Intercepted Calls Reveal Russian Army in Disarray', *New York Times*, 28 September 2022.

87   'Little Russia' is the old Tsarist name for Ukraine.

88   Włodzimierz Odojewski, *Le Crépuscule d'un monde*, tr. from Polish into French by Joanna Ritt and Jacqueline Trabuc, (Paris: Éditions du Seuil, 1966), 54-55. (Translated from the French by Charlotte Mandell).

89   See Mikhail Zygar, *War and Punishment: The Story of Russian Oppression and Ukrainian Resistance* (London: Weidenfeld & Nicolson, 2023), 353.

90   Vladimir Putin, 'On the Historical Unity of Russians and Ukrainians', 12 July 2021, in English on the website of the Office of the President of Russia at http://en.kremlin.ru/events/president/news/66181. The Russian original is available online at http://kremlin.ru/events/president/news/66181.

91   Fiona Hill, 'Putin Has the U.S. Right Where He Wants It', *New York Times*, 24 January 2022.

92   Subtitled version available online at https://www.youtube.com/watch?v=VpB6uPY1r1o.

93   Serhii Plokhy, *The Gates of Europe: A History of Ukraine*, (New York: Basic Books, 2021); Timothy Snyder, 'The Making of Modern Ukraine', September–December 2022. The first lecture is online at https://www.youtube.com/watch?v=bJczLlwp-d8; the following ones are accessible via the scrolling menu.

94   The name 'Rus' seems to derive from a Swedish word meaning 'men who row'. See Serhii Plokhy, *The Gates of Europe*, 25.

95   Plokhy and Snyder disagree about the identity of the author of this myth. In his third lecture (https://www.youtube.com/watch?v=Om_A5TTQMm0&list=PLh9mgdi4rNewfxO7LhBoz_1Mx1Ma-O6sw_&index=3, starting at 33:35), Snyder attributes its origin to the Chernihiv theologian Lazar Baranovych; Plokhy attributes it to the Archimandrite of the Kyivan Cave Monastery Innokentii Gizel, under whose supervision the *Synopsis* in which this story appears was published in 1674 (Plokhy, *The Gates of Europe*, 121). I don't have the expertise required to settle the question.

96   Piotr Akopov, '*Nastuplenie Rossii I novogo mira*' ['The Offensive of Russia and the New World'], RIA Novosti, 26 February 2022,

...   originally online at https://ria.ru/20220226/rossiya-1775162336. html but now inaccessible. The text has been reposted at https://www.discred.ru/2022/02/26/nastuplenie-rossii-i-novogo-mira/#bounce.

97   Timofei Sergeitsev, '*Chto Rossiya dolzhna sdelat s Ukrainoi*' ['What Russia Should Do with Ukraine'], RIA Novosti, 3 April 2022, available online at https://ria.ru/20220403/ukraina-1781469605.html?fb-clid=IwAR1ZIUhDAiRSEdJc5ueqFVoaR1ub3CcuJZlNwlpzKV-Deg6_liLAQfdLVI. An English translation is available on the website of the Center for Civil Liberties (CCL) athttps://ccl.org.ua/en/news/ria-novosti-has-clarified-russias-plans-vis-a-vis-ukraine-and-the-rest-of-the-free-world-in-a-program-like-article-what-russia-should-do-with-ukraine-2/.

98   This translation attempts to preserve the awkwardness and the repetitions of the original text.

99   Timothy Snyder, 'Russia's genocide handbook', 8 April 2022, online at https://snyder.substack.com/p/russias-genocide-handbook.

100   These six video cassettes, in Russian without subtitles, are available in their entirety at https://vha.usc.edu/testimony/23366. The University of Southern California Shoah Foundation is the successor to the Shoah Visual History Foundation, founded by Steven Spielberg, which collected the testimonies of over 50,000 survivors of the Shoah, both Jewish and non-Jewish, between 1994 and 1999. See https://sfi.usc.edu/collecting for details of their methodology.

101   The official document that bears these names, shown towards the end of the USC Shoah Foundation film, is in Russian; I'm transcribing the names as they appear.

102   Hrynevych, 'Babyn Yar after Babyn Yar', 127.

103   Cf. https://en.wikipedia.org/wiki/Kyiv_TV_Tower.

104   Anatoliy Kuznetsov, *Babiy Yar: Roman dokument* [Babiy Yar: A Documentary Novel] (Moscow: Sovietsky pisatel-Olimp, 1991), 328.

105   Hrynevych, 'Babyn Yar after Babyn Yar,' 125.

106   'There is no memorial above Babi Yar': a line from a poem by Yevgeny Yevtushenko used in Shostakovich's Symphony No. 13, 'Babi Yar' – Translator's note.

107   BYHMC and FORMA Architectural Studio, *Analysis of historical and contemporary context*, 192-193.

108   Timothy Snyder, *Bloodlands: Europe Between Hitler and Stalin* (London: Vintage Books, 2011), 227-228.

109   Snyder, *Bloodlands*, 345.

110   The American Jewish Joint Distribution Committee, founded in 1914.

111   Hrynevych, 'Babyn Yar after Babyn Yar', 109.

112   See https://www.billdownscbs.com/2013/07/blood-at-babii yar-kievs-atrocity-story.html for excerpts from the articles and photographs of the journalists and the survivors. Lawrence's article remains more sceptical about the reality of the events than Downs's,

| ... | which allows us to see how unthinkable for a Western mind massacres of such amplitude were, even though they were common practice in Eastern Europe since 1941 and even before that. |

113 Brown, *A Biography of No Place*, 218.

114 Joshua Rubinstein, 'Night of the Murdered Poets', in Joshua Rubinstein and Vladimir Naumov (eds.), *Stalin's Secret Pogrom: The Postwar Inquisition of the Jewish Anti-Fascist Committee* (New Haven: Yale University Press, 2001), 22.

115 Russian acronym for 'The Extraordinary State Commission for the Investigation of the Crimes of the German-Fascist Invaders and Their Accomplices and the Damage They Caused to Citizens, Collective Farms, Public Organizations, State Enterprises and Institutions of the USSR'.

116 Hrynevych, 'Babyn Yar after Babyn Yar', 111.

117 Aleksandr Solzhenitsyn, *Dvesti let vmeste : Chast 2. V Sovietskoe Vremya* [Two Hundred Years Together: Part 2. The Soviet Era] (Moscow: Mir Publishers, 2002), chapter 22. Online without page numbers at http://zeminfo.ru/library/glava22.html. Solzhenitsyn cites as his source '*Khrushchev i evreiskiy vopros*' ['Khrushchev and the Jewish Question'], in *Sotsialisticheskiy Vestnik* [The Socialist Courier] (New York: Russian Social Democratic Labour Party, 1961), no. 1, 19.

118 Rubinstein, 'Night of the Murdered Poets', 38.

119 This information is taken primarily from BYHMC and FORMA Architectural Studio, *Analysis of historical and contemporary context*, 192-193.

120 Hrynevych, 'Babyn Yar after Babyn Yar', 129.

121 BYHMC and FORMA Architectural Studio, *Analysis of historical and contemporary context*, 192.

122 Hrynevych, 'Babyn Yar after Babyn Yar', 136.

123 BYHMC and FORMA Architectural Studio, *Analysis of historical and contemporary context*, 192.

124 BYHMC and FORMA Architectural Studio, *Analysis of historical and contemporary context*, 208.

125 Nakhmanovych, 'A Place of Memory', 294.

126 Personal communication.

127 John Cheyne and William Stokes, 'The Breath of Death is the Gift of Life', Riga, 1953.

128 There are some remarkable exceptions, such as the Ukrainian historians Sofia Dyak, Andrii Usach and Yurii Radchenko, as well as the Canadian-American historian of Ukrainian origins John-Paul Himka.

129 See Plokhy, *The Gates of Europe*, 266-267.

130 Ernest Renan, '*Qu'est-ce qu'une nation?*' ['What is a Nation?'], lecture given in 1882, published in *Discours et conférences* (*Speeches and Conferences*) (Paris: Calmann Lévy, 1887). In English online, tr. Ethan Rundell, at http://ucparis.fr/files/9313/6549/9943/What_is_a_Nation.pdf.

131   Timothy Snyder, *The Reconstruction of Nations: Poland, Ukraine, Lithuania, Belarus 1569-1999* (New Haven: Yale University Press, 2003), 143.

132   Timothy Snyder, *Bloodlands*, 196.

133   Andrii Ussach, personal communication.

134   John-Paul Himka, *Ukrainian Nationalists and the Holocaust: OUN and UPA's Participation in the Destruction of Ukrainian Jewry, 1941-1944* (Stuttgart: Ibidem-Verlag, 2021), 247 and 246-255.

135   Snyder, *Bloodlands*, 196.

136   For these events, see Gerald Reitlinger, *The House Built on Sand: The Conflicts of German Policy in Russia, 1939-1945* (New York: The Viking Press, 1960), 164-167, as well as Per Rudling, 'The OUN, the UPA and the Holocaust: A Study in the Manufacturing of Historical Myths', in *The Carl Beck Papers in Russian & East European Studies*, no. 2107, 2011, 8-10, online at https://pdfs.semanticscholar.org/68b1/c6aa8eca-db92a6f63884af1dd80da594f938.pdf.

137   Personal communication.

138   For these events, see Reitlinger, *The House Built on Sand*, 168-169, and Rudling, 'The OUN, the UPA and the Holocaust', 9-10, as well as Yurii Radchenko, personal communication.

139   Leonty Forostivskyy, *Kyiv pid vorozhymy okupatsiiamy* [Kyiv Under Enemy Occupation] (Buenos Aires: M. Denysiuk, 1952), 76, quoted by Yurii Radchenko, "'*I todi braty z Moskvy I braty-zhydy prykhodyly I obhyraly brativ ukraintsiv do nytky*": *Olena Teliha, Babyn Yar ta evrei*' ['"And then the brothers from Moscow and the Yid-brothers came and stripped the Ukrainian brothers bare": Olena Teliha, Babyn Yar and the Jews'], published online on 27 March 2017 at http://uamoderna.com/blogy/yurij-radchenko/teliha.

140   Personal communication.

141   Andrii Usach, '*Problematychnyy martyrolog : Zhertvy OUN(m) u Babynomu Yaru*' [A problematic martyrology: the victims of the OUN-M in Babyn Yar'], published online on 6 March 2017 at https://uamoderna.com/blogy/usach-andr/problematic-martyrology.

142   Heinrich Himmler, speech to the *Grüpenführer-SS* in Posen on 4 October 1943, document 1919-PS from the Nuremberg trial.

143   As a simple example, see the English Wikipedia page for Olena Teliha at https://en.wikipedia.org/wiki/Olena_Teliha, which claims: 'A lot of her activities were in open defiance of the Nazi authorities.'

144   Quoted by Eduard Dolinskyy, president of the Ukrainian Jewish Committee, during a televised broadcast on 30 March 2016, viewable at https://www.youtube.com/watch?v=dpMcWhEgE1w&t=172s and cited by Radchenko, '*Olena Teliha, Babyn Yar ta evrei*'.

145   Quoted by Radchenko, '*Olena Teliha, Babyn Yar ta evrei*'.

146   Per Rudling, 'The OUN, the UPA and the Holocaust', 26.

147   This extract from *The Falsifiers of History* is quoted by Robert Chandler and Yury Bit-Yunan in their note 66 to Vasily Grossman, *Stalingrad*,

...   942. See also https://en.wikipedia.org/wiki/Falsifiers_of_History. The entire book, translated into English, is available at https:// ucf.digital.flvc.org/islandora/object/ucf%3A5071/datastream/ OBJ/view/Falsificators_of_history__an_historical_note__Text_of_ communique_issued_February__1948.pdf.

148   See for example Snyder, *Bloodlands*, 220; Snyder, *The Reconstruction of Nations*, 162; and Himka, *Ukrainian Nationalists and the Holocaust*, 305-359.

149   Snyder, *The Reconstruction of Nations*, 160.

150   Snyder, *The Reconstruction of Nations*, 160.

151   Snyder, *The Reconstruction of Nations*, 166.

152   These opposing strategies are described in detail in *The Reconstruction of Nations*, 165-167.

153   Rudling, 'The OUN, the UPA and the Holocaust', 10.

154   Petro Balei, *Fronda Stepana Bandery v OUN 1940 roku* (*The rebellion of Stepan Bandera within the OUN in 1940*), Tekna A/T, 1996, 141, quoted by Snyder, *The Reconstruction of Nations*, 165.

155   TsDAHO Ukrainy, 1/20/931, ll.36-39 (1944), quoted by Brown, *A Biography of No Place*, 221.

156   Henry Friedman, *I'm No Hero* (Seattle: University of Washington Press, 1999), 33-37, quoted by Himka, *Ukrainian Nationalists and the Holocaust*, 387-388.

157   These numbers are calculated by Grzegorz Hryciuk, 'Straty ludności na Wołyniu w latach 1941-1944' ['Population losses in Volhynia 1941-1945'], in *Polska-Ukraina: Trudne pytania* [Poland-Ukraine: Difficult Questions], vol. 5, Karta, 1999, 278, quoted by Snyder, *The Reconstruction of Nations*, 170.

158   Snyder, *The Reconstruction of Nations*, 175.

159   TsDAVO, fond 3838, op.1, spr. 57, f. 6, quoted by Himka, *Ukrainian Nationalists and the Holocaust*, 373.

160   TsDAHO, fond 1, op.23, spr. 928, f. 190, quoted by Himka, *Ukrainian Nationalists and the Holocaust*, 373.

161   Testimony of the Jewish partisan Yitzhak Geller in *Sefer ha-partizanim ha-Yehudim* [Book of the Jewish Partisans] (Merhavia: Sifriyat Po'alim, 1958), vol.1, 681, tr. Alan Rutkowski, quoted by Himka, *Ukrainian Nationalists and the Holocaust*, 381.

162   Testimony in Maria Hochberg-Mariańska and Noe Grüss, eds., *Dzieci oskarżają* [The Children Accuse] (Krakow: Centralna Żydowska Komisja Historyczna, 1947), 139, quoted by Himka, *Ukrainian Nationalists and the Holocaust*, 388.

163   AŻIH, 301/3337, 14, quoted by Himka, *Ukrainian Nationalists and the Holocaust*, 389.

164   Snyder, *The Reconstruction of Nations*, 164.

165   DARO, fond R30, opys 2, spr.15, f.126, quoted by Himka, *Ukrainian Nationalists and the Holocaust*, 373.

166　Per Rudling, 'The OUN, the UPA and the Holocaust', 34.

167　See Andreas Umland and Yuliya Yurchuk, 'Introduction: The Organization of Ukrainian Nationalists (OUN) in Post-Soviet Ukrainian Memory Politics, Public Debates, and Foreign Affairs', in 'Issues in the History and Memory of the OUN I', *Journal of Soviet and Post-Soviet Politics and Society*, vol. 3, no 2, 2017, 115-128.

168　Umland and Yurchuk, 'Introduction', 121.

169　See Josh Cohen, 'The Historian Whitewashing Ukraine's Past', *Foreign Policy*, 2 May 2016.

170　Per Rudling, 'Yushchenko's Fascist: The Bandera Cult in Ukraine and Canada', in 'Issues in the History and Memory of the OUN I', 129-130.

171　Personal communication.

172　Oles Yanchuk, *Neskorenyy* [The Invincible], 2000, viewable on YouTube (with partial English subtitles) at https://www.youtube.com/watch?v=lnL2gSrg26A. The film is financed by the Ukrainian Ministry of Culture, Dovzhenko Studios and the Ukrainian Congress Committee of America (UCCA, a structure that since 1940 has gathered together a large number of organizations of the Ukrainian diaspora in the United States, including several groups or associations of veterans of the OUN-UPA). Dr. Askold Lozinsky, president of the UCCA, is credited as a scientific consultant for the film.

173　Personal communication.

174　Włodzimierz Odojewski, *Oksana l'Ukrainienne*, tr. into French by Agnes Wisniewski (Paris: Les éditions Noir sur Blanc, 2003), 138. (Translated from the French by Charlotte Mandell).

175　Personal communication.

176　Artiom Skoropadskyy died on 10 December 2022 after a long stomach illness.

177　'Polite green men': a term ironically employed by the Russian media, along with 'polite people', to refer to the Russian soldiers with unmarked uniforms who took over the Crimean peninsula in February 2014. — Translator's note.

178　Numerous sources have confirmed this Russian financing of the Ukrainian far right; the pro-Russian oligarch Dmytro Firtach (who has now had to flee and seek refuge in Vienna from an American arrest warrant) has been openly accused of serving as an intermediary for the Russian financial backing of the Svoboda ultranationalist party.

179　This incident, filmed and posted online, took place on the edge of Kharkiv, in the village of Velyka Danylivka. The old woman, named Anna Ivanovna, was welcoming Ukrainian soldiers liberating the zone, whom she visibly mistook for Russians; when a soldier took hold of her flag to step on it, she angrily refused to accept the food they offered her. Russian propaganda pounced on the video and broadcast it widely; sculptures of Anna Ivanovna and her flag were erected in Voronezh, in Russia and in occupied Mariupol; her image was

...   reproduced on public buildings throughout Russia. See *'"Luchshe by ia znamenitoy ne byla": Kak ukrainka s sovetskim flagom stala kulturnym fenomenom v Rossii i chto ona ob etom dumaet'* ['"I wish I weren't famous": How a Ukrainian woman with a Soviet flag became a cultural phenomenon in Russia and what she thinks about it'], BBC News/ Russian service, 16 May 2022, as well as 'Babushka Z: The woman who became a Russian propaganda icon', BBC News, 15 June 2022, https://www.bbc.com/news/world-europe-61757667. The video is featured in a Russian-language programme of the Ukrainian media Freedom.ua, viewable at https://www.youtube.com/watch?v=Kr3fP9AgvYM.

180   The online publication of the video presenting this research was unfortunately suspended due to the war. An outline has been published in Nick Axel and Nicholas Korody (eds.), *Babyn Yar: Past, Present, Future* (Leipzig: Spector Books and Babyn Yar Holocaust Memorial Center, 2021), 87-93 and 134-141.

181   Kuznetsov, *Babiy Yar: Roman dokument*, 12-14.

182   Sergei Loznitsa, *Babi Yar. Contexte*, 2021.

183   Karel C. Berkhoff, 'Babyn Yar in Cinema', in Hrynevych and Magocsi, *Babyn Yar: History and Memory*, 240-243. The images filmed by Donskoi were notably used by Michaël Prazan in his 2009 documentary *Einsatzgrüppen. Les commandos de la mort*, where they are presented as authentic images.

184   For a rigorous analysis of this sequence of events, and the parallels with the history of Babyn Yar, see the work carried out by Maksym Rokmaniko and his Center for Spatial Technologies, in collaboration with the BYHMC and Forensic Architecture, at https://forensic-architecture.org/investigation/russian-strike-on-kyiv-tv-tower, as well as the interactive article by Linda Kinstler, 'Who Will Remember the Horrors of Ukraine', *New York Times*, 13 June 2022.

185   This sound installation is the work of the Ukrainian-British artist Maksym Dimidienko. See https://babynyar.org/en/audio-installation for more details and excerpts.

186   This poem was published for the first time in *Novyi Mir*, 39th year, No. 3, March 1963, before being reprinted in posthumous volumes. It is available online at http://sehrg.at.ua/Kyselyov.htm. It should be noted that although he wrote most of his work in Russian, Kiselov, always strongly influenced by Taras Shevchenko, chose a year before his premature death in 1968 to write exclusively in Ukrainian. I am grateful to Andrei Dmitriev for drawing my attention to this author and to this poem in his text *'Des années de contre-vérités corrosives'* ['Years of corrosive counter-truths'], *Le Monde*, 3 May 2022, where the French translation, more poetic and less literal than my own, is by Elena Balzamo.

Image captions

All numbers provided are page references.

All of Antoine d'Agata's photographs were taken in Ukraine between April 2021 and February 2023. The archival photographs were selected and edited by Antoine d'Agata.

6   Kyrylivskyy Hai, Kyiv, January 2022.
10   Advertising poster, Babyn Yar Park, June 2021.
17   Dorohozhychi metro station, Kyiv, July 2021 (thermal camera).
22   Archival image: Soviet prisoners in Babyn Yar, probably on 1 October 1941 (photo Johannes Hähle, negative no. 18, detail. © Hamburger Institut für Sozialforschung).
26   Construction of the 'Crystal Wall of Tears', Babyn Yar Park, Kyiv, June 2021.
31   Lviv train station, March 2022.
32   *Romni* (Roma woman) in a welcome tent for displaced persons, Lviv train station, March 2022.
36   Synagogue, Babyn Yar Park, Kyiv, June 2021.
39   Babyn Yar Park, Kyiv, January 2022.
45   Kyrylivskyy Hai, Kyiv, January 2022.
46   Kyrylivskyy Hai, Kyiv, April 2021.
48   Misha, 'Pavlovka' psychiatric hospital, Kyiv, September 2021.
51   Abandoned institute, Kyrylivskyy Hai, Kyiv, June 2021.
57   Nastia, 'Pavlovka' psychiatric hospital, Kyiv, February 2023.
59   'Pavlovka' psychiatric hospital, Kyiv, June 2021-February 2023.
67   Kyrylivskyy Hai, Kyiv, September 2021.
68   Kharkiv, May 2022.
71   'Pavlovka' psychiatric hospital, Kyiv, February 2023.
73   Between Irpin and Kyiv, March 2022.
76   Antonov International Airport, Hostomel, May 2022.
80-1 Corpses of Russian soldiers collected by Ukrainian forces, Kharkiv *oblast*, May 2022.
84   Bucha morgue, May 2022.
87   Bucha, Irpin and Borodianka, May 2022-February 2023.
92   *Pogreb*, No. 58 Vokzalna Street, Bucha, May 2022.
99   Mala Rohan, Kharkiv Oblast, May 2022.
107   Bullets, shrapnel and various other objects left by Russian forces, Kyiv and Kharkiv *oblasts*, May 2022.
108   Bucha morgue, May 2022.
113   Kharkiv, March 2022.
118   Hostomel, May 2022.
121   No. 144 Yablunska Street, Bucha, May 2022.
128   Bus of refugees, Lviv, March 2022.

131   Burned garage on Sklozavodska Street, Bucha, May 2022.

134   Traces of torture and murder, graves and corpses left after the Russian retreat from Kyiv *oblast*, May 2022.

137   'Pavlovka' psychiatric hospital, Kyiv, February 2023.

138   Kharkiv, May 2022.

141   Abandoned Russian position, Chernobyl Exclusion Zone, May 2022.

148   Sites where the Russian army tortured and murdered five humanitarian volunteers, children's holiday camp, Vokzalna Street, Bucha, May 2022.

151   Archival image: civilian from Severynivka tortured and killed by Russian military intelligence, Motyzhyn, late March 2022 (photo Oleh Bondarenko, detail. © Oleh Bondarenko).

157   Site where a humanitarian volunteer was killed by the Russian army, children's holiday camp, Vokzalna Street, Bucha, May 2022.

163   Exhumation of the corpse of Serhii Ivanovich Kyslytskyy in an abandoned Russian base, Vyshehrad, May 2022.

164   Kyrylivskyy Hai, Kyiv, January 2022.

172-3 Ordinary citizens, soldiers, members of the Territorial Defence and Ukrainian politicians, between May 2022 and February 2023.

179   No. 81 Yurii Illienko Street, September 2021.

180   Archival image: abandoned corpse on Melnikova Street, probably on September 29, 1941 (photo Johannes Hähle, negative no. 3, detail. © Hamburger Institut für Sozialforschung).

185   Archival image: Ruvin Shtein, late 1943-early 1944 (photographer unknown, screen capture from the filmed interview of Ruvin Shtein by the USC Shoah Foundation, detail. © USC Shoah Foundation, University of Southern California).

188-9 Graves of veterans of the Second World War, military cemetery, Dorohozhytska Street, Kyiv, June 2021.

194-5 Found portraits of Jews killed at Babyn Yar, Babyn Yar National Preserve, Herzen Street, Kyiv, October 2021.

198   Morgue No. 1, No. 9 Oranzhereina Street, June 2021.

201   Morgue No. 1, No. 9 Oranzhereina Street, June 2021.

206   Dorohozhychi metro station, Kyiv, May 2022.

212   Archival image: the young Solomon Mikhoels (date and photographer unknown. © Wikimedia commons).

221   Archival image: pogroms in Lviv, June 1941 (filmmaker unknown, photogram from the documentary film *Babi Yar. Context* by Sergei Loznitsa, detail. © Atoms & Void).

227   Archival image: Olena Teliha, born Olena Shovgeniva, while studying at the Mykhailo Drahomanov Ukrainian Pedagogical Institute in Prague, 1923 (photographer unknown).

236-7 Archival images: UPA commanders and fighters, ca. 1943-1949 (photographers unknown, details).

243   Archival image: Ukrainian postage stamp with the image of Stepan Bandera, 2009 (detail. © Wikimedia commons).

246   Demonstration of veterans of the volunteer brigades and far-right activists, Kyiv, 14 October 2021.

251   Dmytro Reznichenko, Kyiv, May 2022.

254   Realist Security Hub shooting range, Yurii Illienko Street no. 46A, Kyiv, June 2021 (thermal camera).

259   Vilkhivka, Kharkiv *oblast*, May 2022.

262   Demonstration of veterans of the volunteer brigades and far-right activists, Kyiv, 14 October 2021.

266   Babyn Yar Park, Kyiv, June 2021.

271   Syrets neighbourhood, Kyiv, September 2021.

273   Yaroslaviv Val Street, Kyiv, September 2021.

276   'Pavlovka' psychiatric hospital, Kyiv, June 2021.

277   *Korpus* 26, 'Pavlovka' psychiatric hospital, Kyiv, June 2021.

281   Lviv train station, March 2022.

283   'Pavlovka' psychiatric hospital, Kyiv, February 2023.

288   Bucha, May 2022.

291   Father Ioann, Horenka, May 2022.

296-7 Detail of a German aerial reconnaissance photo of Babyn Yar and surroundings taken in 1943 and hung in the BYHMC offices, January 2022 (© Babyn Yar Holocaust Memorial Center).

301   No. 25 Olena Teliha Street, Kyiv, June 2021.

302   No. 25 Olena Teliha Street, Kyiv, June 2021.

307   *Tefilla* (Jewish phylactery) found after the war, Babyn Yar National Preserve, Herzen Street, Kyiv, October 2021.

310   Underground pipe with the Babyn Yar stream, Kyiv, September 2021.

317   The television tower reflected in the 'Field of Mirrors', Babyn Yar Park, Kyiv, January 2022.

320-1 Archival images: drone photographs of the Babyn Yar Park, January 2022 (operator Dmytro Stoikov. © Dmytro Stoikov/Babyn Yar Holocaust Memorial Center).

323   Mausoleum of the Kachkovsky brothers, Kyrylivskyy Hai, Kyiv, January 2022.

324   Kyrylivskyy Hai, Kyiv, July 2021.

327   Kyrylivskyy Hai, Kyiv, January 2022.

Acknowledgements

This book was enriched and made possible by many people. The authors would like to express their gratitude:

First of all, to all those, Ukrainians and others, who were willing to speak to us or be photographed. Some are named in the book, others are anonymous. We are deeply grateful for their cooperation, their generosity and their openness.

Then, to the Babyn Yar Holocaust Memorial Center, which supported our investigations in Kyiv, Antoine d'Agata's photographic work and the making of this book; and in particular to Ilia Khrzhanovskiy, Oleksei Makukhin, Maksym Yakover, Oleh Shovenko, Valeriya Didienko, Nadiya Zaitseva, Maksym Rokmaniko, Halina Shokola and Vitalii Lusher, along with all their colleagues.

To the French Embassy in Kyiv: ambassador Étienne de Poncins, Bruno Caussanel, Olivier Jacquot, Frédéric Rousseau and their colleagues.

To the newspaper *Le Monde*, which made possible part of our travels in Ukraine after the start of the Russian invasion: Jérôme Fenoglio, Marie-Pierre Lannelongue, Dominique Perrin, Aurore Salcedo, Lucy Conticello, Dr Élisabeth Roche, Ludivine Dagorn, Florence Aubenas and Thomas d'Istria.

To the *New York Times Magazine*: Kathy Ryan and Shannon Simon.

To the *Guardian*: Kate Edwards and Louis Siroy.

To Magnum Photos and the Magnum Gallery: Giulietta Palumbo, Samantha McCoy, Léa Robert, Pierre Mohamed-Petit and the entire Paris office team.

To Picto Bastille: Christophe Batifoulier and Élisabeth Heiring.

For the postproduction of the photographs, to Jonathan Paredes, Charlie Jouvet and again Giulietta Palumbo. The postproduction of the photographs on pages 80 and 81 was supported as part of the large national project *Radioscopie de la France: regards sur un pays traversé par la crise sanitaire* ('Radioscopy of France: views of a country going through a health crisis') financed by the Ministry of Culture and directed by the Bibliothèque nationale de France.

To Alina Zamirovska for her precious help with the translations of some of the interviews.

To Nataliya Humeniuk, Anton Drobovych, Oleh Sosnov, Konstantin Ilianok, Dmytro Stoikov, Ihor Chekachkov, Rita Burkovska, Anton Shynkarenko, Saveli Barashkov, Darina Solodova, Evhenii Safonov, Kseniya Palfi, Joséphine Huppert (Centre Pompidou press service), Gilbert Brownstone, Luc Delahaye and Gaëlle Girbes.

And finally, with all our hearts, to Rubymaya Jaeck-Woodgate and Tania Bohórquez.

Fitzcarraldo Editions
8-12 Creekside
London, SE8 3DX
Great Britain

ISBN 978-1-80427-112-4

Design by Ray O'Meara
Typeset in Fitzcarraldo
Printed and bound by TJ Books

The publication of this book was supported by
the Babyn Yar Holocaust Memorial Center

Fitzcarraldo Editions